46833

**FRANCIS CLOSE HALL
LEARNING CENTRE**
Swindon Road Cheltenham
Gloucestershire GL50 4AZ
Telephone: 01242 532913

UNIVERSITY OF
GLOUCESTERSHIRE
at CHELTENHAM *and* GLOUCESTER

NORMAL LOAN

1 3 DEC 2006

44706 03/05

13 MAR 1980   12. DEC. 1983   LIBREX

D0239837

THE COTSWOLDS

A New Study

Uniform with this book

DARTMOOR : A NEW STUDY
Edited by Crispin Gill

FCH LEARNING CENTRE
UNIVERSITY OF GLOUCESTERSHIRE
Swindon Road
Cheltenham GL50 4AZ
Tel: 01242 532913

WITHDRAWN

THE COTSWOLDS

A New Study

EDITED BY CHARLES AND ALICE MARY HADFIELD

Contributors:

John W. Murray
A. Brian Hawkins
Christopher M. Swaine
I. F. Smith
Bruce N. Eagles
Kathleen Morgan
Frank H. Garner
Michael W. Ingram
Christopher Cox
Charles Hadfield
David Bick
Lionel F. J. Walrond
Alice Mary Hadfield
David Verey
John Green
Norman Collins

David & Charles : Newton Abbot

ISBN 0 7153 6224 0

© 1973 DAVID BICK, NORMAN COLLINS, CHRISTOPHER COX, BRUCE N. EAGLES, FRANK H. GARNER, JOHN GREEN, ALICE MARY HADFIELD, CHARLES HADFIELD, A. BRIAN HAWKINS, MICHAEL INGRAM, KATHLEEN MORGAN, JOHN W. MURRAY, I. F. SMITH, CHRISTOPHER M. SWAINE, DAVID VEREY, LIONEL F. J. WALROND

All rights reserved. No part of this publication may be reproduced, stored in a retrieval system, or transmitted in any form or by any means, electronic, mechanical, photocopying, recording or otherwise, without the prior permission of David & Charles (Holdings) Limited

942·417
HAD

Set in 11 on 13pt Baskerville
and printed in Great Britain
by Clarke Doble & Brendon Limited Plymouth
for David & Charles (Holdings) Limited
South Devon House Newton Abbot Devon

Contents

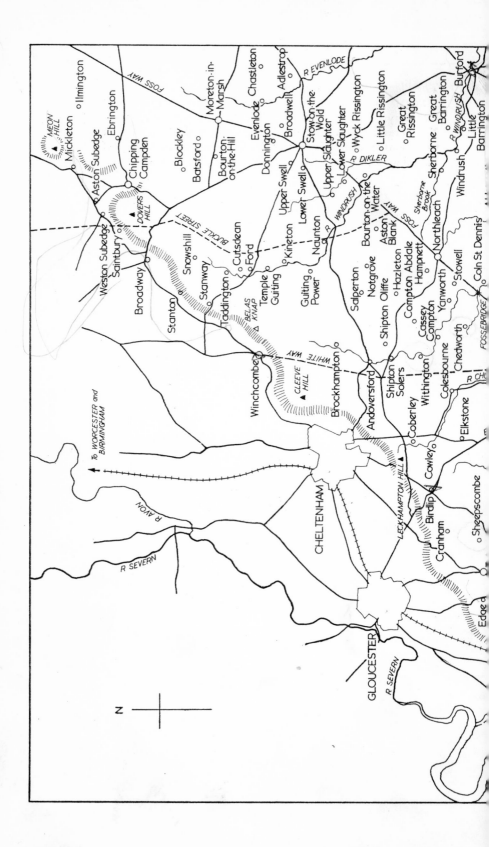

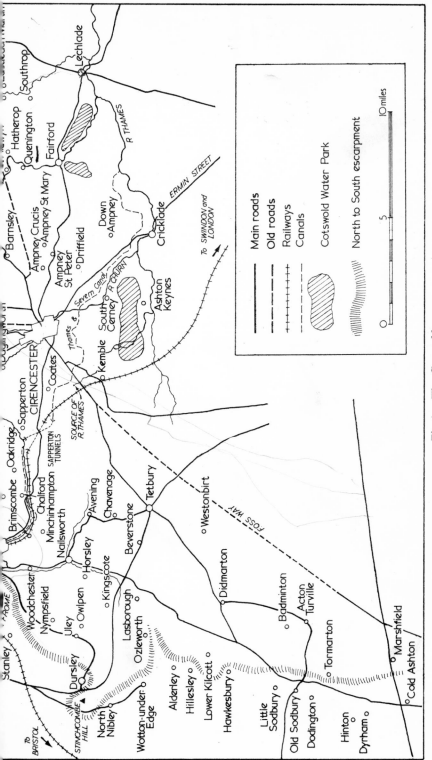

Fig 1. The Cotswolds.

List of Illustrations

Plates

11

GLOUCESTERSHIRE COLLEGE
OF EDUCATION
LIBRARY

Figures in Text

15
16

Introduction

By Charles and Alice Mary Hadfield

THE COTSWOLDS are an upland limestone area in England, mainly in Gloucestershire, of bare, smooth, undulating outline, far enough from any influential centre to have developed their own individuality, and not so remote that they have suffered social decline. The shape of this area, difficult to demarcate, has emerged from the ten lines of research which make up this volume. We define it as a 40 mile long escarpment with wolds falling gently back from it, running from Meon Hill, just north of Chipping Campden, south-west to Stinchcombe Hill below Stroud, and with fingers stretching down from the rough bluff of Stinchcombe to Sodbury and Marshfield. The hill country dies out here and so does its peculiar personality. The noble influences of Bath and Bristol have marked the Avon country from here to the south and east, and though good stone building continues it belongs to a wider culture than Cotswold.

The escarpment is the whole western frontier of the Cotswolds, including the small places which perch on ledges and dips in the upper face, Stanton and Stanway, Didbrook, Leonard Stanley, Wotton-under-Edge. These front the prevailing wind and weather, and look over sheltered, rich valley land and busy highways, but are distinct from both. On the east there is no clear frontier, but a weaving of small rivers which mark off the Oxford downs, the Thames valley and the Berkshire downs from Cotswold. The Cotswold hills slope down from the escarpment edge towards this eastern level and form an upland region which, looked at in an atlas, is roughly 10 miles across from Winchcombe to Stow-on-the-Wold, 18 from Birdlip to Burford, 16 from Painswick to Bibury, 12 from Stroud to Cirencester, and so narrows to the southern dissolution. Here again the distinction is between a tougher, pure tradition, and the richer diverse culture spreading up the Thames valley to Swindon and Oxford, and down from Stratford and the great and ancient wealth of the Midlands.

Limestone is the main feature characterising the Cotswolds hills and Cotswold building. The limestone, and some building, covers a much wider area than that defined here: Somerset, Warwickshire, Oxford-

15

shire, Northamptonshire could all claim a part of it. The Cotswolds are
in Gloucestershire, but there are large stretches of Gloucestershire which
are not Cotswold. Visitors sometimes feel hazy about the region, not
seeing it as an entity. They may go to Chipping Campden, Burford,
Cirencester; some reach Painswick or Minchinhampton. They will have
an impression of grey stone buildings, bare upland, thick woods, pastoral
stream valleys, broken rocky cliffs and quarries, yet be unable to identify
any sense of unity.

   In the Cotswolds the whole is greater than any of the parts, and this
is sometimes hard for a visitor to absorb. The whole is the limestone
foundation moulded by the weather of this particular area to a structure
of wonderfully smooth surface and skyline, with subtle undulations that
grow slowly on the mind's eye. The soil is poor-to-middling which
establishes one element of the unity. Where richer, deeper soil develops to
the north, east and south, the character of landscape and building
changes. Cotswold soil supports stone, grass, crops, flowers and trees of
a clear pale light-bearing colour quality, which is so indigenous that
natives do not often realise it. The upland wolds, of light drained soil,
carry close-rooted spare grass, yellow cowslip, silver barley, blue geranium,
and the delicate hardy blue harebell; pale stone walls cross the contours,
pointed by hawthorn bushes, creamy white all May, and windbreaks
and clumps of rustling light green beech. Dark elms create a strong visual
contrast. Upon this homogeneous landscape, the farm buildings and
villages have been built, century after century, of stone quarried from
the hills, of the same light bearing quality, and following the local
contours for labour saving or for the shelter they provide. Scarcity of
water has often grouped them. Their origin has nearly always been a
natural one. Castles have not been as influential as good grazing for
sheep. So the character of the Cotswolds has been shaped by a strong
blending of wolds and villages, colour and outline, of a subtle, penetrating
beauty, unlike any other region in England.

   Each of the ten lines of approach in these pages reveals an entity
different from the region beyond it. In a few cases such as farming,
processes or statistics have included over-the-border-areas, but the
individual entity remains clear and intact. The contributors examine the
formation of the area, its land, regional climate, occupations, small
society and groups, their history within the area, their culture, work and
contribution to their setting, and the growth and character of the modern
scene. The Cotswolds have never been cut off from the mainstream of
English life and history, yet they have retained their own identity.

   Today the Cotswold region, whose inaccessibility was once so sure a

Page 17 (above) *Winter at Seven Springs*; (below) *Bisley*

GLOUCESTERSHIRE COLLEGE
OF EDUCATION
LIBRARY

Page 18 (above) *The hill country of Nailsworth;* (below) *a lonely high wold village, Ford*

defence of its regional character, has become increasingly popular. Is the local life vigorous enough to maintain itself? Will people want to go on living in plain houses and villages, often in lonely country, and remain content in small communities? Is there enough employment to keep them there, sufficient housing and schools? Do the authorities care? Can footpaths, hedges and rough thicket shelters for insect and bird survive? This book explores Cotswold characteristics in their slow formation and their modern expression, and sets binoculars on the future.

B

1

Geology and Physical Environment

J. W. Murray and A. B. Hawkins

THE COTSWOLD HILLS have attracted the attention of geologists since the early part of the nineteenth century. In 1834 Murchison published the first book on the area, *An Outline of the Geology of Cheltenham.* This was followed in 1844 by a larger second edition revised by Strickland & Buckman. The Geological Survey published the Cheltenham memoir in 1857. Richardson produced a detailed account of the area in 1904. More recently Dreghorn has published a popular account of the whole Cotswold area (1967). In addition to these books there are numerous papers published in the *Quarterly Journal of the Geological Society of London,* the *Proceedings of the Geologists' Association, Proceedings of the Cottswold Naturalists' Field Club* and the *Proceedings of the Bristol Naturalists' Society.*

Stratigraphy and Conditions of Accumulation

All the rocks exposed at the surface in the Cotswolds are of Jurassic age :

Generalised succession of Jurassic strata

	Upper Jurassic	Purbeck Beds Portland Beds Kimmeridge Clay Corallian Beds Oxford Clay and Kellaways Beds
Represented in the Cotswolds	Middle Jurassic	Cornbrash Great Oolite Series Inferior Oolite Series
	Lower Jurassic	Upper Lias Middle Lias Lower Lias

Beneath the Jurassic are the clays, marls and sandstones of the Trias. These are never seen at outcrop in the Cotswolds but they are known from borehole evidence to be present at depth throughout the entire area.

In Fig 2 the main Cotswold mass is delimited by the lower boundary of the Inferior Oolite Series and the upper boundary of the Great Oolite Series. To the north and west is the low land of the Severn valley underlain by Lower Lias and Triassic deposits. To the south-east the Cotswold Limestones are overlain by Upper Jurassic clays.

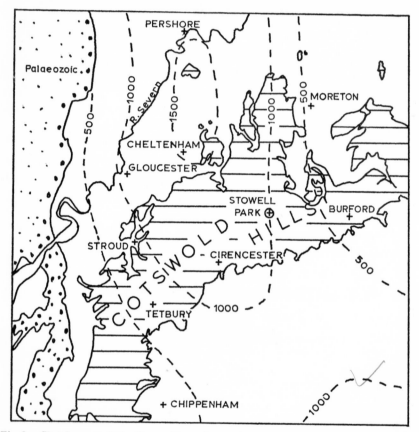

Fig 2. Sketch map of the Cotswolds to show selected geological boundaries together with contours on the pre-Permian basement (depth below sea level in metres).

Data from boreholes have been used to construct topographic maps of the surface beneath the Permian and Triassic rocks (Kent, 1949; Green & Melville, 1956; Tectonic maps of Great Britain and Northern Ireland, IGS, 1966). A summary of these maps is presented in Fig 2. The thickness of the Mesozoic rocks in general is greatest in a basin centred between Pershore and Cheltenham. This basin extends southwards beneath the

Cotswold Hills, which run across it obliquely. The thickest succession of Middle Jurassic rocks is at Cleeve Hill near Cheltenham. To the north-east and south-west the rocks thin, and this is clearly shown in Fig 5.

The Lias

Lower Lias clays form the low land in the Severn valley at the foot of the Cotswold escarpment. There are few exposures, so the thickness is not known very accurately : probably 500–1000ft in the centre of the basin around Cheltenham. One of the best places to see this formation is on Robins Wood Hill, south of Gloucester (Tuffley Old Brickworks, SO/836149). Shales in the lower part of the quarry belong to the *davoei* and *ibex* zones. In the central part of the quarry the shales are of uncertain age, but in the upper part there are limestones with *Amaltheus*, which are of the Middle Lias *margaritatus* zone (Ager, 1956). Above are shales and siltstones also of Middle Lias age (*spinatum* zone).

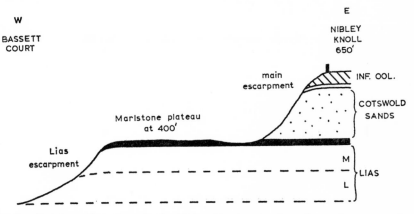

Fig 3. Sketch section through the Cotswold edge to show the main scarps controlled by the Inferior Oolite and the subsidiary terrace and scarp formed by the Middle Lias Marlstone.

The Middle Lias thickens from 100ft at Wotton-under-Edge to 250ft in the central Cotswolds. It consists of clays in the lower part capped by a silty limestone, the Marlstone, which forms a hard resistant band around 15ft thick. At Stinchcombe near Dursley, where it is exposed in a quarry (ST/735995), fossils are abundant, particularly bivalves, belemnites and large nautili. This is the type locality of the rhynconellid *Gibbirhynchia micra* Ager (Ager, 1954). Because the Marlstone is so hard it forms an escarpment and plateau at the foot of the main Cotswold scarp (Fig 3). This is best developed between Wotton-under-Edge and Dursley and from Cheltenham to Chipping Campden.

OXSTALLS CAMPUS LIBRARY
GLOUCESTERSHIRE COLLEGE
OF ARTS AND TECHNOLOGY
OXSTALLS LANE
GLOUCESTER GL2 9HW

The Upper Lias rests with a slight non-sequence on the Marlstone. Occasionally a condensed horizon has been observed at the base, but the lack of exposure limits the information available. Much of the Upper Lias is composed of silts and fine sands of the Cotswold Sands. These are exposed in a lane cutting leading from North Nibley to the quarry on Nibley Knoll. The thickness is 120ft at Nibley but a maximum thickness of 230ft is known from Stinchcombe. North of Stroud the Sands thin rapidly and give way to the Upper Lias Clay, which thickens northeastwards to reach 270ft at Cleeve Hill. It then thins again towards Moreton-in-Marsh. Above the Cotswold Sands in the South Cotswolds is a series of condensed beds known collectively as the Cephalopod Bed because of the abundance of ammonites and belemnites.

An interesting feature of the Upper Lias deposits is that detailed stratigraphic correlation based on ammonites has shown that the sands, clays and Cephalopod Bed are diachronous (Buckman, 1889). In Fig 4

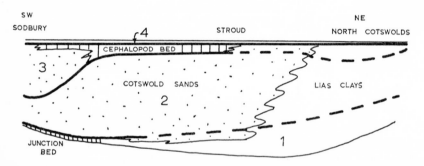

Fig 4. Diagram to show the relationship between the lithological facies and the time-lines defined by the ammonite zones (adapted from Kellaway and Welch, 1948; zonal boundaries are shown as thick lines).

the time planes are seen to cut across the lithological boundaries. For convenience the ammonite zones have been grouped. In group 1 the condensed junction bed of the southern Cotswolds is equivalent to clays and the lower part of the Cotswold Sand at Stroud, and to clays in the North Cotswolds. The second group constitutes the lower part of the Cotswold Sands at Sodbury, the whole of the Cotswold Sands in the Wotton to Stroud area, and clays in the North Cotswolds. Group 3 is represented by the upper part of the Cotswold Sands at Sodbury plus the Cephalopod Bed from Sodbury to Stroud, sands north of Stroud, and clays in the North Cotswolds. Finally, group 4, which is the *opalinum* zone, extends across the entire area as a sandy limestone.

The southward migration of Cotswold Sand deposition during Upper

Lias times has always presented a problem of interpretation. Boswell studied the petrography of the sands and decided that their source must have been Brittany. Arkell (1933) suggested that the river which transported them to the site of deposition flowed up the Bristol Channel. Kellaway & Welch (1948) considered that the Malvern-Bath axis caused the accumulation of sand from Dursley south to the Dorset coast. Recently, Davies (1969) has carried out a detailed sedimentological study. He considers that the Cotswold Sands accumulated as back bar, bar, fore bar and tidal channel deposits. He interprets the Cephalopod Bed as a platform interior sand such as is found on the modern Bahama platform.

Inferior Oolite Series

Table 1

DETAILS OF THE INFERIOR OOLITE SERIES GENERALISED FOR
THE WHOLE COTSWOLDS
(* Indicates the absence of rocks of this age)

Stage	Ammonite Zones	Formation	Limestone-Type	Group
	Parkinsonia schloenbachi	*Clypeus* Grit	oolitic, shelly and fragmentary	
	Strigoceras truelli	non-sequence*	*	Upper
	Garantiana garantiana	Upper *Trigonia* Grit	shelly	Inferior
	Strenoceras niortensis *Teloceras blagdeni*	unconformity*	*	Oolite
Bajocian	*Otoites sauzei*	*Phillipsiana* Beds *Bourguetia* Beds		Middle
	Witchellia spp	*Witchellia* Grit Notgrove Freestone	oolitic	Inferior
	Shirbuirnia spp	Gryphite Grit	sandy, shelly	Oolite
	Hyperlioceras discites	*Buckmani* Grit Lower *Trigonia* Grit	sands and shelly shelly	
	Ludwigella concava	unconformity Tilestone Snowshill Clay Harford Sands	*	
Upper Aalenian	*Brasilia bradfordensis*	Upper Freestone Oolite Marl	oolitic variable	Lower Inferior
	Ludwigia murchisonae	Lower Freestone Pea Grit	oolitic pisolith	Oolite
	Ancolioceras spp	Lower Limestones	oolitic	
	Tmetoceras scissum	*Scissum* Beds	sandy, shelly	

This series forms the main escarpment of the Cotswolds, and it also forms the plateaux of Cleeve Hill and the North Cotswolds. Details of the succession are listed in Table 1. Nowhere are all the formations present in one outcrop. Following the long period of primarily clastic sediment accumulation in the Lower Jurassic, the Middle Jurassic is characterised by an essentially limestone or carbonate succession. The transition from clastic to carbonate can be seen in the Cephalopod Bed and the *opalinum* sandy limestones. Most of the Lower Inferior Oolite is made up of oolitic limestones with a sparry calcite cement. These form massive beds with large-scale false bedding indicating the build-up of oolith banks, and small-scale current bedding representing ripples. Fossils are sparse because the water was shallow and subject to high-energy wave disturbance. However, within the sequence there is the very different rock type represented by the Pea Grit. It takes its name from the presence of rounded algal-carbonate growths known as pisoliths, which are set in a matrix composed of shell debris (bioclasts) and fine grained carbonate cement (micrite). The Pea Grit is scarcely represented in the south Cotswolds, but in the central area, especially around Crickley and Cleeve, it is well developed and reaches a thickness of at least 27ft. It is often richly fossiliferous.

Between the Lower and Upper Freestones is the Oolite Marl, which consists of soft marls and various limestones including fine-grained shelly and oolitic types (biomicrite, micrite and oomicrite). Fossils are common in some of the marl bands.

The highest beds of the Lower Inferior Oolite are the Harford Sands, Snowshill Clay and Tilestone. These are preserved only in the core of the Cleeve Hill 'syncline' where they reach a thickness of 42ft. Elsewhere in the Cotswolds, if they were originally deposited, they were removed during the period of slight warping and erosion which took place at the end of Lower Inferior Oolite times. Thus, there is an unconformity between the Lower and Middle Inferior Oolite.

The slight warping led to the development of very gentle fold-like structures, 'synclines' being developed at Painswick and Cleeve Hill, and an 'anticline' at Birdlip. Middle Inferior Oolite deposits are preserved only in the two 'synclinal' areas. At Painswick the succession ranges from the Lower *Trigonia* Grit to the Notgrove Freestone, while at Cleeve it extends to the top of the *Phillipsiana* Beds (Fig 5).

Further slight deformation and erosion preceded the deposition of the Upper Inferior Oolite. Two ammonite zones, *Teloceras blagdeni* and *Strenoceras niortensis*, are not represented in the succession. The Upper *Trigonia* Grit is a richly fossiliferous shelly limestone (biomicrite) with

Trigonia and *Acanthothyris*. Wherever it is exposed, it rests on an erosion surface in the underlying rocks. This is marked by the presence of borings of the bivalve *Lithophaga* and by the concentrations of oysters which commonly are cemented to the erosion surface. The *Clypeus* Grit rests conformably on the Upper *Trigonia* Grit but there is a non-sequence or break in time between the two. Several limestone types are represented in the *Clypeus* Grit and fossils are commonly abundant.

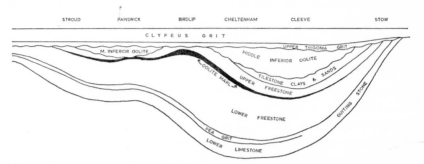

Fig 5. Diagram to show the relationship of the members within the Inferior Oolite Series. The vertical scale is much exaggerated and gives a false impression of the degree of folding (modified from Arkell, 1933).

The Inferior Oolite series shows a thickening in the Cheltenham–Cleeve Hill area which coincides with the axis of the basin of Mesozoic sediments shown in Fig 2. However, there is no reason to believe that the topography of the sea floor during Inferior Oolite times in any way resembled a basin. The Lower Inferior Oolite oolitic sands (oosparites) probably formed submarine shoals in a high-energy, tropical, marine or slightly hypersaline sea. The Pea Grit has been interpreted by Arkell (1933) as representing a coral reef, but corals are not very common. It seems probable that the environment was sublittoral with perhaps a few feet of water. It was too disturbed to permit algae to form a continuous cover on the sediment surface but not so disturbed to prevent the growth of the algae on the shell fragments to form pisoliths (Murray, 1969).

The Harford Sands and Snowshill Clays represent a brief return to clastic deposition, although the Tilestone is an oolitic limestone.

During Middle Inferior Oolite times fine sand was being contributed to the area and the limestones are mainly shell debris types. These probably formed under shallow-shelf sea conditions with a water depth greater than 20ft and, therefore, too deep for the formation of ooliths. The only oolitic phase was during the Notgrove Freestone time.

Likewise shallow-shelf sea conditions probably existed during Upper *Trigonia* Grit and *Clypeus* Grit times, although during the latter period shallowing of the sea is indicated by the presence of ooliths and intra-clasts (fragments eroded from penecontemporaneous sediments).

To summarise, throughout Inferior Oolite times the sea was shallow. Therefore, the greater thickness of sediments observed in the Cheltenham–Cleeve Hill area is due primarily to more rapid subsidence of the sea floor, with which sedimentation kept pace. At the edges of the basin, around Moreton-in-Marsh and the Mendip region, subsidence was much slower and the succession is thinner.

Great Oolite Series

This series shows even greater variety of formations and each has received a local name. Only recently, through the very thorough survey by Arkell & Donovan (1951), have the details of the complexities been revealed. The total thickness (approximately 200ft) does not vary much through-out the Cotswold area but individual formations thicken, thin and die out laterally. There is no evidence that the general basinal subsidence or the slight warping observed in the Inferior Oolite had a continued influence in Great Oolite time. A regional study of the Bathonian in southern England has shown that the Cotswold area formed part of a

Table 2

CORRELATION OF THE GREAT OOLITE SERIES IN THE COTSWOLDS
The cycles are numbered A, B, C, D, from bottom to top, with 1 = clay, 2 = oolitic limestones and 3 = porcellaneous limestones (adapted from Arkell & Donovan, 1951). See also Fig 6

Bath Area	Wotton Area	Minchinhampton Area
Forest Marble D_1 Bradford Clay	D_2 Wychwood Beds Acton Turville Beds	Wychwood Beds Bradford Fossil Bed
C_2 Bath Stone C_2 Bath Lower Rags	C_3 Petty France White Limestone Kemble Beds	Kemble Beds (in Forest Marble facies)
C_1 Upper Fuller's Earth (Lansdown Clay) Somerset Fuller's Earth Rock	B_3 Tresham Rock B_2 Hen's Cliff Oolite and Boxwell Rock B_1 Hawkesbury Clay Cross Hands Rock	White Limestone Flaggy Oolite A_3 Minchinhampton White Limestone A_2 Minchinhampton Weatherstones
acuminata Beds Lower Fuller's Earth	*acuminata* Beds Lower Fuller's Earth	A_1 *acuminata* Beds Lower Fuller's Earth (Stroud Clay)

slowly subsiding shelf sea north of the more rapidly subsiding Dorset Basin (Martin, 1967).

Arkell & Donovan recognised three main facies : clays, argillaceous to porcellaneous limestones (usually evenly bedded), and current-bedded shelly oolitic limestones. These three facies are seen to be repeated in a regular vertical sequence from clays to oolithic limestones, to porcellaneous limestones. Altogether four of these cycles can be recognised, and these are shown in Table 2. Cycle D includes the Lower Cornbrash as the uppermost unit. Examination of Fig 6 shows that the clay in

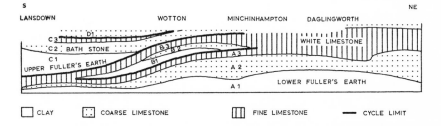

Fig 6.   Diagram to show the relationship of the members in the Great Oolite Series (adapted from Arkell and Donovan, 1951). Cycles as in Table 2.

each cycle stretches progressively less far north and that the oolitic limestones reach progressively further south. The main direction of deposition appears to be towards the south-west. It seems probable that the clay bands represent shelf seas receiving muddy sediment, that periodically oolith banks prograded into these seas from the north-east and that in the lee (ie north-east) of the oolith banks there were more sheltered clear waters in which corals and brachiopods flourished.

Quarries

Numerous quarries exist along the Cotswold scarp. None of them is actively worked at present and all are becoming overgrown to a greater or lesser extent. The majority of the quarries were worked to supply stone for local buildings. The Lower Limestone and the Lower and Upper Freestones of the Lower Inferior Oolite are oolitic limestones which do not split in any preferred direction. They can be readily cut into cubes or carved if desired. Consequently, they were formerly much in demand as building stones. Most of the scarp quarries are in these rocks. Probably the best known example is the main quarry on Leckhampton Hill, which supplied much of the stone used to build Cheltenham.

Fewer quarries were worked on the dip-slope of the Cotswolds. One that is still actively worked for shelly and oolitic limestones of the Great Oolite Series is Pike Quarry, Horsley (ST/815986). Simonds Quarry, Burleigh (SO/862014), is used as a builder's yard but can be entered with permission. There are numerous shallow workings, now completely overgrown and usually forming conspicuous copses. These mainly provided fissile limestone of the Great Oolite Series. When fresh, the stone is usually cream-coloured, but with time the stones from different localities weather to varying tints of buff to brown. The houses are commonly roofed by the greyer stone tiles from the Stonesfield Slate.

Many of the large Cotswold fields are separated by stone walls. Some of the stones will have been picked up by the farmers but generally they were obtained from narrow quarries at the edge of the fields. Shallow workings of this kind may be seen along the B4058, from the scarp edge near Wotton-under-Edge to Kingscote and further north around Trougham Common.

As there are too many quarries to describe in detail, the following localities have been selected because they show particularly fine sections.

Dursley (ST/749978)

To the west of the town is a steep hill called the Broadway. On the north side of the road is an old quarry worked at two levels. The lower quarry is cut in Lower Inferior Oolite. From the base upwards it shows massive oolitic Lower Limestone, then 9in of nodular and marly material which may be equivalent to the Pea Grit. Above is a series of hard oolitic beds separated by marly partings forming the Lower Freestone. Open gulls are well shown here. The floor of the upper quarry is probably the level of the unconformity, for the rocks above are of Upper Inferior Oolite age (see Figs 5 and 7). These are the Upper *Trigonia* and *Clypeus* Grits. Both formations are fossiliferous.

Correlation of these beds with Leigh's Quarry on Selsley Common is shown in Fig 7, with the roadside quarry at Stanley Wood (SO/826017) shown in between.

Selsley Common

On Selsley Common to the south-west of Stroud there are numerous small workings and a famous quarry known as Leigh's Quarry (SO/826025). This is not visible from the road; it lies 200yd north of Selsleyhill Farm.

Gulling is clearly seen and some of the gulls are infilled with hardened

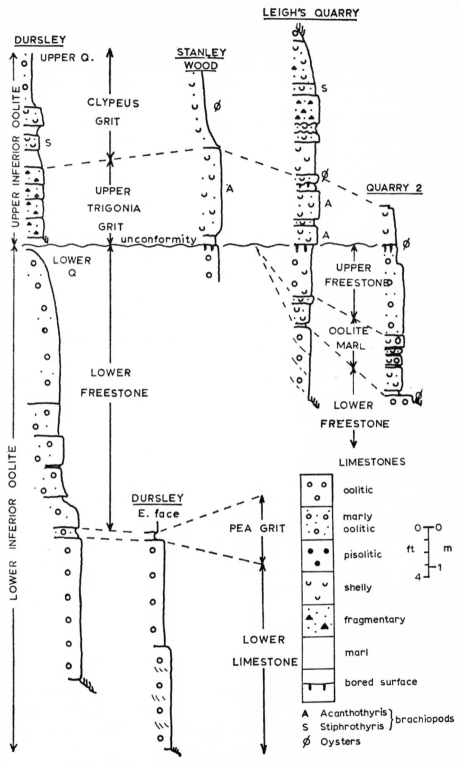

Fig 7. Quarry sections in the South Cotswolds (from Murray, 1969).

breccia. At the foot of the quarry is oolitic Lower Freestone, which shows large-scale cross-bedding. Above is the softer Oolite Marl, which forms a hollow in the cliff. This is followed by oolitic limestone of the Upper Freestone. At the top of this is a prominent bored surface encrusted with oysters. This is the unconformity or erosion surface cut into the Lower Inferior Oolite. Above are the shelly and fossiliferous Upper *Trigonia* and *Clypeus* Grits of the Upper Inferior Oolite (Figs 5 and 7). The section at Quarry 2 on Selsley Common (SO/829033) is given for comparison (Fig 7).

Leckhampton Hill (SO/939185)

This locality is famous for its quarries cut in the Inferior Oolite. The section in the main quarry extends from the Upper Lias through the Lower Inferior Oolite. It is best to examine only the lower part of the succession in this quarry. The Lower Freestone and Oolite Marl are more readily seen in the South Quarry, while the 'Ragstones' are accessible in the top quarry (Fig 8).

In the main quarry the Upper Lias Clay is usually to be seen in small temporary exposures close to the ruined buildings. Above are the *Scissum* Beds, which are shelly and sandy limestones. The Lower Limestone starts with a hard ferruginous shelly limestone and passes up into shelly rubbly limestones. The Pea Grit contains pisoliths, which are subspherical algal growths, roughly the size of a pea—hence the formation name. These beds are richly fossiliferous. The overlying Lower Freestone is an oolitic limestone in which fossils occur mainly as fragments.

The South Quarry displays a fine section of Lower Freestone. The oolitic limestone is cross-bedded with steep foresets dipping mainly to the south-west. Within these large units, which represent submarine oolith banks, there is a small-scale cross-bedding representing former ripples and small sand waves. At the southern end of this quarry the Oolite Marl can be reached. It consists of soft and hard beds of marl and marly limestones which are richly fossiliferous. Careful examination of the screes is usually rewarded by the find of well-preserved brachiopods. The section in this quarry is capped by an oolitic limestone, the Upper Freestone.

A footpath runs in a north-easterly direction across the hilltop to a small working known as the Top Quarry. Just below the floor of this quarry the top of the Upper Freestone may be seen in the cliff. This is the highest bed of the Lower Inferior Oolite exposed at Leckhampton. The top of the Upper Freestone is an unconformity representing a period

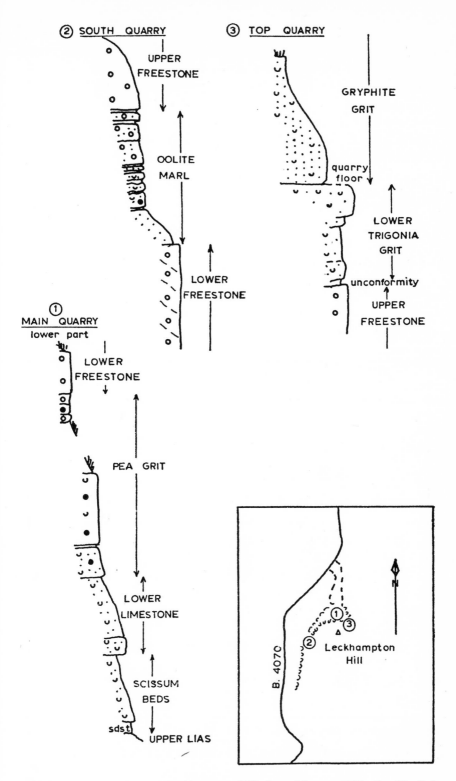

Fig 8. Quarry sections at Leckhampton Hill (from Murray 1969). See Fig 7 for key to ornament and scale.

of time when the sediment ceased to accumulate and was probably eroded to some extent. The first rocks above the unconformity are the shelly limestones of the Lower *Trigonia* Grit and these form the floor of the Top Quarry. The remainder of the succession is Gryphite Grit, a shelly limestone with abundant *Gryphaea sublobata*. These two formations belong to the Middle Inferior Oolite. No Upper Inferior Oolite is visible at this locality.

Structure

Hancock (1969) has recently discussed the structure. The regional dip of the Middle Jurassic sediments is 1° to 2° to the east or south-east. Two principal fault directions are recognised, 10° north of west

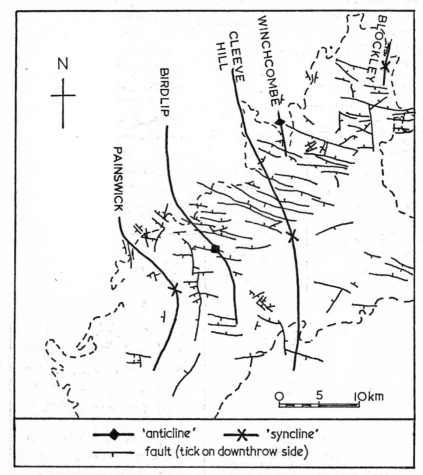

Fig 9.　Structural features of the Cotswolds (adapted from Hancock, 1969).

Page 35 *Native inhabitants:* (above) *common toad;* (centre) *pasque flower, Pulsatilla vulgaris;* (below) *adder*

Page 36 *Native inhabitants:* (above) *little ringed plover at nest;* (centre) *large blue butterfly, female laying eggs;* (below) *meadow saffron, Colchicum autumnale*

and north to south (Fig 9). The east-west faults have longer traces and are commoner. They are thought to be normal faults with an average throw of 65ft in each conjugate system.

Three fold-like structures occur within the Inferior Oolite. These are the Painswick syncline, Birdlip anticline and Cleeve Hill syncline. These folds formed during the deposition of the beds. There is no measurable difference of dip across them and it is only on diagrams such as Fig 15, with a large vertical exaggeration, that they become apparent. In the field they are shown up by the variation of bed thickness and the effects of the unconformities. The Winchcombe anticline and Blockley syncline are Tertiary folds.

Of great local significance are the superficial structures. These formed during the Quaternary, the most recent geological period. The most common are cambers, which occur where competent permeable beds such as the Inferior Oolite overlie the incompetent impermeable Upper Lias Clays. Some of the clays, when in a very moist state, are squeezed out by the overlying weight, and hence the upper beds will be lowered progressively near the scarp or valley slopes. These features can be very important in topographic appreciation as they round off hilltops which would otherwise be more angular. As the beds camber down the hillside they obtain a new dip often completely different to the regional dip. Further, owing to gravitational movement, tension stresses will open up zones of weakness such as joints to form gulls. These are mainly infilled fractures. They may be narrow or many yards in width. Eventually blocks of the competent bed will separate downslope to form isolated masses. Associated with these two movements, the strata between the gulls will rotate about their own centre of gravity, forming a steeper angle than the camber dip. This localised oversteepening is known as dip and fault structure. This may produce very steep dips with no relationship to the regional dip.

Two other superficial movements exhibited in the Cotswolds are slips and valley bulges. The former occur when the weight of the rock near a steep slope becomes too great for the underlying strata to support. Like cambering, slips usually occur when the incompetent strata become very moist, so weakening their resistance to shear, resulting in an unstable situation that is relieved by a gravity slip. Again the dip of the disturbed beds has no relationship to the regional dip.

Valley bulges occur where the differential weight of the strata on the valley sides compared with the valley floor causes lateral movement of the underlying deposits into the valley. This can produce a bulge which may show highly disturbed structure.

c

All these features can be seen in the Frome Valley. Fig 10 shows a diagrammatic section from Maiden Hill through Doverow Hill into the Frome valley. Cambered and gulled Inferior Oolite with dip and fault structure occurs on the south side of Maiden Hill. Between here and Doverow Hill, the Cotswold Sands have an apparent diminished thickness, while the almost level platform is formed by the Middle Lias Marlstone. In Doverow Hill Wood the Inferior Oolite outcrops in a quarry at 469ft, approximately 200ft lower than the same strata on Maiden Hill. This has been lowered by the Doverow Hill Slide (Ackerman & Cave, 1968). Another slide separates the strata in the Brickpit Quarry from that of Doverow Hill.

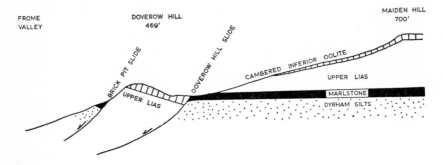

Fig 10.   Diagrammatic section of the superficial structures in the Doverow Hill area
(based on Ackermann and Cave, 1968).

These structures have been proved to be Quaternary in age (Hawkins & Kellaway, 1971, and papers listed in Kellaway, Horton & Poole, 1971). During this period the cold and wet climate produced vast quantities of water from melting snow and ice which gave high pore-pressure conditions compared with those of today. The resultant instability was relieved by the superficial movements.

The Relief of the Cotswolds

The interbedded nature of the limestones and clays influences the relief, drainage, soils and settlement. The relief of the Cotswolds is dominated by its steep scarp slope. Whilst south of Hawkesbury this is only 250ft high, in the Cheltenham region it rises 700ft and forms a distinct boundary with the Severn vale. This steep slope rises within a mile from the Lower Lias Clay to the scarp crest. To the east the dip-slope varies between 8 and 20 miles (Fig 11). As the regional dip of the

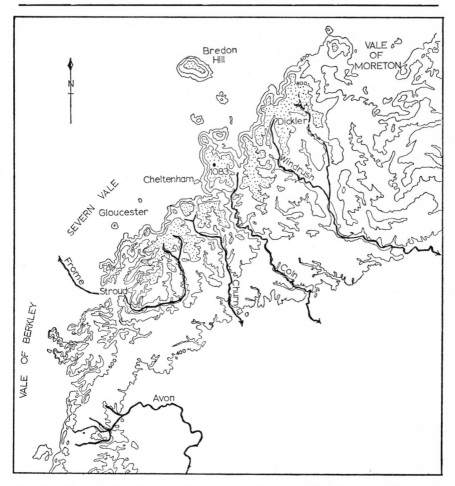

Fig 11. Generalised relief map. Contours are shown at 400, 600, and 800ft: areas over 800ft stippled.

Jurassic rocks is steeper than that of the river profiles, the dip-slope valleys pass eastwards from older to younger strata.

In the north the main scarp-forming rock is the Inferior Oolite, while in the south this becomes thinner and the presence here of the Great Oolite, in a limestone facies, means that this horizon forms the highest relief. The differential permeability of the beds cause springs and swallets. The varying height of the water table during changing weather conditions is reflected in streams lengthening as winterbornes or being reduced in length and volume over the permeable beds due to underground seepage. The water table is a subdued reflection of the relief and, consequently, with an easterly dip there are few big springs on the scarp slope. However, localised lowering of the permeable beds by cambering may help to increase spring discharge.

The soils of the Cotswolds vary greatly in character, depending mainly on their origin. Most are derived directly from the bedrock, but in the valleys alluvial deposits and scattered glacial deposits form a varied base material. In general, however, the limestones weather to give a thin brashy soil, which is referred to by the Soil Survey in their forth-coming memoir as the Sherborne Series. This soil, frequently reddish-brown in colour, may be low in calcium carbonate, due to leaching. The dry nature of the soils made them excellent sheep country, but nowadays their friable nature is utilised mainly for arable farming. On the clays the soils are deeper and their base less well defined. However, these Evesham Series of the new Soil Memoir are less well drained, and although arable farming is frequent, permanent pasture for summer grazing is characteristic.

Many of the village sites are also related to the geology and relief, being situated either at bridging sites, as spring settlements or in the valleys around shallow wells.

With two such pronounced relief features as the scarp and dip-slope, each will be described in turn. Those interested in examining the area in more detail should take the Ordnance Survey Sheets and One Inch Geological Sheets into the field, while explanations of some areas can be found in Dreghorn (1967).

Scarp Face and Dip-Slope

In order to help the reader, the scarp face will be described in a traverse from the north-east to the south-west. The River Stour valley, through the Vale of Moreton, forms a natural termination to the Gloucestershire Cotswolds.

Hidcote Hill (854ft) to the west of the Vale of Moreton is almost separated from the main Cotswolds by a tributary of the Knee brook, the Marlstone saddle being just below 500ft. In a similar manner Meon Hill (637ft) is now an outlier, although here the hill cap-rock is the Marlstone. The scarp in the Dover's and Long Hill region is really a spur, here separated from the main dip slope by the Chipping Campden Brook. At Broadway, the scarp rises from about 300ft on the Lias Plain to 1,048ft. The headwaters of the Badsey Brook have eroded a small combe south of Broadway. Geomorphologically this is still a youthful feature, with only a little flat land on the floor in the Lias clay. Between Broadway combe and Winchcombe the scarp, capped by Inferior Oolite, is generally above 900ft. However, at Lynes Barn Farm it is almost breached by the headwaters of the rivers Isbourne and Windrush, forming an air gap at 767ft.

The Winchcombe embayment has been eroded by the headwaters of the River Isbourne along the line of the Winchcombe anticline. This structure has facilitated erosion, resulting in a broad, undulating clay floor to the combe with steep eastern and western slopes up to 15°. The size of the enclave is accentuated by the Cleeve Hill spur and the outliers of Oxenton, Alderton and Bredon. From the hill fort on Nottingham Hill (915ft) the view across the Severn vale to the Malverns is very impressive. Langley Hill (901ft), capped by Inferior Oolite, is separated from Nottingham Hill by the Prescott saddle at about 560ft; indeed, this probably would have been lower if the Marlstone band was less resistant. Between the main spur and the Marlstone-capped outlier of Dixton Hill (537ft) is a Liassic vale, followed by the main railway line. To the northwest, Oxenton Hill (734ft) forms another outlier. The southern and south-western limits are fault controlled, but with the southerly dip, erosion has produced gentle slopes here compared with the scarp slope. Alderton Hill (674ft) is capped by the Upper Lias and consequently has a shorter potential life span than those capped by Inferior Oolite.

The largest of the Cotswold outliers, Bredon Hill, rises to almost 1,000ft in the north-west, where steep scarp slopes of 20° occur. The slopes are sometimes accentuated by the blackwalls of old slips. Beneath the Inferior Oolite, the Upper Lias Clay has a hummocky nature where it has been affected by a series of rotational slips. Bredon Hill has good examples of cambering and gulling. Dreghorn (1967, p 85) suggests that the King and Queen stones, petrified oolite breccia, are a gull deposit. Minor surface depressions can be observed on the dip slope, and they probably follow the line of sagging associated with large gulls. During the intense cold of the glacial periods, when the hill would have been surrounded by ice, frost heave caused disturbance of the upper brashy oolitic limestone, producing involutions which can now be seen in some quarry faces.

The highest point of the Cotswolds is Cleeve Hill, 1,083ft. From here the panoramic view on a clear day makes the walk worthwhile. Here, owing to the depositional syncline, the Inferior Oolite has the thickest succession anywhere in the Cotswolds. Southwards to the River Chelt the scarp trends north-south and forms the eastern boundary of the town of Cheltenham.

Immediately south of the A40, which runs up the River Chelt valley, the scarp is dominated by Leckhampton Hill (967ft). Here, as elsewhere in the region, the Marlstone forms a platform near the foot of the Cotswolds. Above this the impermeable Upper Lias clays are overlain by the waterbearing strata of the Inferior Oolite, and, consequently, many successive slips have occurred on steep slopes, giving them a hummocky appearance. The upper slopes are dominated by the old quarry walls; the quarrying began in the latter part of the eighteenth century. To the non-geologist, the Devil's Chimney is the most outstanding feature of this area. This rock pinnacle, of Lower Freestone, was probably left by the quarrymen as some sort of monument. The suggestion that it was left because it was of inferior stone is doubtful, as poor quality stone would not be so localised. Such a pinnacle is inherently unstable, and in this case erosion along the vertical joints will speed its destruction and hence, by the end of the century, Cheltenham may have lost its famous landmark. The typical exfoliation weathering of massive oolitic limestone has produced thick screes around much of the non-quarried hill, where slopes are often about 30°, approximately the angle of repose. Although some open joints can be seen at Leckhampton Quarries, these are better exhibited at Salterley Grange Quarry, together with cambered, gulled, and dip and fault structures. Charlton Kings Common, the steep northern slope of Leckhampton Hill, also exhibits superficial phenomena. Sagging associated with the gull and dip and fault structure produces a hummocky scarp edge. Old slip masses, such as Mountain Knolls Wood at the eastern end, now appear as almost isolated masses (Dreghorn, 1967, p 101).

Two miles to the south-west is Crickley Hill. Here the famous craggy slope is noted as being one of the finest exposures of Pea Grit in Britain. The strata here are almost horizontal, clearly demonstrated in the Devil's table, a naturally eroded bedding plane surface. Generally, the beds, although well jointed, have not cambered much, but in the quarry to the north this structure becomes more pronounced. From Barrow Wake splendid views across the Severn vale can be enjoyed without leaving one's car if parked on the A417 between Air Balloon Inn and Birdlip. Beneath Barrow Wake and to the south of the A436, hummocky ground reminiscent of successive slips dominates the lower slopes. Evidence of recent movements causing fresh backwalls of 2 to 3ft is visible. The fact that the land is below the main spring line is indicated by the ridged and furrowed nature of the better cultivated fields even on 5° slopes. Elsewhere the hummocky wet fields have rough pastureland.

To the west of Birdlip is the Witcombe embayment. Here the floor of the combe, below 350ft, is formed of Lower Lias, from which the southern end rises with slopes up to 20° to over 900ft in Witcombe Wood. To the west the scarp slope descends from 984ft on Birdlip Hill to a little over 750ft at The Buckholt, where the headwaters of the Painswick brook, a tributary of the Frome, have incised back nearly to the scarp edge. This leaves a narrow ridge connecting with the Great Oolite-capped High Brotheridge (927ft) and Cooper's Hill. Fiddler's Elbow Quarry on the edge of the A46 exhibits many features of superficial movement, with dips up to 65°. The Painswick brook, running approximately parallel with the scarp slope, will in time separate High Brotheridge, Painswick Hill and Scottsquar Hill from the main Cotswolds.

To the south the relief is influenced by the changing thickness of the varying geological formations. The Great Oolite becomes more important and frequently forms the scarp crest, with a subsidiary scarp overlooking the Inferior Oolite platform.

Painswick Hill (929ft) is a visitor's paradise, with shady off-road parking and brushwood and forested slopes to wander over. The Lower Inferior Oolite in Painswick Beacon Quarry dips westerly up to 40° owing to the cambering of the Inferior Oolite in the Holcombe valley. However, to the south in Catbrain Quarry the beds dip eastwards into the Painswick valley, giving a false impression of an anticlinal structure. In the northern part of the quarry the 9–15in wide gulls have been infilled with debris frequently very rich in ooliths, while the smaller 3–6in gulls have remained as voids. Dip and fault structure is observed here but better seen at the southern end of the quarry, where gulls up to 7ft wide are infilled with reddish-brown silty sand and angular oolitic fragments. Owing to the superficial structures, the beds have a vertical displacement up to 10ft, resembling faulted strata. A careful examination of the joint surfaces reveals calcite veining, frequently with horizontal ridges. These are interpreted as depositional features associated with the level of the water table during the Pleistocene. Hancock (1969) pointed out that they were formed before the superficial movements.

The views from Scottsquar Hill and Haresfield Beacon (713ft) are again excellent, although from the former visibility may be obscured by the wooded hillsides. South in the woods on Maiden Hill is an old quarry exhibiting superficial displacements, which have previously been described. This is an excellent area for examining these structures and realising how unstable the area must have been during the rapid incision of the River Frome.

North of the River Frome small tributary valleys such as Painswick, Slad and Toadsmoor have their own particular beauty. In this deeply incised area the rocks on the valley sides have suffered Pleistocene movements as a result of rapid incision and oversteepening beyond their stable equilibrium. This is also common to the south, as in Burleigh Quarry on Minchinhampton Common.

To the south-west of Stroud is Selsley Common (689ft) and Bown Hill (763ft). Again from here the views across the Severn vale are excellent and it is a popular spot for visitors. In this region, especially in Stanley Wood, the scarp is probably at its steepest, with slopes of 25°. This lower but steep scarp slope continues southwards and contrasts with the higher more gentle slope of the north Cotswolds.

At Uley the headwaters of the River Cam have eroded a valley with an almost north-south alignment, similar in direction to the Painswick and Slad valleys. The steeper slopes here of the scarp and of the outliers of Cam Long Down and Downham Hill are due to the weak cohesion of the Cotswold Sands. Slips have also accentuated the slope angle. Higher up the slope, Fuller's Earth mudflows have covered some of the original floors of the tributary valleys.

South of Uley the Dursley spur, like that at Cleeve Hill, breaks the line of the Cotswolds. This spur is in process of destruction and at one point is only just wide enough to take the A4135.

If the visitor walks to Stinchcombe Hill (719ft) on a clear day, he is rewarded with views of the vale of Berkeley. Below can be seen the wide Marlstone platform on which many of the settlements such as Stinchcombe, North Nibley and Wotton-under-Edge are situated (see Fig 3).

In this region the scarp crest is capped by Great Oolite and consequently the scarp slope is broken into a series of steep slopes and platforms. Thus at Wotton-under-Edge the Marlstone scarp is followed by the dip-slope terrace before the steep rise over the Cotswold Sands. On these steep slopes strip lynchets are common because of their easily worked friable soil. Above, the slope flattens on to the dip-slope of the Inferior Oolite before rising again west of The Ridings over the Fuller's Earth on to the Great Oolite dip-slope.

To the south of Wotton-under-Edge two other deep valleys cut the scarp edge before the scarp takes an almost north-south alignment, forming a fairly straight wall overlooking the Bristol coalfield. The northern of these valleys, Ozleworth Bottom, is asymmetric, with subsidiary valleys on the north but steep slopes to the south. An examination of the northern slopes shows that many of the valleys are floored with mudflows, the one south of Newark Park originating in a large slip just west of the park house. The southern side of the valley also has large slips, clearly exhibited at Hens' Cliff.

Dip-Slope

The undulating topography of the dip slope with its characteristic drainage of dry headwater valleys and its area of good farm land rich in big estates will not be described in the same detail as the scarp slope, although some description will be made of interesting river valleys.

Rivers

The Dikler valley, north-west of Stow-on-the-Wold is greatly influenced by the geology. The valley begins in the area of Springhill House and for 2 miles to the Jockey Stable Cottages it follows a dry depression eroded through the Inferior Oolite and floored with the Cotswold Sands. In this section through Bourton Downs the sands are sufficiently permeable and above the normal water table that only in wet weather does this portion of the valley become a winterborne. Below here the valley continues within the Cotswold Sands, but a surface stream is generally present; presumably it is here that the valley floor intercepts the water table. South of The Warren an east-west fault lowers the Inferior Oolite to form the bedrock at the valley floor and once again the stream passes underground. Hence between Hinchwick and Banks Fee Farm the dry valley in the Inferior Oolite becomes broader. Downstream at Banks Fee Farm, when the river reaches the base of the Inferior Oolite, it becomes a surface feature flowing through Stow-on-the-Wold.

The valley of the River Windrush begins at Oat Hill (921ft) on the southern side of the Broadway combe. Whilst it does not form a clear scarp saddle, the valley through the Inferior Oolite has no catchment area. This, and similar examples, is considered by some to be an indication that the rivers originated on the Welsh hills. However, it is more probable that these air gaps were cut during the glacial period. It is known that ice penetrated the vale of Moreton to the east and the Severn plain to the west. Whilst the thickness of this ice is not known, it is likely that melt water eroded the valleys, thus causing many of them to be 'misfits'.

South of Field Barn, where the floor of the valley is about 750ft, there are several streams which form the headwaters of the River Windrush. Between Temple Guiting and Naunton the valley is characteristically asymmetric, being steeper on the east, owing to uniclinal shifting. Downstream the river flows through the village of Bourton-on-the-Water, situated where the River Windrush leaves the valley to join the flood plain of the Dikler.

In the same way as the River Windrush begins near the Broadway combe, the Coln rises near Brockhampton just south of the Winchcombe embayment. From here the River Coln continues to flow on the Upper Lias until Withington. The steeper eastern side of the valley is influenced by the uniclinal shift, while the size and shape is controlled by the cap-rock and disposition of the strata due to faulting. South of Withington the river flows over the Inferior and Great Oolites and consequently is narrower and more steeply sided. The sinuous valley takes a south-easterly course and, since the dip of the strata is steeper than the gradient of the river, it flows over progressively younger rocks. Where the A433 crosses the Coln lies the village of Bibury, a settlement of special attraction.

Richardson (1930, p 41) drew attention to the changing position of the headwaters of the Ampney brook. Generally it is near where the A433 crosses the valley, but during wet periods, when the water table is higher, the Winterwell extends the stream about 3 miles up the valley. In dry periods the stream above Ampney Park can become almost water-less; the permanent source is the Ampney Springs with a discharge of over 3 million gallons a day. Once the stream leaves the Great Oolite it becomes permanent.

To the west the headwaters of the River Churn rise near the scarp within a mile of the Lilley brook, a tributary of the Severn. The river begins at Seven Springs, 1½ miles south-east of Leckhampton Hill; some people consider this to be the source of the Thames. Running south-wards, the Churn valley is gentle-sided on the Upper Lias and, as with the Coln, the width and nature of the valley are much affected by the east-west faulting. South of Cowley the river turns eastwards, parallel to the fault orientation, until at Colesbourne it returns to a southerly course. Like many of the Cotswold streams it receives water from springs but loses water by seepage. Richardson (1930, p 42) records gauging by Simpson who in 1859 measured a 2·9 million gallons a day discharge at Colesbourne on the Upper Lias. The discharge had diminished to 0·4 million gallons per day at North Cerney on the Inferior Oolite, less than 4 miles downstream.

Avon and Frome Valleys

There is insufficient space to describe all the Cotswold valleys but mention must be made of two others, the Bristol Avon and the Stroud Frome.

In the country between Tetbury and Wootton Bassett it is frequently difficult, without reference to the map, to know whether the streams flow into the River Thames or River Avon. The streams to the south and west of Wootton Bassett flow to the Avon, whereas those to the north-east flow to the Thames. The source of the River Avon is again a topic of dispute. Some authorities quote Joyce's Pool at Didmarton, and others Cow Down Springs. It is interesting to note that the Ordnance Survey differs with the scale of its maps. On the 1in sheet Cow Down Springs is put in blue yet the wet course is taken another mile upstream. On the $2\frac{1}{2}$in sheet Joyce's Pool is shown in blue as the source. Once again, it is the problem of the winterborne, the spring discharge depending on the height of the water table. The present writers, however, would prefer to consider the River Avon beginning in one of the streams near Little and Old Sodbury within $\frac{1}{2}$ mile of the scarp.

The River Frome valley begins approximately 100yd south of the Witcombe embayment in the scarp face, although there is no marked saddle in the hillside. From here the valley in the Inferior Oolite, usually about 200ft deep, runs southwards to Sapperton, where it turns westwards and deepens. This wooded valley is very attractive, with much of the land belonging to large estates. In the section through Francombe Wood Valley bulge structures have been described by Ackermann & Cave (1968). The floor of the valley is here on Inferior Oolite, seen in some swallow holes. This rock has been penetrated, owing to differential lateral move-ment of the incompetent Upper Lias silts and clays, to give a bulge 25ft high. The fact that this bulge is still present indicates little erosion in this part of the valley and stresses the recent nature of some of these superficial movements.

Like the Bristol Avon, the River Frome begins on the dip-slope before turning west and eroding a deep valley through the scarp slope. In neither case is the reason for this known.

Notes to this chapter are on pages 299–300.

2

Wild Life

C. M. Swaine

THE COTSWOLDS comprise an escarpment of oolitic limestone with a rich diversity of habitats occupied by plants and animals in great variety. The vegetation is strongly influenced by the nature of the climate and soil conditions, while animals are directly or indirectly dependent upon plants for concealment, shelter, breeding places and food. Every type of vegetation, therefore, tends to have its characteristic population of animals.

A living community, however, is never a completely stable association. Its composition is in a dynamic state and any considerable change in the conditions of life inevitably results in a major adjustment in the living population.

This automatic process of reorganisation is named *seral change* and the final result, reached, perhaps, after a long period in which the community is 'left to itself', is termed the *natural climax*. This, over most of the Cotswolds, appears to be some kind of deciduous forest, with beech the predominant tree. Something approaching the natural climax is seen today in the beautiful beechwoods along the western edge of the escarpment, but even these are not in their primeval state, and there is really no truly natural vegetation left on the Cotswolds.

Man is the greatest disturbing influence and the usual effect of human technology has been to stop or redirect the process of seral change, with the consequent setting up of unnatural equilibria. These *deflected climaxes* are to be seen all over the Cotswolds. Larch plantations, grazed downland, roadside verges, trout streams, lawns and, most extensive of all, the various types of farmland are all instances of more or less man-made climax communities. Past and present processes leading to this situation may now be outlined.

Origins of Wild Life

The Cotswolds, like the rest of Britain, acquired most of their present-day species by recolonisation, following wholesale exterminations during the Pleistocene ice ages.

The last of four glaciations began some 70,000 years ago and ended rather abruptly about 8000 to 10000 BC. The southern fringe of the ice reached South Wales and the Bristol Channel, but the Cotswolds were free from glacier ice except for a rather small incursion in the north.

At various intervals during the Pleistocene there were land connections between southern England and Europe. A considerable surface of dry land was also present at times off southern and western Ireland and in the Irish Sea. All these unglaciated regions presumably served as 'refuge areas' for certain kinds of plants and animals which later spread back into Britain as the ice and tundra conditions finally receded northwards.

It seems unlikely that the western refuge areas contributed much to the present-day Cotswold flora and fauna, but it is possible that such western species as the rusty-back fern, western gorse, greater and lesser horseshoe bats and the rare large blue butterfly fall into this category. (See Appendix, p 300, for scientific names.)

By far the greatest number of species, both plant and animal, now found in this part of England, arrived here across the land connection in the south-east, a link with the Continent of Eurasia which was finally severed by a rising sea level about 5500 BC.

By that time, when Britain became an island, more than 90 per cent of our modern land and fresh-water species had spread from north-western Europe into this country, and the Cotswolds lay well in the path of the advancing wave of life.

The current British distribution of many species of plants and of some animals shows a marked south-eastern tendency, thus reflecting their origins from that direction (Fig 12). A few good examples of plants in this category which occur on the Cotswolds are traveller's joy, pasque flower, wild parsnip, common broomrape, nettle-leaved and clustered bellflowers and the bee orchid.

Animal examples are more difficult to find, largely because insects, birds and bats may have flown across to Britain after submersion of the land bridge. However, butterflies such as the white-letter hairstreak, chalk-hill blue, Adonis blue and the dragonfly *Orthetrum cancellatum*, show distribution similar to those of the plants mentioned above, and perhaps for the same reason (Fig 12).

Once Britain became separated from Europe further arrivals of plants and of non-flying animals must have been few until man began, accidentally and intentionally, to introduce one new species after another.

By 3000 BC Neolithic man was becoming numerous in Britain, and about this time forest clearance increased rapidly in importance. Cultivation of the land appears to have developed first on the light easily managed chalk soils and it seems very probable that the oolite of the Cotswolds, so similar to chalk in many ways, was treated similarly at about the same time. By the Bronze Age, some 1500 BC much of the Cotswolds had probably been cleared of its open forest, and various weeds of cultivation became increasingly numerous as the centuries passed. Dock, cornflower, good King Henry and ratstail plantain are all examples of early arrivals.

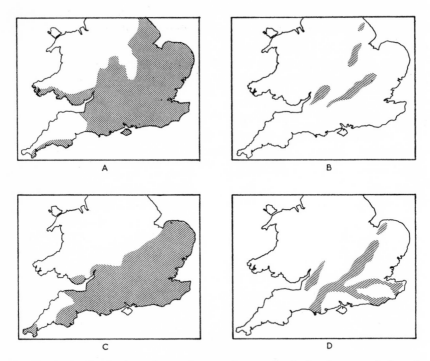

Fig 12.   Main distributions of two plants and two animals showing a marked south-eastern tendency. (A) Wild Parsnip (*Pastinaca sativa*). Widespread in the south-east. Common on the Cotswolds; (B) Pasque flower (*Pulsatilla vulgaris*). Restricted to chalk and limestone (strongly calciphile); (C) Black-lined Orthetrum dragonfly (*Orthetrum cancellatum*). Common in Cotswold gravel pits; (D) Chalk-hill blue butterfly (*Lysandra coridon*). Restricted to chalk and limestone. Locally common on the Cotswolds.

In Roman times a number of other plants appeared for the first time : corn marigold, corn-cockle, scarlet pimpernel and ground elder are cases in point. Species introduced still more recently, which have spread to the Cotswolds, include the Oxford ragwort, first noted at Oxford in 1794, the pineapple weed, introduced in the nineteenth century and now abundant, and Canadian waterweed, currently plentiful after its arrival in Britain in 1842.

During the same period the region has also acquired its quota of animals brought into Britain by human agency. Of the majority no detailed records exist, for the arrival of small animals in timber and other merchandise often passed unnoticed in the early stages of colonisation. Well known examples are cockroaches, bacon beetles and clothes' moths.

More is known of the history of larger animals. House mice, fallow deer and pheasants were perhaps all brought in by the Romans. The Roman pavement at Woodchester, near Stroud, depicts a ring-necked pheasant, but it is not certain that the birds were actually imported at that time.

More important invasions were by black rats in the twelfth century AD and brown rats 600 years later. No black rats are found on the Cotswolds today, but they once formed the main reservoir of bubonic plague which infected our forebears. The Black Death in 1348 may have killed as much as half the human population of Gloucestershire, thereby creating such a shortage of labour on the Cotswolds that a major shift took place from cereal growing to sheep rearing, thus promoting the rising wool trade.

Relatively recent arrivals include the little owl, grey squirrel and American mink. The first two of these were released in Britain late in the nineteenth century and reached Cotswold country about 1910 and 1930 respectively. The mink has been spreading in Britain following escapes from fur farms and by the end of 1971 had been noted on at least four Cotswold streams.

Very few animal species have crossed unaided into Britain since the submergence of the land connection some 7,500 years ago. Birds are naturally the most likely to do so and two recent conquests of England have provided new species for the Cotswolds also. The little ringed plover, formerly a very rare vagrant to Britain, was first found breeding in this country in 1938 and colonised gravel pits on the Cotswolds in 1952. The collared dove, reaching England in 1955, had spread to various parts of the Cotswolds by 1963 and is now a common bird.

Insects which cross to Britain and reach the Cotswolds more or less regularly include the painted lady, red admiral and clouded yellow butterflies, the silver-Y moth and the humming-bird hawkmoth. Most of these insects fail to survive the English winter, but they illustrate ways in which our country may still acquire new species without the intervention of man.

The events of the past million years which have had the greatest influence on the development of Cotswold wild life may, therefore, be summarised broadly as comprising four critical phases :

(a) Glacial or sub-glacial conditions which left relatively little plant and animal life in the region. This period ended 10000 to 8000 BC.

(b) The final retreat of the ice, closely followed by plant and animal colonisation, mostly across the land connection from Europe. This phase lasted from about 9000 to 5500 BC.

(c) The submersion of the land connection about 5500 BC, leaving Britain as an island.

(d) The rise of human population leading to an ever-increasing influence on wild life, the primary effects being due to forest clearance and to cultivation.

The Cotswolds had been formed in a shallow sea, followed by elevation above the water, long before the ice ages of the Pleistocene period. Jurassic limestone is about 130 to 150 million years old, and the effects of the calcareous nature of Cotswold rocks must have been felt throughout the four phases referred to above. This influence on plant and animal life is still so great that its general importance deserves some attention.

Effect of Limestone on Wild Life

Like chalk the oolitic limestone contains a very high proportion of calcium carbonate. This has marked effects on both physical and chemical properties of soils, which tend to be light, well aerated, well drained and markedly alkaline. These soil conditions account for the rarity or total absence on the Cotswolds of certain plants such as bell heather, bilberry, ling and wavy hair-grass, which are intolerant of limy material in the soil and are often known as 'calcifuges'. On the other hand, various so-called 'calciphile' or 'calcicole' plants are more or less restricted to base-rich soils such as those of this district. An even larger number of species appear to thrive better and to be more abundant on such soils, while not being absolutely restricted to them. The Cotswolds comprise one of the finest areas in Britain for 'calciphile' vegetation, and the more important of these plants are listed in Table 3.

Table 3

IMPORTANT CALCIPHILE FLOWERING PLANTS

Pasque flower	Basil thyme
Cotswold penny-cress	Clustered bellflower
Hairy violet	Squinancywort
Chalk milkwort	Wayfaring tree
Common rock-rose	Small scabious
Common buckthorn	Woolly thistle
Kidney vetch	Dwarf thistle

Page 53 (above left) *Head of Minerva found at Kingscote churchyard,* (right) *Head of Minerva, left side;* (below) *Quenington: the wonderful Norman tympanum over the north doorway of the parish church. One opinion holds that it illustrates Rev, xx, 2–13, with Satan bound, one figure rising out of the sea, one from Hell out of the mouth of Satan, and the other from death. The face in the sun represents God the Father*

Page 54 (left) *Deserted medieval village, Lower Ditchford, near Blockley;* (below) *Stow-on-the-Wold, the market place showing the cross and Edward's House*

Purple milk-vetch	Lily of the valley
Horseshoe vetch	Angular Solomon's seal
Sainfoin	Broad helleborine
Dropwort	Violet helleborine
White beam	Musk orchid
Spurge-laurel	Bee orchid
Bastard toadflax	Fly orchid
Yellow-wort	Burnt-tip orchid
Felwort	Pyramidal orchid
Deadly nightshade	Upright brome
Dark mullein	Tor-grass
Knapweed broomrape	Crested hair-grass
Large wild thyme	Meadow oat
Marjoram	Downy oat

Some species have been omitted on the grounds that they are less consistently calciphile, and a few more are excluded on account of their rarity or extremely local Cotswold occurrence.

The dependence of animals on limestone and chalk soils is usually more indirect, as illustrated by the following Cotswold examples. The chalk-hill blue and Adonis blue butterflies depend for their larval food chiefly on the horseshoe vetch and are thus found in the habitats of this plant. The rufous grasshopper occurs almost exclusively on calcareous slopes but seems not to depend on any one food plant. The reason for its restricted habitat is thus not so obvious as in the case of the butterflies, and a fully satisfactory explanation cannot be given at present. The glow-worm is widespread and quite a common beetle on the Cotswolds. Although not limited to calciphile vegetation, it is certainly more plentiful there. This insect feeds on small snails which do best on lime-rich ground where material for their shells is readily available. The glow-worm is therefore most often found where its food is plentiful.

The direct and indirect importance of limestone in the lives of plants and animals will emerge frequently in the following consideration of the various major habitats of the Cotswold hills and valleys.

Woodlands

The wooded country of this district falls into two main groups—the semi-natural beechwoods of the steep *escarpment face* and a variety of mixed deciduous woodlands, much more extensively influenced by man, on the long Cotswold *dip-slope* which falls gently eastwards.

The best scarp edge beechwoods are found between Birdlip in the north and Dursley to the south. They lie almost entirely on the inferior oolite and strongly resemble the 'beech-hangers' of the south-eastern

D

chalk downs. Their tall grey trunks support the dense canopy so typical of beech trees, and both the shrub layer and the ground vegetation are often very scanty. The major reason for this is that the canopy cuts off a great deal of the light, whose intensity at ground level in summer is often below 5 per cent of full illumination and may fall as low as 1 per cent. Beech trees also produce deep leaf-litter and their fine roots are massed close to the surface of the soil thus tending to prevent the growth of small plants.

Provided that the light intensity is not too low, however, a characteristic ground flora develops. The dominant plant is usually sanicle or ivy, but may be dog's mercury. Sanicle does well on rather well-drained sloping ground; ivy often forms dense mats in deep shade and by no means always ascends the trunks of the trees. Mercury is less plentiful in these steep woods than in those of the dip slope.

Table 4

CHARACTERISTIC FLOWERING PLANTS OF THE ESCARPMENT BEECHWOOD GROUND FLORA

Stinking hellebore	Yellow birdsnest
Wood anemone	Yellow archangel
Hairy violet	Woodruff
Wood dog violet	Wall lettuce
Wood-sorrel	Herb paris
Spurge-laurel	Broad helleborine
Common enchanter's nightshade	Common helleborine
Ivy	Common twayblade
Sanicle	Birdsnest orchid
Dog's mercury	Lords and ladies
Wood spurge	Wood melick
Common wintergreen	

Other species of more or less frequent occurrence are included in Table 4, but in addition to these there are a few which call for special comment. The broad helleborine, included in Table 4, is common in some beech-woods, and there is always a chance that the rarer narrow helleborine, also white-flowered, may be overlooked among plants of the commoner orchid. There are no recent Cotswold records of this plant. The very rare red helleborine is known from a few localities, mostly in or at the edge of escarpment beechwoods. It seldom flowers in deep shade and can easily be missed when in the vegetative state.

Two saprophytes occur commonly under the beeches. These are the birdsnest orchid and the yellow birdsnest. Both are devoid of chlorophyll and subsist on leaf mould by means of an association with fungi, a 'mycorrhizal' relationship, found also in many other plants, in which each partner benefits by the activity of the other.

The animal life of the escarpment beechwoods tends to be somewhat scanty, chiefly on account of the sparseness of the ground vegetation. Most of the species of deciduous woodland birds (see Table 5) are present, but populations are small. One bird found here and there in these steep woods, but otherwise very local on the Cotswolds, is the wood warbler, whose spring arrival is heralded by its shivering song uttered high in the canopy of young leaves. This bird avoids dense ground-vegetation for nesting purposes and so finds suitable sites in the beech-hangers.

Table 5

TYPICAL BREEDING BIRDS OF THE COTSWOLD DECIDUOUS WOODLAND

Sparrowhawk	Goldcrest
Pheasant	Spotted flycatcher
Woodpigeon	Redstart
Stock dove	Robin
Turtle dove	Blackbird
Cuckoo	Song thrush
Tawny owl	Mistle thrush
Green woodpecker	Long-tailed tit
Great spotted woodpecker	Marsh tit
Lesser spotted woodpecker	Coal tit
Tree pipit	Blue tit
Wren	Great tit
Hedge sparrow	Nuthatch
Garden warbler	Tree creeper
Blackcap	Chaffinch
Whitethroat	Jay
Willow warbler	Carrion crow
Chiffchaff	

For the visitor who is prepared to search closely for smaller animals, some interesting discoveries can be made. Several species of snail which thrive in old woodland on limestone are to be found. These include *Pomatias elegans*, a terrestrial relative of the winkles, which spends much of its life buried in leaf mould; *Ena montana* (the butlin snail) which is a central European species found in the south and south-east of Britain; and *Clausilia rolphii*, a close relative of the smaller door-snail (*C. rugosa*), but much less common and more restricted in distribution.

Fascinating as are some small forms of life, the majority of naturalists concentrate their attention on larger or more easily observed creatures. Large insects are not a notable feature of the scarp edge woodlands. .

Butterflies tend to be scarce, except along the margins and rides, because their ground-living food plants are not plentiful. Two insects, however, which live in the foliage of the trees may be noted. The oak bush-cricket is the only British member of the Order Orthoptera which is fully tree-living. It is quite common on beech as well as on the oak, which appears in its English name. When seen at rest on a tree trunk in the gloom of an August beechwood, this delicate green insect seems almost to glow in the dim light. Beech leaves form a common food of the lobster moth caterpillar, quite numerous in these woods. This grotesque larva must present a fearsome appearance to a small hungry bird and, like the related puss-moth caterpillar, reinforces its self-defence by squirting formic acid at the intruder!

Thus if the escarpment beechwoods tend to be somewhat impoverished in species of plants and animals, they compensate for this, partially at least, by their stately beauty and by the presence of some scarce and unusually interesting forms of wild life. The mixed woodlands of the Cotswold dip-slope, now to be considered, are generally much richer in plant species, and, therefore, support a greater variety of animals large and small.

The dip-slope woods are mostly situated along the sides of the main valleys where the soil is deeper than on the scarp face. Although beech will do well in this situation, many of the woods have been radically altered by human interference, and the variety of tree species is much greater. The prime result is that more light reaches the ground than in pure beechwood, with the consequent development of a rich and varied flora beneath the trees.

Characteristic species in the shrub layer, which is very well developed, include the wayfaring tree, dogwood, spindle-tree, privet and hazel, all more or less calciphile species. Brambles and wild roses may be present in varying density, while traveller's joy is an abundant climber in well lit clearings.

Dominant plants in the ground flora, often forming dense carpets, are dog's mercury and sometimes enchanter's nightshade but, in all, between seventy and eighty species of herbaceous flowering plants may be said to occur more or less frequently in the fieldlayer of these mixed deciduous woodlands. They include many delightful spring flowers such as wood anemone, bluebell, various violets, bugle, ground ivy, wood spurge and yellow archangel.

In May and June lily of the valley and the very local angular Solomon's seal come into bloom. These not infrequently grow together, and the Cotswold woodlands are among the few places where the latter plant may be seen in quantity. By July deadly nightshade is in full bloom. This highly poisonous plant, with its dull purple bell-shaped flowers and large shiny black berries, is of common but rather local occurrence. High summer sees a profusion of rose-bay, hairy Saint John's wort and nettle-leaved bellflower contributing pink, yellow and blue to the colour scheme. By late August and throughout September the last and perhaps the loveliest of woodland flowers is to be found. The beautiful meadow saffron, so often misleadingly called 'autumn crocus', blossoms abundantly at this late season, the pale mauve flowers emerging leafless from the ground in woodland rides and clearings.

As summer fades into autumn, interest in wild flowers may fade also, but a new search can now develop as an increasing number of 'toadstools' appear in the woods. Fungi are active all through the summer, but a great many produce their fruiting bodies only or mainly in the autumn. As many as fifty species or more of the larger fungi may be found on a single visit to one of the richer woods at this season. The notorious death-cap toadstool, perhaps the most poisonous of fungi, is not uncommon in some years, especially in beechwoods where other allied species, also poisonous, are often present at the same time. Another fungus charac-teristic of our beechwoods and, indeed, often found under quite small clumps of trees, is the earth star (*Geastrum triplex*), which opens to a five- or six-pointed star revealing the spore-containing 'puff-ball' within.

With so great a wealth of plant life in the dip-slope woodlands, a wide range of animals may be expected. Birds are abundant and more than thirty species are regular and more or less common in spring and summer. Table 5 lists these birds, many of which, however, are not restricted to woodland habitats.

Other birds occur more sparingly. Several pairs of buzzards nest in the central and north Cotswolds and may be found for a considerable distance down the dip-slope. The scarp face cliffs in the west are too low to attract these fine raptors and virtually all Cotswold nests are in tall trees. The hobby is not a true woodland species, but small woods and clumps of trees on the sides of the main valleys provide breeding places for a few pairs of this beautiful little falcon.

Wood warblers are scarce in the dip-slope woods, probably because the ground flora is too dense, but they occur in a few beechwoods. Willow tits are uncommon but widespread, and the elusive hawfinch is reported from time to time. Woodcock have bred in woods of the central Cotswolds for some years, but appear to be few in number, while nightingales and nightjars turn up irregularly and are never numerous, the latter favouring recently cleared ground.

GLOUCESTERSHIRE COLLEGE
OF EDUCATION
LIBRARY

Woodland mammals are quite well represented. Foxes are plentiful, as may be expected in hunting country. The badger is even more of a woodland species and is common all over the Cotswolds. Much important research into the life history and habits of this interesting animal was carried out by Ernest Neal in woods near Rendcomb in the early 1940s.

Grey squirrels are abundant in deciduous forest, but our native red squirrels, after a long period of decline, finally disappeared from the Cotswolds between 1945 and 1950. The common rodents in the woods are the wood mouse and bank vole. Dormice may occur in some places where hazel is present, but there appear to be no satisfactory recent reports of this pretty little creature.

The larger wooded areas of the central Cotswolds support a good population of fallow deer. The little muntjac has also been reported occasionally from 1960 onwards and roe deer appear to have spread on to the Cotswolds about the same time. Neither of these smaller species is yet common.

Noticeable and attractive woodland insects include certain butterflies. The most widespread of these is the speckled wood, while four species of the fritillary group are found more or less regularly in these habitats. The first to appear in spring is the pearl-bordered fritillary, followed in June by the more local small pearl-bordered. In some woods the large and handsome silver-washed fritillary is not uncommon in July and high brown fritillaries appear about the same time, but seem to be of very local occurrence. Three other butterflies are to be seen here and there. The rarest of the three on the Cotswolds is the white admiral, for which there seem now to be few localities. Purple and white-letter hairstreaks are local but not uncommon. The former favours old oak trees, not necessarily in woods, and the latter is often to be seen feeding on bramble flowers in the vicinity of elm trees.

The long list of woodland moths includes such large species as the lime, poplar, eyed and privet hawkmoths, the attractive leopard moth, whose caterpillar lives inside the branches of trees, and the handsome lunar hornet clearwing, which mimics a large wasp or hornet in appearance. Its larva is also a wood-feeder, living within willow or poplar stems. The caterpillars of another and smaller species, the orange-tailed clearwing, live inside the stems of the wayfaring tree and the emergence holes are usually the first indication one finds of the presence of this insect.

Woodland margins often provide the richest variety of plants and animals, especially if the adjacent ground is calcareous downland. The intermediate marginal land between these two communities is much favoured by butterflies of both habitats and the chirp of the dark bush-cricket is a familiar sound during late summer in some places. Birds such as the lesser whitethroat, grasshopper warbler, bullfinch and tree pipit find suitable breeding places here, while plants of this scrubby grassland include the fly orchid, woolly thistle and deadly nightshade.

Oolitic Downland

Downland communities tend to be present on the Cotswolds wherever there is steep uncultivated ground free from woodland. They are therefore most commonly found along the western slopes of the escarpment overlooking the Severn, and on the sides of the innumerable little dry valleys or 'bottoms' of the Cotswold dip-slope. The ground in these areas is so steep that cultivation has proved impracticable or too costly, and such terrain has therefore been used for many centuries as rough grazing for sheep and cattle, a privilege shared, until the 1950s, with a multitude of rabbits.

Soils on the downs are of the type termed *rendzina*—shallow, well drained, alkaline and fertile, with rich topsoil grading directly to the parent limestone beneath. Under these conditions of soil and grazing a highly typical flora develops, consisting basically of grassland with a large number of other characteristic species.

Dominant grasses are sheep's fescue, red fescue, upright brome and tor-grass, according to the degree of grazing pressure. Other grasses commonly present include the meadow and downy oats, crested hair-grass and quaking-grass.

Many of the characteristic downland plants were included in Table 3, which gives a list of species that thrive on the Cotswold limestone. Some of these deserve special mention at this point.

Several plants are almost exclusively calciphile. These are exemplified by chalk milkwort, clustered bellflower, bastard toadflax (which is a partial parasite on roots of various herbs), and the beautiful pasque flower. The latter, quite a rare plant in Britain, occurs in a number of Cotswold localities, in one of which some thousands of flowers may be seen in April.

Several orchids are also very typical of oolitic downland habitats. Purple and green-winged orchids are early flowerers; the frog and bee orchids bloom in June; pyramidal and scented orchids are also plentiful but blossom a month or so later. Two other June-flowering species are much less common. The burnt-tip orchid occurs in only a few places and is nowhere plentiful, but the little musk orchid is often abundant in its scattered Cotswold localities, although quite rare in Britain as a whole.

The downland orchid season does not end until September, for the autumn lady's tresses puts out its tiny white flowers as summer draws to its close.

The highest land on the Cotswolds is the summit of Cleeve Hill (1,083 feet). Much of this large area is clothed in a limestone flora related to that already described, but one special feature is worthy of note. A small area near the summit carries an overlay of sandy material and this has been colonised by ling, which is a well known calcifuge plant (p 52). Elsewhere on the Cotswolds it can survive, with poor growth, only on ground sufficiently leached out by rain to impart a neutral or acid reaction to the soil.

Grazing is the natural grassland equivalent of lawnmowing in the garden, and if it is relaxed on any area of downland seral changes (p 48) set in. The finer grasses tend to disappear in the face of coarser species such as upright brome and especially the aggressive tor-grass, which has already succeeded in smothering many downland slopes. These grasses also gradually eliminate most of the typical downland herbs referred to above, and one of the problems of nature conservation on these hills is to ensure that adequate grazing is available at the right time to preserve interesting downland communities.

In 1954 the virus epizootic disease of myxomatosis decimated the formerly abundant rabbit population of the Cotswolds, as elsewhere in Britain. This removal of an efficient 'lawnmower' was a major ecological event which may have delighted the farming community but which raised some apprehension in the minds of naturalists. Plant and animal communities, however, are very resilient and some adjustment took place in time.

Buzzards and stoats, which often kill rabbits, declined somewhat in numbers but then recovered, and the resourceful fox seemed to take the loss of rabbits in its stride. Greater effects, however, were produced in the downland plant communities, especially as the virtual disappearance of rabbits coincided with, or followed, a period of reduction in the use of downland for the grazing of farm stock. Many plants became scarcer and more patchy in distribution in competition with coarse grasses, and this in turn has influenced the numbers of dependent animals.

Good examples are provided by the kidney vetch, horseshoe vetch and common rock-rose. The first of these is the larval food plant of the small blue butterfly; the second is required by the caterpillars of the chalk-hill and Adonis blues, and rock-rose sustains the young of the brown Argus butterfly and also those of a pretty little green moth, the Cistus forester which is often abundant on those slopes where common rock-rose is plentiful. It is evident that if these food plants are exterminated by invading tor-grass, the butterflies must also disappear.

An even more interesting case is given by the very rare large blue butterfly, which used to occur at a number of downland sites on the Cotswolds. The extraordinary life history of this insect involves egg-laying on wild thyme flowers and the transport of the tiny caterpillar by ants of certain species into their nests. Here the caterpillar feeds upon the ant larvae, finally pupating near the surface of the ants' nest.

Unfortunately wild thyme is often a casualty of downland invasion by coarse grasses, or of change in land utilisation by man, and this is sufficient to break the life cycle of one of Britain's rarest butterflies. It is doubtful whether any sites for the large blue butterfly remain on the Cotswolds, and a recent survey suggests that the Adonis blue also may have disappeared. However, the large blue is a particularly elusive insect and colonies may yet be found. Table 6 lists butterflies which are typical of the oolitic downland of the Cotswolds.

Table 6
SOME BUTTERFLIES OF THE COTSWOLD DOWNLAND

Species	Food plants
Marbled white	Various grasses
Meadow brown	Various grasses
Small heath	Various grasses
Dark green fritillary	Violets
Duke of Burgundy fritillary	Cowslip, primrose
Small blue	Kidney vetch
Brown Argus	Common rock-rose
Common blue	Birdsfoot trefoil, clovers
Chalk-hill blue	Horseshoe vetch
Adonis blue*	Horseshoe vetch
Large blue*	Wild thyme
Small copper	Dock, sorrel
Green hairstreak	Various herbs and shrubs
Dingy skipper	Birdsfoot trefoil, etc
Grizzled skipper	Wild strawberry, bramble, etc
Small skipper	Various grasses
Large skipper	Various grasses

In addition, certain migrant butterflies may be encountered, and also common species not especially associated with this habitat. The grayling butterfly is surprisingly scarce.

* Present status uncertain.

Another group of insects commonly associated with downland is the Acrididae or grasshoppers. Some kinds occur in rich grassland or even in quite damp places, but six species are to be found more or less plentifully on calcareous banks, roadside verges and in other dry grassy places. English names for these insects are not widely used and only their scientific names are unambiguous. The six species, all quite easy to identify, are given in Table 7.

Table 7
COTSWOLD DOWNLAND GRASSHOPPERS

Common field grasshopper	*Chorthippus brunneus*
Meadow grasshopper	*C. parallelus*
Common green grasshopper	*Omocestus viridulus*
Mottled grasshopper	*Myrmeleotettix maculatus*
Rufous grasshopper	*Gomphocerippus rufus*
Stripe-winged grasshopper	*Stenobothrus lineatus*

The first three in Table 7 are common over most of Britain, with the common field grasshopper preferring dry places, the meadow grasshopper found in all types of grassland, and the common green grasshopper thriving best in rich grass, and thus found along the lower edge of the downland slopes and in their moister hollows. The mottled grasshopper is really a species of heathland and sandy places, but the drier downland habitats, especially if stones break the surface, provide suitable places for this pretty little insect. The last two species in Table 7 are both closely associated with chalk or limestone vegetation and are thus the two most typical of, although not the most abundant on, the Cotswold slopes.

Visitors to these hills not infrequently remark upon a magnificent snail they see. This is the Roman snail, the largest British land species, found commonly, if somewhat locally, in this district, where it occurs in open woodland and on hedgebanks as well as on downland. Its English name reflects the belief that the Romans introduced it to Britain, but its shell is known from pre-Roman deposits.

Several smaller snails are common in the limestone grasslands, those of the genus *Helicella* often swarming in immense numbers after rain, and found glued to plants such as wild carrot and yarrow during dry periods. Anyone wandering at dusk through such places is almost sure, at the right season, to see the tiny green lights of the many glow-worms which feed upon small and medium-sized snails. The glow-worm is not a 'worm' but a beetle, and it is the wingless females which glow brightly, thereby attracting the males.

Limestone downland is not notable for its vertebrate animals. Rabbits are tending to increase again, especially where bushy ground or adjacent woodland is available, and here also is found the bank vole. In the grassland proper the field vole replaces the latter.

Depending on the extent to which bushes and scattered trees are present, and upon the density of the ground vegetation, certain birds may breed on the downland. The willow warbler is probably the most usual, but grasshopper warblers may be present if coarse grasses grow among bushes. Tree pipits prefer somewhat sparser vegetation, and the woodlark is intolerant of any but a thin cover of grasses and other plants. Woodlarks, for reasons not known, appear to have deserted their few Cotswold 'edge' localities since 1962, the decline setting in before the severe winter weather of early 1963, which cannot, therefore, be entirely to blame.

A characteristic but not always welcome vertebrate member of the downland fauna is Britain's only poisonous snake, the adder. It occurs also in woodland clearings and is widespread on the Cotswolds. The grass-snake and slow-worm (really a legless lizard) also may be found, but they are not typical of these dry banks, and prefer moister localities such as parks and gardens, the vicinity of streams and other 'mesophytic' habitats.

Agricultural Land, Roads and Villages

Farming on the Cotswolds is considered in another chapter. Here we are mainly concerned with those marginal habitats for wild life which inevitably accompany the cultivation of the land, together with the immediate environment of human dwellings.

The Cotswolds are crossed by few major roads but there is an extensive network of minor ones. Roadside verges in the open country often assume many of the characteristics of the downland discussed in the previous section. In other places the vegetation is much thicker. Most verges are adjacent to farming land and, therefore, tend to harbour weeds ot agricultural importance. This, together with the need to preserve a clear view along the roads, necessitates regular maintainance. Modern methods of spraying with selective weedkillers and of cutting the vegetation tend to reduce the variety of plant life and, therefore, of the animals which depend upon it. Verge plants such as marjoram, sainfoin and the lovely blue meadow cranesbill are much less in evidence than in former years. Whinchats and stonechats have disappeared, and the tree pipit and even the whitethroat are less plentiful than they were.

Birds closely associated with the agricultural land itself include the corn bunting, of local but widespread occurrence on these hills, and the lapwing, which is thinly distributed and much scarcer than it used to be. Stone curlews once inhabited the high open areas but disappeared many years ago. Scattered hedgerow trees encourage the breeding of kestrels and little owls, while the beautiful barn owl may still be seen wavering through the dusk like a big pale moth.

The brown hare is the most conspicuous mammal of the farm fields, the field vole and mole probably the commonest. Hares increased considerably after the decline of the rabbit population which resulted from myxomatosis. The pretty little harvest mouse, one of the tiniest of mammals, may once have been widespread in Cotswold cornfields but there appear to be no recent records.

Many weeds of agriculture are now less common than they were, for modern farming is efficient in eliminating them from growing crops and in screening out their seeds from those of crop plants. Gone are the days of red poppies in the cornfields and one may search in vain for corn-cockle, Venus's looking-glass and the pheasant's eye. However, not all farm weeds are in decline. Wild oats find intensive cereal-growing in their favour, for their fruits are very like those of cereal crops and they are no longer checked so regularly by the old practices of rotation.

All these plants and animals are in some way dependent on human activity. Several others are even more closely associated with us, thriving in and around the farm buildings and villages of the Cotswolds. Most noticeable are the birds. The various tits, nuthatches and robins which visit bird-tables are found in many other habitats, but house sparrows, swallows and house martins are closely and mainly reliant upon man, at least for their breeding places. In some villages swifts nest in the roofs of the old houses, darting at speed into the irregular crevices left between the old stone roofing-tiles. The increasing use of modern manufactured tiles has already greatly reduced the number of breeding colonies on the Cotswolds. A recent arrival is the collared dove (p 51), now occurring at many farms, villages and small towns. It thrives where grain and other seeds are available in quantity, as in hen-runs, farmyards or, in general, where seed-eating birds are kept in captivity out-of-doors.

Comparable associations with man are shown among mammals by house mice and brown rats. Both of these are perhaps still all too common in and around Cotswold farms, but recent records of mice trapped inside village houses seem to suggest that the house mouse is less common —perhaps much less common—than it used to be. Most such reports now refer to the wood mouse which comes in from the autumn cold, sometimes in numbers, and not infrequently accompanied by bank voles and even common and pygmy shrews! Interesting reports have also been made in a few places of the large and handsome yellow-necked mouse, which may well be more widespread on these hills than is generally supposed.

The picturesque old houses on the Cotswolds are built from the local stone, which varies much in building quality from place to place. There are, therefore, many old open quarries scattered over the hills. When left to themselves these acquire a number of calciphile plants such as yellow-wort, fairy flax, horseshoe vetch, carline thistle and weld. Two species are found on loose stony ground. The limestone polypody, a fern, grows here and there on small oolitic screes, as in the Postlip quarries on Cleeve Hill. The Cotswold penny-cress is a rare British plant, virtually restricted as a native to the northern Cotswolds where it occurs, sometimes abundantly, in patches of loose stone in the old quarries, on the tops of ancient stone walls and in equivalent habitats.

Some of the best Cotswold stone comes from underground, especially from the old tunnels in the vicinity of Nailsworth but also in other 'edge' localities. These former mines, penetrating far underground, form the winter resorts of several species of bat, the most characteristic being the lesser and greater horseshoe bats. The former is the commoner and more widespread in Britain, but is not plentiful on the Cotswolds. The greater horseshoe bat has a restricted distribution both on these hills and in the country as a whole. Of the small British population, perhaps no greater than 500 individuals, some three-fifths live in Gloucestershire, and many of these are on the Cotswolds.

Other species of bats found in this district are the pipistrelle, whiskered bat, noctule, barbastelle and common long-eared bat, but records of these animals are all too sparse and more data is needed. Indeed, mammals in general tend to be 'under-recorded' as compared with birds and flowering plants.

Fresh-water habitats

Important aquatic habitats on the Cotswolds are provided by the rivers and artificial lakes of the dip-slope and by the extensive system of man-made gravel pits which have become so important a feature of the upper Thames drainage system in recent years.

The chief rivers run in a south-easterly direction to join the infant Thames. For most of their course they traverse the oolitic limestone country, but some, notably the Evenlode and Windrush, have cut deeply down to the underlying lias deposits, and this is also true of the shorter streams which flow westwards off the Cotswolds into the River Severn.

The water of all these rivers is alkaline in reaction and this has its usual marked influence on flora and fauna. Most reaches of the dip-slope streams are fringed with alders, while willows, especially the crack willow and osier, are also common. The water flows steadily but gently, and fast stretches are unusual. Small meanders are frequent and the depth of water varies from a few inches over stone and gravel to several feet in the deeper pools, where the bottom is muddy.

Marginal vegetation is often dominated by a dense growth of reed-grass and yellow flag, with marsh marigold flowering in profusion in early spring. If the current is not too strong, branched bur-reed is plentiful in somewhat deeper water, while the most important hydrophyte is a species of water crowfoot, *Ranunculus pseudofluitans*, which forms thick masses trailing down the centre of the stream. In the fast stony reaches, usually no more than a few yards in extent, the only aquatic vegetation may be a few algae, chiefly species of *Vaucheria* and *Cladophora*, and the lime-loving liverwort, *Pellia fabbroniana*, which grow attached to stones.

Aquatic animal life is well represented in these waters. The fresh-water shrimp is so abundant that it must form an important source of food for fish and other small carnivores. A much larger crustacean is the fresh-water crayfish, which is common in the better aerated stony reaches. Crayfish are intolerant of pollution and are restricted to waters rich in dissolved salts.

Mayflies and caddis flies are plentiful, their young stages under the water, the adults to be seen at the right seasons in flight or resting on the vegetation. The largest and most noticeable of the common mayflies is the green-drake, whose nymphal stages live in burrows in mud and gravel at the bottom of the streams. Dragonflies are not particularly abundant along the Cotswold rivers, but the two handsome damsel-flies of the genus *Agrion* may be mentioned. The males are jewels of insects, their bodies and wings marked with dark turquoise-blue. *Agrion virgo*, with wings all turquoise, is often the commoner, but *A. splendens*, whose wings carry turquoise bands, may occur with it or replace it where the water flows more slowly and the bottom is muddy.

Many of these streams are periodically stocked with trout, and there is an interesting trout farm, open to visitors, at Bibury. The only other 'game' fish to be found is the grayling, occurring in the upper Thames and some of its tributaries such as the Evenlode, Coln and Windrush. Salmon seldom if ever nowadays penetrate to these waters, for the polluted lower reaches of the Thames form an effective barrier to the migrations of this fish. For the same reason eels are rare on the Cotswolds Various 'coarse' fish occur, chief among them being roach, chub, dace, gudgeon and pike. Perch, bream and bleak are also present in some localities. Minnows and bullheads are common and there are some records of that primitive fish-like creature, the brook lamprey.

Many species of birds may be seen along the Cotswold streams, but few are characteristically river species. The moorhen and mallard are the commonest of these and breed in considerable numbers. Herons feed along the quieter stretches, but heronries are few and tend to be temporary.

Reed warblers are found only in the lower reaches of the Thames tributaries, and sedge warblers are scarce in these river valleys.

Two water birds are of special interest as they owe their presence on the Cotswolds to the activities of man. The grey wagtail and, in particular, the dipper require fast-flowing broken water, and in this part of England such habitats are restricted to the vicinity of weirs, mill-races and the outlets of artificial pools. Both these birds breed in such places and are found along a number of Cotswold rivers.

Lakes have been constructed in several of the dip-slope valleys. An interesting example is Rendcomb Lake between Cheltenham and Cirencester, which was made in the 1860s by damming the River Churn.

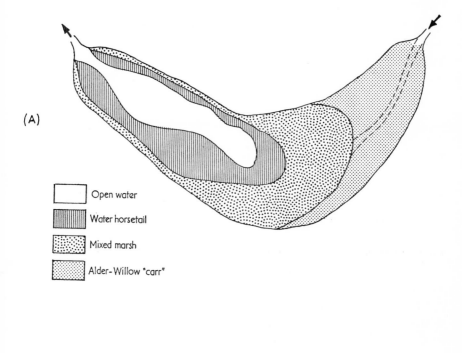

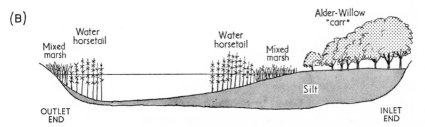

Fig 13. (A) plan, and (B), longitudinal section of an artificial lake, showing silt deposition from the inlet and consequent zonation of vegetation (based on Rendcomb lake near Cirencester).

Such pools always tend to silt up at the upstream end and frequently it is possible to see zones of vegetation correlated with depth of water. This is represented in Fig 13, the diagram being based on the simplified history of Rendcomb Lake. The upstream end, in these circumstances, eventually becomes a type of wet alder-willow woodland known as 'carr'. Its ground flora consists of such plants as marsh marigold, meadowsweet and yellow flag and, in high summer, may become an almost impenetrable tangle of nettles, goosegrass and bittersweet.

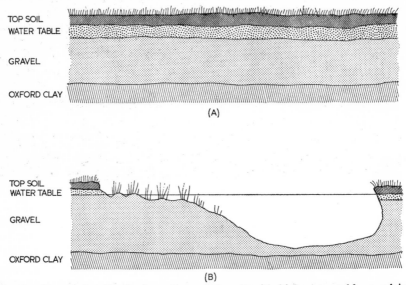

Fig 14. Gravel pits. (A) Section of gravel deposit with high water table, overlying impervious bed of Oxford clay; (B) Results of shallow excavation (*left*) and 'wet-dig' method by drag-line (*right*).

The Cotswolds carry no natural lakes, but along the lower or eastern fringe of the dip slope there are now a large number of open stretches of water formed artificially as a result of the extraction of gravel on a grand scale.

These gravel deposits lie astride the main Cotswold rivers near to where they discharge into the upper reaches of the Thames. The gravel consists of disintegrated oolitic limestone which obviously had its origin higher up the Cotswold slope. It was presumably brought down during the glacial and post-glacial periods and now overlies the geologically younger Oxford clay. This clay bed impedes drainage so that the gravel is full of water. The water table lies close to the surface of the ground, and when gravel is removed, the excavation fills at once with water, unless extensive pumping is employed (Fig 14).

Page 71 (above) *Sheep grazing near the source of the Windrush at Field Barn Farm, Taddington;* (below) *Early spring harrowing by the escarpment at Leckhampton*

Page 72 (above) *Cotswold barns, walls and wolds at Salperton;* (below) *Donnington Brewery, Stow-on-the-Wold*

From the point of view of natural history, the method of extraction of gravel profoundly influences the animal and plant populations which develop in the pits. A superficial excavation produces the best results in the first instance. Shallow pools of various sizes are separated by islands and peninsulas of gravel and this combination favours the development of varied wild life (Fig 14).

The gravel is at first bare, and the water virtually devoid of plant life, but early colonisers are soon on the scene. Windborne fruits and seeds, such as those of coltsfoot, sow-thistles and willowherbs, are among the first species to arrive, shortly followed by a greater variety of land and marsh plants. The shallow pools soon develop an extensive growth of water crowfoot, water forget-me-not, celery-leaved buttercup, common water-plantain and other plants. Hornwort, water milfoil and the water-weed *Lagarosiphon majus*, recently introduced from south-east Africa, are common submerged species.

The immersed parts of water plants provide food and shelter for animals of various kinds. Many species of crustacea and insects are early immigrants to this underwater world. Chief among the latter are numerous kinds of water beetles, water boatmen, the water scorpion and the water stick-insect. Dragonflies become plentiful and include some local and scarce species.

One of the earliest dragonflies to colonise is the black-lined Orthetrum, very much a south-eastern species in England (see Fig 12). At later stages the big Emperor dragonfly may also be found and a few pits have supported colonies of the blood-red Sympetrum, which appears to be associated, for no obvious reason, with false bulrush plants or with the water horsetail. In all some fifteen or more species of dragonfly may be sought in and around these waters.

Frogs, toads and newts also colonise shallow parts of the pits, toads usually spawning in deeper water than frogs. Records of the three British species of newt in Cotswold waters are few, but it is probable that all three—the great crested, smooth and palmate newts—occur in some of the gravel workings.

On the bare gravel which may surround and intersect the shallow water, the processes of colonisation and seral change involve a large number of wasteland and semi-marsh plants, including grasses and other herbs which encroach from surrounding farm fields. Among the early arrivals are myriads of willow seeds, mostly belonging to the osier, the crack willow and to members of the sallow group. These tree-seeds are of the utmost importance for, if allowed to grow, they eventually colonise the whole of the gravel area, forming a kind of willow 'carr' (p 70). This may be

E

regarded as the climax vegetation (p 48) of the habitat, for the high water table effectively prevents the elimination of willows by forest trees which would otherwise lead to a more complex type of woodland.

Probably the commonest way of extracting gravel now in use is the dragline or 'wet-dig' method, in which the gravel is scraped from the bottom of the water, down to the Oxford clay, and piled at the waterside for removal by lorry (Fig 14). The result is a pit with practically vertical sides, so that no shallow margins are available for colonisation by plants and animals.

Nevertheless a pit of this type is still of natural history interest. Not only do the steep sides provide good nest-sites for kingfishers and sand martins, both quite common in this part of the Cotswolds, but many ducks and other aquatic birds, shortly to be considered, are attracted to the surface of a large sheet of water. Furthermore, these lakes tend to develop a rich underwater life, thereby creating suitable conditions for the establishment of a large population of fishes of various kinds.

The speed with which most species of fish appear in these waters indicates that introduction by man is the major source of colonisation. Some pits have been stocked with trout, and various kinds of 'coarse' fish are to be found in others. The chief species are carp, roach, rudd, bream, tench, perch and pike. The latter is a ferocious carnivore and large specimens may cause havoc among the young of ducks and grebes.

To a majority of naturalists the bird life of the gravel pits is of primary interest, and it depends in large measure on the degree of colonisation by plants. Large expanses of deep water often lack emergent vegetation but attract many coot and duck, especially in winter. Considerable numbers of pochard, wigeon, tufted duck, mallard and teal often accompany the coot, while shoveler and pintail are much less common. A few goldeneye appear in most winters and there are occasional reports of smew, goosander and of several scarce species.

Gulls have always been frequent autumn and winter visitors to these pits, but of recent years a large winter roost, chiefly of black-headed, common and lesser black-backed gulls, has started to build up near South Cerney. Other winter visitors include slavonian and black-necked grebes, while the great crested grebe appeared early in the history of these waters. It did not start to breed for some years, however, until sufficient cover had developed to offer protection for the nests. This grebe is now quite common as a nesting bird in the larger pools.

Expanses of bare gravel with adjacent shallows form the breeding ground of the little ringed plover (p 36), of which a number of pairs now nest annually in the gravel pit area. This bird is intolerant of vegetation near the nest so that its persistence in this district depends upon the continuing provision of areas of bare gravel.

The margins of the shallow water, with variable quantities of plant life, attract migrant wading birds, which drop down to feed. These include common, green and wood sandpipers, snipe and jack-snipe, greenshank, ruff and several species better known on estuarine mud or the sea shore —dunlin, sanderling, ringed plover and others. Redshank and lapwing breed in or near several of the pits, but snipe appear not to do so at present.

As the marginal vegetation grows thicker and willow bushes become established, reed buntings, sedge warblers and occasional pairs of yellow wagtails begin to breed, while the establishment of small reed-beds encourages the nesting of the reed warbler, a bird which often also uses tangles of willow herb and other plants among small willows. At this stage coot, moorhen and mallard breed in large numbers, a few nesting tufted ducks may be present, and little grebes will use pools too small or too overgrown to attract the larger great crested grebes.

Still further increase in the density of vegetation may result in a decline in the number of species of birds and of other forms of wild life, especially if willows grow thickly in and around the shallow water of the pits.

A principle which has been implicit in much of this account of Cotswold wild life emerges once more. Communities of plants and animals are dynamic systems and are constantly adjusting to changing conditions. It is for man to decide how he wishes these changes to develop and to act accordingly. The establishment of reserves or refuge areas is not in itself enough to protect our dwindling heritage of wild plants and animals. These places must be managed according to scientific principles, and in this field there is wide scope for work to be done by conservation bodies at all levels, and by an interested and well informed public.

The Cotswolds lie largely in Gloucestershire, but the adjacent counties of Somerset, Wiltshire, Berkshire and Oxfordshire are also involved. The whole area is now covered by the system of County Naturalists' Trusts, whose primary concern is with the various aspects of protection and conservation of wild life. Several natural history societies are also established in the region, and these perform the equally important and complementary function of studying and reporting on the plants and animals of the district. These organisations welcome as members all those who are interested in the study and conservation of the wild life of the Cotswolds, one of the loveliest areas of outstanding natural beauty in our country.

Notes to this chapter are on pages 300–1.

3

From Prehistory to A D 1500

I. F. Smith, Bruce N. Eagles and Kathleen Morgan

Prehistory

I. F. Smith

Mesolothic and Neolithic Age

THE FIRST human communities[1] to frequent the Cotswold Hills arrived some 7,000–8,000 years ago,[2] when small bands of hunters and food-gatherers began to exploit the resources of the forest which had grown to dominate the landscape after the final glacial episode of the Ice Age. Their camp sites and hunting grounds are known only from scattered Mesolithic flint implements in the arable fields of the present day. To date, some three dozen find-spots are recorded, nearly all from parishes in the southern and mid-Cotswolds where flints of this kind have been deliberately searched for.[3] A provisional assessment of the finds suggests territorial partition between two populations.[4] Hunting rights in the southern Cotswolds may have been appropriated by people of Maglemose affinities coming in directly from Somerset and Wiltshire, and ultimately of Scandinavian origin. The mid-Cotswolds seem to have been claimed by other groups, who had perhaps wandered in from areas farther east and whose remoter connections were with the Sauveterrian of France. In this area there are also traces of a third group, known from an insular flint-working tradition named after a site at Horsham (Sussex); this tradition seems to have evolved after submersion of the former land connections prevented further contacts with the Continent, around 6000 BC.

Chipped flint axes, the Mesolithic tree-felling and wood-working tools, are rarely found in the Cotswolds, probably because all flint had to be carried from Wiltshire or Berkshire or collected from river gravels. Broken axes are therefore likely to have been re-used to make smaller implements. Despite this lack of direct evidence, it can be assumed that Mesolithic people made at least small clearings in the forest round their camp sites; wider clearances may have been effected by fires, spreading accidentally from hearths or used deliberately to drive game or even to concentrate food supplies by providing improved grazing for herbivores.[5]

Many clearances would have been transitory, leaving little or no permanent alteration in the environment. But the circumstance that flints of

Mesolithic and Neolithic types occur together quite frequently as surface finds hints at the possibility that ready-made openings may have offered attractive conditions for the initial establishment of early farming communities. With the appearance of the first farmers, during the latter part of the fourth millennium BC,[6] the process of systematic clearance began in earnest. Analysis of snail fauna from a Neolithic occupation surface underlying the chambered tomb at Ascott-under-Wychwood has shown that by c 2800 BC the forest had been replaced by dry short-turfed grassland.[7] Comparable evidence from sites outside the Cotswolds suggests that burial monuments were customarily constructed in clearings, and it may be inferred that each of those plotted on Fig 15 represents a patch of Neolithic arable or pasture.

Information about the local Neolithic economy comes almost entirely from the chambered tombs; in addition to bones of domestic animals, mainly those of cattle, with smaller numbers of sheep or goats, pigs and dogs,[8] querns incorporated in the structures of two or three tombs suggest some cereal growing.[9] Occasional remains of wild animals are reported,[10] but in general hunting seems to have contributed little to the diet.

The single excavated Neolithic settlement in the Cotswolds is the one already mentioned, at Ascott-under-Wychwood, where, in the part of the occupied area that had survived, there were hearths, pits, scattered fragments of pottery and worked flints, but no structural traces of dwellings.[11] Apart from other buried sites of this kind still awaiting discovery, the positions of Neolithic settlements are likely to be revealed only by concentrations of flints on the surfaces of arable fields, like those recorded from Long Newnton,[12] from Hazel Wood, Avening,[13] and from many fields in and around the parish of Swell.[14] Systematic search for such sites has yet to be undertaken.

The necessity to import all material used for stone tools, either in the form of flint nodules or as finished or semi-finished goods (in the case of axes), ensured frequent contacts with communities outside the region. Some flint axes, at least, are likely to have been products of flint mines situated in the chalklands of southern or eastern England; the petrological identification of the igneous or metamorphic rocks of which other axes are made shows that these originated in Northern Ireland, the Lake District, North Wales, Cornwall, and from sources as yet unlocated.[15]

Neolithic and Bronze Age Monuments

At least eighty-five Neolithic tombs can be identified in the area covered by Fig 15; only those for which there seems to be satisfactory evidence have been included on the map.[16] They constitute the main group of the Cotswold-Severn chambered tombs, one of the most important concentrations of Neolithic monuments in the British Isles, and consist essentially of one or more megalithic burial chambers (rooms walled and roofed by massive stones, with provision for access from the exterior) incorporated in long barrows (more accurately, long cairns). At the

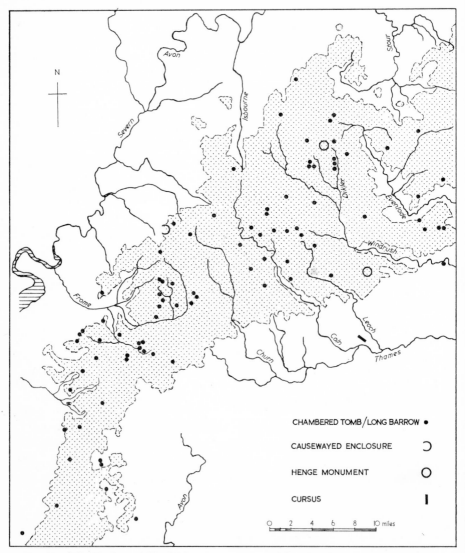

Fig 15.   Distribution of Neolithic monuments, mainly after *Trans BGAS* LXXIX. Stipple indicates land above 400ft OD.

present day the two 'show' barrows of Belas Knap and Hetty Pegler's Tump alone provide an adequate impression of the architectural refinement and engineering skill displayed by these monuments, which generally have cairns 100–200ft in length, sometimes surviving to a height of 10ft or more. Comprehensive information about local patterns of distribution, topographical siting, chamber plans and finds is available in a recent detailed survey.[17] The tomb at Ascott-under-Wychwood is dated about 2800 BC;[18] this seems likely to represent a central date for the period of construction of the group as a whole.[19]

Analysis of architectural components suggests that, while some tombs may be of unitary design, others are composite monuments, betraying signs of additions and alterations.[20] This evidence for remodelling, coupled with the implications of the rite of multiple successive burials and the fact that some tombs remained in use until c 2000 BC or later,[21] reflects not merely the prolonged importance of these monuments as burial and, probably, cult centres but also stability of the communities concerned.

Numbers of burials recorded from individual tombs range from four to twenty-six; almost without exception, skeletons are fragmentary and disordered, a condition that may have arisen partly from initial storage of bodies elsewhere and partly from disturbance when chambers were reopened to admit further burials—or to remove portions of those already there.[22] In view of the possibility that the contents of chambers may sometimes have been cleared out more thoroughly, it cannot be assumed that skeletons found represent the total numbers of individuals interred. Though persons of all ages are normally represented, predominance of males may suggest that burials were those of selected members of a community.[23]

Fragments of pottery and other artefacts exhibit a general similarity to those of the 'Windmill Hill culture' of southern England, but the structural components of the tombs may derive from more than one funerary tradition. Immediate antecedents for the long cairns which cover the megalithic chambers are to be found in the earthen ('unchambered') long barrows of the chalklands of southern and northeastern England. In some instances the long cairns may have been constructed over existing chambers of quite different origin.

The existence of a monument characteristic of the 'Windmill Hill culture' was made known in 1971 when excavation revealed a causewayed enclosure within the area of the Iron Age hill fort on Crickley Hill.[24] Preliminary results suggest that an area of about 3 acres was defined by three lines of interrupted banks and ditches; deliberate levelling, attested by layers of limestone slabs packed into one of the ditches,

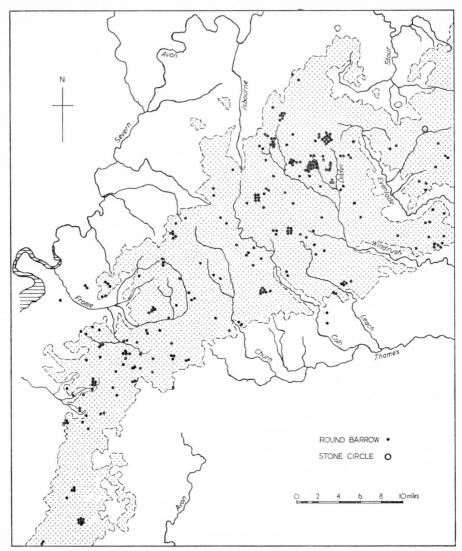

Fig 16.   Distribution of Bronze Age monuments, mainly after *Trans BGAS LXXIX*
(A few of the unexcavated round barrows may be earlier or later than Bronze Age).
Stipple indicates land above 400ft OD.

is a normal feature of these enclosures.[25] The other Neolithic ceremonial
monuments, henges at Condicote[26] and Westwell,[27] and the cursus at
Lechlade, are all likely to belong to the latter part of the third millennium
BC or the beginning of the second; of like date are pits containing Late
Neolithic pottery at Lechlade,[28] Cam,[29] and Bourton-on-the-Water.[30]

The circle of standing stones at Rollright[31] (Fig 16), situated in the
vicinity of a chambered tomb, suggests that places of Neolithic burial

retained their sanctity into the earlier centuries of the second millennium, as does the frequent siting of round barrows in proximity to chambered tombs.[32] The comparatively small number of round barrows in the Cotswolds may also reflect the strength of tradition amongst the established population and a reluctance to adopt the new rite of burial in single graves.[33] Beaker immigrants were few, to judge from the small quantity of beaker pottery recorded,[34] and it is perhaps significant that around one-third of the beakers come from secondary burials or deposits in chambered tombs.

Beaker and Bronze Age

Beaker and Bronze Age settlements are unknown, apart from those implied by surface flints;[35] the distribution of round barrows indicates the opening of new areas on the limestone during the second millennium, some of them perhaps as offshoots from existing settlements of earlier origin. For the first time there is now substantial evidence of occupation on the gravel terraces north of the Thames, where some of the numerous crop-marks of ring-ditches visible on air photographs must mark the sites of ploughed-out barrows.[36] A couple of richly furnished burials in barrows at Snowshill and Marshfield,[37] and a few stray finds of bronze axes and spearheads, show that the occupants of the Cotswolds shared to some extent in the wealth of the Early Bronze Age 'Wessex culture'. The paucity of metal implements attributable to the latter phases of the Bronze Age makes it difficult to discern patterns of trade.[38] A discovery of more than local significance was made on West Littleton Down, Tormarton, in 1968, when a gas-pipe trench revealed the skeletons of two young men with fragments of the spearheads that had killed them still embedded in their bones; they had died around 970 BC.[39]

Iron Age

The construction of hill forts from about the 6th century BC, or possibly a century or two earlier,[40] their siting in positions of strategic or tactical advantage, and the implied concentration of communities within and near their defences, testifies to social, and perhaps also terri-torial, reorganisation during the Iron Age.[41] The seventeen hill forts spaced out along the edge of the Cotswold escarpment, half of the total number shown in Fig 17,[42] are indicative of intensive occupation in this area, where steep-sided spurs offered ideal situations for the creation of strongholds. Areas enclosed vary from $2\frac{1}{2}$ acres to 120 acres; the majority

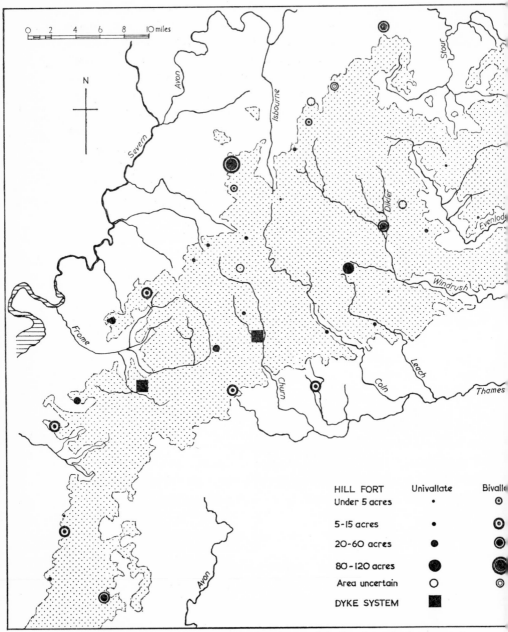

Fig 17. Distribution of Iron Age defensive sites, mainly based on the inventory for Gloucestershire compiled by the Royal Commission on Historical Monuments (England). Stipple indicates land above 400ft OD. Note: monuments situated west of the Cotswold escarpment are not included.

fall within the range of 5 to 15 acres. Just over a third of the hill forts are bivallate (have two ramparts, each with an outer ditch). The double defences seem to have been planned from the outset in some instances, but in others the outer rampart appears to be a later addition. At Sodbury Camp (Fig 16) work on the outer rampart and its ditch can be seen to have stopped just before completion. Excavation reveals that univallate forts may also have complex histories. That on Leckhampton Hill was apparently abandoned after an episode when part of the rampart was damaged by burning of the incorporated timbers. But at Crickley Hill the first rampart, destroyed in the same way, was rebuilt and the entrance elaborated; subsequently this rampart too was burnt.[43]

Plans of buildings found in 1972 inside the fortification on Crickley Hill represent two phases: an orderly arrangement of rectangular structures 28ft to 80ft long, replaced by a circular house 48ft in diameter.[44] Traces of open settlements are recorded from a few places in the uplands,[45] but house-plans are otherwise known only from lower-lying sites on the river gravels. At Lechlade[46] an isolated house was defined by a circle of posts, 20ft in diameter; it may have been rebuilt at least once. Internal post-holes could have supported looms or other domestic equipment and there may have been a porch outside the entrance. At Langford Downs,[47] nearby, two probable houses of similar plan, one of them 48ft in diameter, had stood within small ditched enclosures. They were in use during the first century BC. Round houses are also known from Salmonsbury,[48] a large settlement at the confluence of the Dikler and the Windrush enclosed within double ramparts and ditches of hill-fort proportions. Crop-marks in the parishes of Lechlade, Fairford and Kempsford suggest the existence of a series of unfortified Iron Age settlements along the uppermost reaches of the Thames comparable with those known in the Oxford region.

Amongst the scanty finds of Iron Age metalwork three are of special interest. Large hoards of iron currency bars from Salmonsbury[49] and from the hill fort on Meon Hill[50] seem to represent a concentrated form of wealth stored within these strongholds. Riches of a more personal nature accompanied two of the burials in the small inhumation cemetery near Birdlip.[51] The famous ornamented bronze mirror had been placed in the carefully constructed grave of a woman, together with two bronze bowls, ornaments and other valuable possessions. The larger of the bowls was inverted over the skull; the remains of a bronze-mounted wooden bucket were found in a similar position in the grave of a man whose iron weapon (now lost, perhaps a dagger) lay by his left side. Other examples of ornamental metalwork are the embossed bronze bands from a wooden

GLOUCESTERSHIRE COLLEGE
OF EDUCATION
LIBRARY

bucket found on Rodborough Common,[52] a terret from Fairford,[53] and a red-enamelled harness-mount, probably from Sudeley or its vicinity.[54]

The archaeological record for the Iron Age in the Cotswolds is still too scrappy, and the existing evidence too ambiguous, to show whether population changes took place during the first millennium BC. Clear indications of the advent of at any rate a new ruling class are presented by the establishment at Bagendon, near Cirencester, of a capital of the Belgic Dobunni in the first two decades of the first century AD. Excavation of a limited area within the several hundred acres controlled by the great system of dykes at Bagendon,[55] revealed the site of an industrial establishment where iron, bronze and lead were worked, and silver coins (as well as silver-plated forgeries) were minted. Prosperity founded on trade enabled the ruling class to enjoy a high standard of living, as testified by imported goods (wine, fine tableware from Italy and Southern Gaul, glass vessels from Italy, Egypt or Syria). Known houses were, however, still of the traditional round plan, here with substantial stone foundations and doors that could be latched.

Another dyke system, comparable to that at Bagendon and controlling some 200 acres, exists on Minchinhampton Common; its significance for the history and political organisation of the Dobunni is unknown.

Romano-British and Early Anglo-Saxon Occupation
Bruce N. Eagles

Dobunni

Inscribed coins offer some clues to the final stages in the political history of the Dobunni. Coins issued by Anted and Eisu during the decade preceding the Roman Conquest were found at Bagendon. Marked differences in style and distribution between the coins of their successors, Bodvoc and Corio . . , suggest that by c 43 the tribe had split into two factions. The Romanised lettering on Bodvoc's coins points to him as the ruler most likely to have led that part of the tribe which, as related by the classical historian Cassius Dio, surrendered to Aulus Plautius, commander of the Emperor Claudius's army when he landed in Kent in 43.[56]

Roman Frontier and Defences

By 47, when Plautius's term as provincial governor came to an end, the western frontier of the new province extended along the Foss Way, a line covered by probable and possible auxiliary forts, generally some 15 miles to the west, eg at Kingsholm, near Gloucester (Glevum).[57] The Dobunni, therefore, were from this time exposed to the resistance of other British tribes, now led from Wales by Caratacus, a son of Cunobelin. Bodvoc at least, may have welcomed the inevitable Roman garrison.

Parts of Roman military defences have been excavated since 1961 at three different places in Cirencester (Corinium), an important crossing of the River Churn.[58] A sector underlying the later civilian defences on the south-west side may link with similar evidence from The Sands, Watermoor, by the later Silchester Gate. If this is so, and further excavation provides the crucial close dating evidence required, this may be the site of a half-legionary fort, typical of the earliest years of occupation. A smaller fort, probably a successor, found under the basilica in the centre of the town may have been for the Ala Thracum or Ala Indiana cavalry units, recorded on tombstones. This fort appears to have been garrisoned until the early Flavian period, by which time all Roman troops had been withdrawn from the Cotswolds and the region had passed under civilian government. At Gloucester the Second Legion had replaced auxiliary units in 49 and was itself succeeded in 64 by the Twentieth. Chance finds of pottery, coins and military equipment suggest a fort or marching-camp at Kingscote.[59] Dorn[60] may have been a fort at this time. Claudian occupation is recorded at Rodborough.[61] Corio . .'s domain apparently disappeared in this military occupation. It is possible, however, that Bodvoc, cooperating with the Romans, encouraged the Dobunnic aristocracy to absorb a Roman way of life. The remarkable early civilian development of Cirencester certainly suggests such a willing fusion. Imperial policy, ever bent on the 'Romanisation' of newly conquered provinces, had achieved a notable success.

Civilian Development in Cirencester

In the later first century, not long after the abandonment of the latest fort and the consequent levelling of ramparts and filling of ditches, Roman surveyors laid down a street grid. This rigid pattern divided the core of the new town into fifteen rectangular *insulae*. Ermin Street, from Gloucester to Silchester, and Akeman Street, from St Albans (Verulamium), met a mile outside the town by the Foss Way from Leicester, and the Foss Way from Bath, placing Cirencester at a vital junction.

Excavations, particularly since 1960, have provided many details of

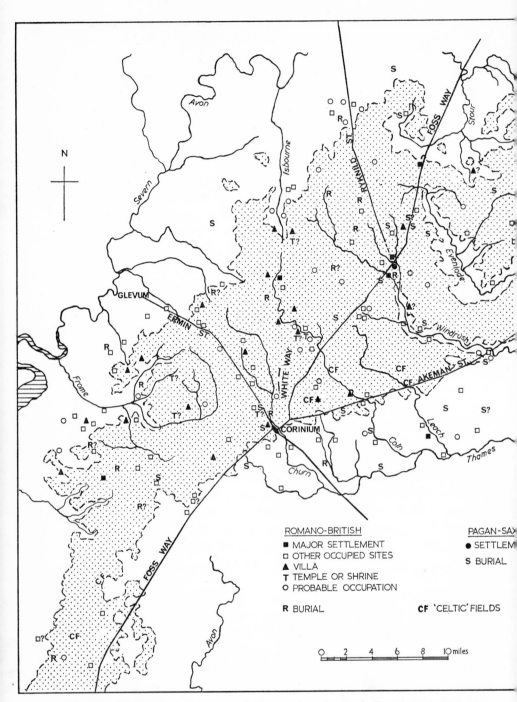

Fig 18. Distribution of Romano-British and early Anglo-Saxon sites. Romano-British sites based mainly on the inventory for Gloucestershire compiled by the Royal Commission on Historical Monuments (England). Stipple indicates land above 400ft OD. Note: monuments situated west of the Cotswold escarpment are not included.

the town's development, although the rescue nature of much of this work has inevitably prevented total examination of most buildings. The forum, the basilica (known since 1897), many houses and shops, the amphitheatre outside the town to the south-west, all date in their first design to the later first century. Designers of the original basilica mistakenly ignored the soft fill of the underlying fort ditches; it collapsed and was competely rebuilt.

Many private houses, first built in timber, were, as in most towns in Roman Britain, rebuilt in stone as the second century progressed. The general availability of local limestone probably hastened this development. Excavation in Insula V in 1961 showed piecemeal modernisation of messuages near the forum with a strict adherence to property boundaries, which appear to have survived for centuries. Many buildings, particularly the larger ones, exhibit a most complicated structural history. Private houses with colonnaded frontages and fine mosaics, such as that with a hare in a central roundel, found in 1971, matched the luxury of public buildings. Veneers of coloured imported marbles covered the walls of the basilica.

We now know that during the later part of the second century a defensive earthen rampart and ditch were made. Excavation shows a stone watch-tower on the north-east side and the monumental Verulamium Gate to belong to this first phase. At the same time, the River Churn, diverted into the ditch, was crossed by a stone bridge outside the Gate. The rampart was later cut back to receive a stone wall, enclosing 240 acres. In the fourth century external bastions were added and the town was defended by professional soldiers operating *ballistae* (heavy catapults).

Reorganisation of provincial administration by Diocletian (284–305) probably made Cirencester already a regional capital, also capital of a new province of Britannia Prima. Much rebuilding now took place. The most notable project known is the enlargement of the forum, fitting for the second largest city in Britain.

Other Settlements

Other Romano-British settlements in this area never approached Cirencester in size or sophistication. Even the larger of them were unwalled and, as far as is known, did not boast pubic buildings, although there is evidence for temples, and large houses with painted walls and heated rooms are found. Paved roads are recorded at Kingscote (a settlement of over 50 acres) and Wycomb (in Whittington parish: 28 acres). At Dorn (10 acres), similar roads may relate to a fort on the same site

as the settlement. Bourton-on-the-Water (at least 55 acres in all), Lower
Slaughter (25 acres), and Wycomb began in the Iron Age, while others
apparently originated in the wake of the Roman army. Subsequent
development could be strongly encouraged by traffic along the trunk
roads—Lower Slaughter and Dorn on the Foss Way and Bourton at
its junction with Ryknild Street, Asthall (Oxon)[62] on Akeman Street—
but Wycomb and Kingscote are distant from these routes. The roads
known at these two places cannot be traced much beyond the settlement
limits. It seems strange that none of the occupied sites along Ermin Street
and the southern part of Ryknild Street developed significantly, although
many small places are known alongside all the roads and doubtless many
more await discovery. Several of the larger settlements are also close to
river crossings, most notably Asthall and Bourton on the Windrush. A
smaller one at Coln St Aldwyn's is by the Coln. North of the Thames,
extensive areas of superimposed crop-marks represent ploughed-out
occupation of many periods often linked by ditched tracks. At Rough-
ground, Lechlade, a probable Iron Age hut and Romano-British buildings have been identified in one such complex, though without tracks, of
more than 20 acres.

Villas

Numerous Roman villas form a major element in the pattern of rural
settlement in the Cotswolds. S. Lysons excavated five in the late eighteenth
and early nineteenth centuries, and revealed some of the finest mosaic
pavements in Roman Britain. By 1900 eleven others had been partially
uncovered. Recently, two of these sites (Great Witcombe and Chedworth)
have been re-examined and villas at Frocester and Whittington newly
excavated, allowing detailed study of structural development. At Frocester
there are traces of a formal garden.

Mrs H. E. O'Neil's excavations in 1948–51 show three periods in the
Whittington villa. The first, in the second century, survived only as a
small bath suite. Towards the middle of the fourth century a winged
corridor house was built. Additions shortly afterwards included a large
hall and extended kitchen. Most corridors and rooms had mosaic pavements, mainly with geometric designs, all of the fourth century. Excavation of the villa at Frocester by Capt H. S. Gracie, began in 1961 and
is still in progress. Here, buildings constructed c 275 were soon enlarged
and added to (c 360), remaining, with repairs, until the fifth century.
A double-ditched enclosure surrounded the villa. Earlier buildings lay
to the south-east. The large villa at Chedworth was discovered by chance

Page 89 *Old roads:* (above) *the White Way near Compton Abdale;* (below) *Buckle Street*

Page 90 *Road Transport:* (above) *a Great Western Railway double-decker bus running between Stroud and Chalford, 1905;* (below) *a two-horse delivery waggon outside an inn in the Stroud district before World War I*

in 1864. Excavation followed and the extensive remains were restored.
(The villa is now open to the public.) Between 1958 and 1965 the late
Sir Ian Richmond recovered further important details. In the early
second century the villa was made up of three separate blocks, arranged
to form a rectangle but open at the east. Later the plan was integrated
and enlarged and in the fourth century covered some 2 acres. A
nymphaeum (shrine of the water-goddesses) was built over the spring which
supplied the villa with water. Tessellated floors of the fourth century
were found in at least fifteen rooms and many corridors. Certain rooms
in the north wing, formerly thought to be a fulling establishment, are
better interpreted as a bath suite. The most complex villa was at Woodchester. Between 1793 and 1796 Lysons excavated some sixty-four rooms
and there were many others. Marble statues adorned rooms and corridors,
and the famous mosaic depicting Orpheus and the beasts is the finest in
Britain. Periodically, the pavement, which remains buried *in situ*, is
uncovered and opened to the public.

The pattern of rural settlement, as so far recorded, can be seen in
Fig 18. Many of these sites have been identified only in recent years and
the picture is far from complete, particularly in the south-western part
of the area. Numerous settlements lie along the river valleys: those by
the River Coln will serve as an example.

Valley of the River Coln

On a direct line it is some 20 miles between the source of the Coln
at Brockhampton and its confluence with the Thames at Lechlade. In
the lower reaches several settlements known from crop-marks are likely
to be partly of Romano-British date. At Coln St Aldwyn's, where Akeman
Street crosses the river, settlement debris has been found along the road
on either bank. A mile beyond, a villa, known since c 1670 but ill-recorded,
nestles in a sharp bend near Bibury Mill. 'Celtic' fields once existed on
Ablington Downs. Several occupied sites are known near the villa at
Chedworth and close by was a temple, with colonnaded portico, excavated
1864–5 and 1930. Lysons excavated another villa at Withington in 1811.
Between Withington and the source, several sites are close to the large
settlement at Wycomb. The distribution of Romano-British occupation
along the Coln seems to illustrate the interdependence of villas and native
settlements, some of which may have been colonate.[63] The valley may
have been linked directly with Cirencester, if a length of bank in North
Cerney parish is in fact the raised *agger* of a Roman road (the White
Way).

F

Celtic Fields

'Celtic' Fields, only remnants of which generally survive, are now known at Aldsworth (70 acres), Badminton (70 acres), Bibury (30 acres), Eastleach (10 acres) and Tormarton (50 acres). Within Barnsley Park, some 120 acres of fields and 4 acres of dry-stone walled closes are associated with Romano-British buildings.

Roman Religious Sites

Cirencester provides the best evidence for the worship of the official Roman Pantheon.[64] A temple to Mercury is implied by reliefs and a stone head. Minerva is represented by a head and torso (not of the same statue), and Diana by a bronze statuette of provincial workmanship. Jupiter Dolichenus, north Syrian and the only Oriental god known in the region, native deities including *Genii* personifying the locality (seen on an inscribed altar) or cloaked (*cucullati*) as godlets of fertility, and the Mother Goddesses in triad, were among other deities worshipped in the town.

In the countryside Mars dominates as god of agriculture. Altars are recorded from Bisley-with-Lypiatt and King's Stanley; a fine bronze statuette from Wycomb; and a relief from Colesbourne may represent him. An oolite head of Minerva (see p 53) from Kingscote is by a local sculptor.[65] *Genii cucullati*[66] are found widely, eight of thirteen reliefs known in Britain being from Gloucestershire. At some shrines the deities are crudely portrayed; two such carvings from Chedworth and Lower Slaughter probably represent minor local gods. Miniature bronze votive objects include a ploughshare and sword from Cleeve Hill, Southam,[67] and axes from Wycomb and Woodchester.

Evidence for Christianity

There is very little evidence for Christianity. At Cirencester a word-square, probably of the second or third century and incorporating PATERNOSTER A(lpha) O(mega), was found in 1868.[68] At Chedworth a Chi-Rho was scratched on the *nymphaeum*, thereby Christianising the shrine.

Recently, several schools of mosaicists have been recognised in Roman Britain.[69] One of the most important worked from Cirencester in the fourth century, specialising in pavements with Orpheus in a central medallion or with saltire designs. Mosaics with Orpheus are found in Cirencester and at Barton Farm, Chedworth, Withington and Wood-chester villas. These wealthy villa-owners would have served the new provincial council in Cirencester. In view of the meagre evidence for Christianity, it is interesting to notice that the Orpheus theme had been early adopted by the Church and that other motifs in the pave-ments at Chedworth and Withington could be possibly of Christian significance.

End of the Roman Era

At present only very limited evidence of the end of Roman Cirencester is available. It seems from the dearth of rubbish and coins (which apparently went out of circulation in Britain c 430)[70] on the worn floor of the forum that public buildings were maintained and cleaned until well into the fifth century. A large inhumation cemetery near the amphi-theatre, currently under excavation, remained in use until after 400.[71] Five bronze buckles,[72] decorated in the chip-carved style characteristic of late Roman military dress, suggest that the town was garrisoned until the early part of the century. The absence of grass-tempered pottery and of fine wares imported from the Mediterranean suggests that the town may have been largely deserted by the later fifth century. A skeleton was found where it had rotted in the last ditch cut alongside Ermin Street.[73] This must mean that town life had then ceased.

In the countryside grass-tempered pottery has been found on the Romano-British fields at Barnsley, at the villa at Frocester and over the residual foundations of a Roman building at St Peter's, Frocester.[74] Two late Roman military buckles derive from the villas at Spoonley Wood at Sudeley, and Chedworth. These finds hint that several villas, at least, continued in use until well into the fifth century.

Anglo-Saxon Settlements and Burials

Only the slightest traces of early Anglo-Saxon settlements are so far recorded. At Bourton[75] clay loom-weights were found in a hut by the Foss Way in 1931. Another hut was excavated at Spelsbury (Oxon) in 1938.[76] Lastly, objects of the mid-Saxon period and later were found in the deserted medieval part of Whittington village, close to the Roman villa.[77]

Pagan Saxon burials occur widely[78] (Fig 18), and particularly, but not entirely, east of the Foss Way. At Poulton (Akeman Street), Stow

(Foss Way) and Stratton (Ermin Street) inhumations are close to Roman roads. At Bourton burials were cut into the surface of the Foss Way. At Bourton again, and at Cirencester[79], they are close to Roman settlements, while a barrow with a primary cremation burial of the seventh century is near the site at Asthall. At least two burials in the cemetery at Barton Farm, west of Cirencester, were cut through a mosaic pavement. The large cemetery at Fairford apparently overlies Roman occupation of some sort.

It is difficult to interpret the significance of the proximity of Roman and pagan Saxon remains at these places. At present, early Saxon cemeteries in Gloucestershire have been little studied. Generally, fifth-century graves have not been identified, although some at Fairford are of this period. Until all the grave goods have been examined, it is impossible to discover how early the Saxon penetration took place. It is likely, however, that the battle of Dyrham in 577[80] marks not the beginning but merely a stage in the long-drawn-out settlement of the county.

A comparison of the pagan Saxon burials with those of rural Roman Britain may prove worthwhile. Thus contracted burials at Foxcote, Withington, which have been taken as Saxon, may be late Romano-British; the combs as grave goods and the strap-end from yellow clay above the burials fit the early fifth century and contraction is more typical of Romano-British than Saxon interments. Two contracted burials at Broadwell, by the Foss Way, may be of similar date. In certain instances the differences between Romano-British and Saxon traditions and grave goods may be more apparent than real.

The parish of Withington has been the subject of a classic study of the relationship between the Romano-British and medieval landscape.[81] Future research seems likely to show that the two periods are closely linked in much of the Cotswolds.

700 to AD 1500
Kathleen Morgan

West Saxons and Middle Angles

THE SETTLEMENT of the Cotswolds by the Saxons had been in progress for over 100 years in AD 700. In the south-eastern part, in the Thames valley and around Cirencester, the early settlement was by the West Saxons, but later the region was probably more widely settled by the Middle Angles, and in the north Cotswolds the place-names show mainly

Anglian influence. It seems likely that the Anglo-Saxons to some extent took over the already existing settlements, making use of land that had already been cleared and following the main Roman arteries of communication—the Foss Way, running through Cirencester and north across the Cotswolds, and Ryknild Street running from Watling Street to join the Foss Way at Bourton-on-the-Water. The predominantly Anglo-Saxon origins of the place-names of the Cotswolds, however, would suggest that the Saxon period saw the basic settlement of the region as it exists today. It has been calculated that 133 parishes in the Cotswolds may be regarded as early centres of settlement. These are spread fairly evenly over the area, but it would seem that the Cotswold plateau was settled before the more heavily wooded valleys. On the plateau the soil was thin and not very productive but it was probably also easier to clear and cultivate with primitive implements. The presence of water was obviously a very important factor in the siting of settlements, and they were therefore often situated on the spring line where the limestone rests on the Lias clay—for example, Broadwell and Westcote in the north Cotswolds—or on the gravel beds beside the streams, such as Bourton-on-the-Water and Moreton-in-Marsh, which provided a dry base for settlements with water easily available. The steep Cotswold scarp, stretching from Chipping Campden to Chipping Sodbury, was the most heavily wooded part of the region and had little early settlement, and when these wooded areas were cleared settlements tended to be smaller.

The early Cotswold communities seem to have been large villages rather than scattered farmsteads. Because the uplands were not very productive, cultivation was extensive and units of farming larger than in more productive areas. Charters of the eighth and ninth centuries show that open field agriculture was the common practice. In its earliest form this was a two-field system with the fields cultivated and left fallow in rotation, and held in common by the members of the community whose farms consisted of scattered strips in the fields. The two basic elements in Cotswold farming were sheep and grain. The sheep were particularly valuable on the uplands, where they helped to prevent erosion and to fertilise the poor, thin soil; but even at this early period they were also kept for the value of their wool. It has been suggested that Cotswold wool may have been used for some of the woollen cloths exported from Mercia to Europe in the time of Offa, King of Mercia, in the eighth century. The estates of which there is evidence in the Saxon period, mainly ecclesiastical ones, show an emphasis on the upland areas that provided extensive sheep pastures, and place-names such as Shipton indicate the importance of sheep in some parts of the Cotswolds. On the whole, meadow for cattle was always scarce, except in the south-east in the lower-lying parts of the Thames valley, and cattle did not form an important element in the early agriculture of the area.

Cirencester and Winchcombe

Although it is thought that the earliest Saxon settlements were around Cirencester, the town did not regain, before the Norman Conquest, the position it had held in the pre-Saxon period as the most important town in the Cotswolds. It is suggested that it was too far south and too near the border of Wessex to become a centre for the predominantly Mercian people who settled in the Cotswolds. The Danish army was at Cirencester in 878 and possibly contributed to its decline. Winchcombe, however, was in a good position to control the northern approach to the Cotswolds, and by the eighth century it was the centre of the kingdom of the Hwicce, an under-kingdom of Mercia thought to have been created by Penda of Mercia in the seventh century and combining the two elements, Saxon and Anglian, of the early settlers of the Cotswolds. The Mercian King Coenwulf founded a monastery at Winchcombe about 798, which became one of the principal landowners in the north Cotswolds. The town became the administrative centre of a wide area, possibly as part of a division of Mercia on a military basis for defence against the Danes, though Winchcombe seems to have held its prominent position before the Danish raids. The area dependent upon Winchcombe was about 1,200 acres, lying mainly on the northern uplands of the Cotswolds, the area of the present county of Gloucester being divided into two units based on Winchcombe and Gloucester. The term 'Wincelcumbescire' occurs in an agreement between the Bishops of Hereford and Worcester, and the shire existed as a separate unit perhaps until the early eleventh century when, by about 1017, it had become merged with Gloucestershire. The town of Winchcombe at this time was a borough with some evidence of urban development, in contrast to the rest of the Cotswold communities, which were almost entirely agricultural. Towards the end of the eleventh century 151 burgesses were recorded at Winchcombe, and it has been estimated that this could represent a population of about 900.

Christianity and Ecclesiastical Organisations

Reference has already been made to the monastery at Winchcombe and to ecclesiastical estates in the Cotswolds; the introduction of Christianity to the area is obscure, but there is evidence of Christian influence before the end of the seventh century. The Venerable Bede records that two rulers of the Hwicce about 675, Eanhere and Eanfrid, became Christians with their followers. Towards the end of the seventh century Ethelred, King of Mercia, and Oshere an under-king of the Hwicce, granted land for the foundation of a monastery at Withington, and another charter of Ethelred, granting land at Malmesbury Abbey, refers to Teta's minster, which has been identified as being at Tetbury. During the next few hundred years surviving charters show that a large amount of land passed into the ownership of religious communities. The cathedral church of Worcester acquired land in the north part of the Cotswolds, around Blockley and Upton, and with Gloucester and Evesham Abbeys was among the largest landowners in the region by the end of the Saxon period. Gloucester Abbey's estates lay mainly in the central part of the plateau, and those of Evesham Abbey in the north around Stow-on-the-Wold. The monastery at Winchcombe, which adopted the Benedictine rule about 969, was the only large monastery actually situated in the Cotswolds. A monastery at Cirencester, founded about 820, apparently never acquired the same importance; it did not adopt the Benedictine rule, and appears to have been very small before its refoundation in the twelfth century.

The other monasteries mentioned above did not survive the Norman Conquest as monastic communities, and minsters recorded at Stanway and Blockley may not have been truly monastic institutions. They possibly represent the beginnings of a parochial system in the form of a group of priests attached to a central 'mother' church and serving a wide area which remained to some extent a unit even when other churches were established within it. Thus Stanway church for example still had associations with Lower Lemington church in the thirteenth century, and both Bourton-on-the-Hill and Moreton-in-Marsh were probably originally part of Blockley parish. Little evidence exists of parochial organisation in the Cotswolds in the Saxon period, but it was likely to have been for the most part of this rudimentary nature. A priest was recorded at Woodchester in 896, and the survival of Anglo-Saxon stonework and sculpture in some churches, particularly in the area around Cirencester, indicates the existence of parish churches. Many more may have existed, too primitive to have survived, but it would be unrealistic to picture the Saxon Cotswold villages as self-contained units each with its parish church and priest. This was a form of organisation still in the process of development at the time of the Norman Conquest.

Domesday's Evidence of the Cotswolds

The Domesday Survey of 1086, which often records information both for that date and for 1066, gives a more detailed picture of the development of the Cotswolds than may be gathered from the scattered references in pre-Conquest sources. The survey is arranged according to the landholders, describing each estate, the hundred in which it lay, the amount of land, and sometimes details of its manorial organisation. The size of estates was given in hides, which is the normal unit of land in records of this time, representing originally the size of an average peasant holding, but varying considerably in acreage from one part of the country to another. The information recorded in Domesday usually includes the number of tenants and how many ploughs they have, and the number on the lord's demesne, that is the land retained in his own hands, with the number of serfs; details of meadow, woodland and mills are often given, and finally the value of the manor in 1066 and 1086. The information is not comprehensive nor is it always consistent; nevertheless it gives a unique picture of the country at the end of the eleventh century, and it is possible to draw certain conclusions about the development of the Cotswold region from the information contained in Domesday.

The survey shows that the majority of the Cotswold villages were in existence, by name, at the time of the Norman Conquest. Some names which are recorded before 1086 do not appear by name in Domesday but may sometimes be recognised as included under other places. For example, Coates is not mentioned by name but its area is apparently included in the entries for several nearby places. Some Domesday placenames survive now only as small hamlets or even single farms, and others have not been identified at all. The names that are recorded in the Cotswolds, as in the county as a whole, are spread fairly evenly over the region. It is evident that a large area of the Cotswolds was under cultivation; apart from a belt of wood along the escarpment, only scattered references to woodland occur. Nor is there much evidence of assarted land indicating recent clearance of woodland. Within the Cotswolds regional differences can be seen. It has been calculated that the density of plough-teams varies from about three to five to the square mile, which is similar to the rest of the county, the highest density being in the south-east corner around Cirencester, and south-east of Winchcombe, and the lowest on the Cotswold plateau. Here the number of ploughs supported by a manor was often the same as or only slightly higher than the number of hides, whereas on the heavier soils presumably a higher number of ploughs was necessary, and there was also frequently a higher population to be supported. Most of the north Cotswold villages had only very small areas of meadow, but the places in the valleys had larger amounts, notably South Cerney in the Churn valley with 100 acres, and the Ampneys on the Ampney Brook with 60 acres, while on the Leach, Kempsford and Lechlade had unspecified amounts of meadow which, from its value, would appear to have been considerable. The absence of references to pasture in the Cotswold manors can only be explained as a deliberate omission.

It is difficult to calculate population from the people recorded in Domesday, but it seems that the population was highest in the south-east part of the Cotswolds and around Cirencester, and it has been calculated that the population varied from about six to eleven people to a square mile. On the plateau, where there were generally fewer plough teams, the proportion of land retained as demesne was often higher, and the number of tenants holding land freely, that is for rent rather than labour service, smaller than elsewhere. The proportion of serfs to ploughs on the lord's demesne has been calculated as two or three, and over the whole county, including the Cotswolds, the proportion of serfs was higher than the average. One indirect indication of population and the prosperity of a place is to be found in the number of mills recorded there, though the siting of water-mills was obviously dictated mainly by the existence of suitable streams. Some places in the eastern sloping valleys—for example, Lechlade and Kempsford—had three or more mills, but in the western sloping valleys, and particularly those of the Frome valley, they were most numerous, the highest number being eight at Minchinhampton. This was to be a very significant factor in the later development of the Stroud valley when the mills, which in Domesday were almost certainly exclusively for grinding corn, began to be used for fulling in the woollen industry. Taken as a whole the development and prosperity of the Cotswolds in 1086 was similar to that of the county and, indeed, of the West Midlands in general.

Turning from the land itself and the people who worked it to the landholders, Domesday confirms the extent of monastic influence in the Cotswolds. The cathedral church of Worcester and the abbeys of Winchcombe, Evesham and Gloucester were the largest landholders in the Cotswolds in 1086. In all, an area of perhaps about 400 hides appears to have belonged to religious bodies. The land of the cathedral church of Worcester included large manors at Bibury and Withington in the central part of the Cotswolds, as well as Blockley farther north. Winchcombe Abbey's estates were fairly compact, around and south-east of the town of Winchcombe, and to some extent intermingled with those of St Peter's Abbey, Gloucester, while Evesham Abbey's lands were mainly concentrated in the north Cotswolds. Some ten more religious communities had smaller holdings scattered over the area. Three of the secular land-holders—Roger of Iver, Roger de Lacy, and William Gozenboded—had lands comparable in size with the ecclesiastical ones, but a large number had only small estates in the Cotswolds.

Among the tenants recorded in Domesday there are several references to priests, usually included with the peasant population, but occasionally, as at Fairford and Bibury, noted separately as holding a certain amount of land. Some thirty-eight priests were recorded on the Cotswold manors, four places having more than one. Stanway was said to have a 'monasterium', which may imply the presence of more than one priest. Of the other places with more than one—Ampney, Guiting and Sidding-ton—all either were at one time or still are more than one parish, while Bisley, where two priests were recorded, may have included Stroud. The recording of a priest at a place may usually be taken to indicate the existence of a church, but the information in Domesday is not always complete. It does, however, suggest that the parochial organisation was still in process of formation, and that, as the architecture of many of the existing churches shows, it was during the next 200 years that many villages first acquired a parish church.

At the beginning of the Norman period the Cotswolds were extensively settled and cultivated, supporting a considerable population. The area was highly organised on a manorial basis, though it would be inaccurate to think of a neat division in which manors coincided with parishes; they varied in size and organisation, some having large demesnes and numerous tenants, others being apparently only single farms. Arable farming was the main source of livelihood, Winchcombe was the only borough and Cirencester had the only recorded market. Communications were by the Roman roads and the ancient Cotswold ridgeway, and also by the saltways which ran from Droitwich in Worcestershire through the Cotswolds to Lechlade, Cirencester and Sodbury. These roads were to remain the main thoroughfares throughout the Middle Ages.

Medieval Growth of Boroughs and Markets

In the next few hundred years one of the major changes in the Cotswolds was the growth of boroughs and markets, and the beginning of urban development in certain parts of the region. Domesday records that a new market had been established at Cirencester; its position at the meet-

ing of three of the main arteries of traffic—the ancient saltway called
the White Way, the Foss Way, and Akeman Street—made it an obvious
commercial centre, and in the years following the Norman Conquest it
replaced Winchcombe as the most important town in the Cotswolds.
Burgesses were recorded there in 1133 and by the thirteenth century
the merchants and artisans were strong enough to resist the claims of
the abbey of Cirencester in a long struggle over the services claimed
by the abbey from its tenants. Ten times as much tax was paid by
Cirencester as by Winchcombe in 1171; eighty-two taxpayers were named
there in 1327 and the assessment of £12 was three times that of Winchcombe, where only a few non-agricultural trades appear among the
names of taxpayers. That town declined in importance during this period,
though the abbey with its large estates and particularly its interest in the
woollen industry saved it from complete obscurity.

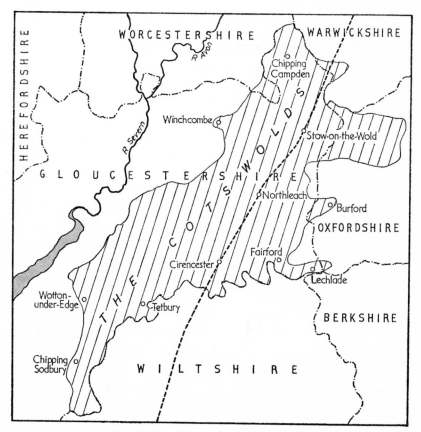

Fig 19.   Medieval Boroughs and Market Towns.

During the twelfth and thirteenth centuries more markets were established in various parts of the Cotswolds, and though most remained only small, some developed into centres of local trade and some achieved borough status. Lechlade, Fairford and Minchinhampton, perhaps influenced by their proximity to Cirencester, and Burford on the River Windrush, had burgesses in the thirteenth century. Lechlade also had the advantage of being on the highest navigable part of the Thames. However, none of these grew very much, though Burford became a prosperous centre of the woollen industry. Minchinhampton was not regarded as a borough after 1300, and another small market town established at Painswick had only seven burgesses by 1334. Tetbury and Chipping Sodbury on the road between Cirencester and Bristol reflected the growing commercial importance of both those places, especially of Bristol. Tetbury was described as an ancient borough in 1287, and Chipping Sodbury was created as a market and fair by the lord of Old Sodbury, William le Gros, about 1227. Further north a market was established by the Abbot of Evesham at Stow-on-the-Wold at the point where the Foss Way is crossed by the main Cotswold ridgeway. Stow never became a borough, but it remained an important centre of trade in the north Cotswolds, and though the term burgess was not used there, Stow had a number of non-agricultural tenants, and references to merchants were frequent in the fourteenth and fifteenth centuries. In 1226 the Abbot of Westminster secured a grant of a weekly market in his manor of Moreton-in-Marsh, lying on the Foss Way. Though Moreton does not appear to have been a borough at any time, it did have a large number of non-agricultural tenements called burgages. Between Stow and Cirencester the Abbot of Gloucester set up the market town of Northleach on his manor of Eastington close to the Foss Way about 1230, and in the 1180s a borough was established at Chipping Campden in the north Cotswolds on the White Way. Wotton-under-Edge was a borough in the reign of King John but according to tradition it was destroyed by fire and did not regain its status until 1253, when Lady Berkeley obtained a new grant of a market and fair.

Trades

The initial impetus to the growth of these small towns was trade, based largely on the agricultural products of the Cotswolds, but some of them became equally important as the centres of the small crafts and industries that began to develop with increasing prosperity. There is evidence of cloth, leather and shoe industries in Stow-on-the-Wold in the fourteenth century, as well as the rural industries directly associated with agriculture. Cirencester had in 1327 people occupied as goldsmiths, dyers and tailors, and similar occupations are found in the other small towns at the same period. Bourton-on-the-Water, which never had a market, perhaps because the Abbot of Evesham, who was the lord of Bourton, did not wish it to compete with his market at Stow, was from the fourteenth century a centre of several trades and small industries. From this time also references in various Cotswold parishes to quarries, stonemasons and tilers indicate the exploitation of the local limestone for building. Quarries in Barrington, Sherborne and Windrush were providing stone for buildings in London and Oxford from the fourteenth century as well as for local building. The cloth and woollen industry (which is discussed in detail in Chapter 6) were already beginning to develop by the late twelfth century when the earliest fulling mill was recorded at Temple Guiting. In the next few hundred years this was to become the major factor in the growth of the Cotswold towns and in the eventual urbanisation of the Stroud valley. However, most of the Cotswold towns grew only slowly (or in some cases declined) and retained their essentially rural character. In 1267 Northleach had eighty burgage plots, Chipping Campden had seventy-six about 1273, and Fairford and Chipping Sodbury sixty-eight and 177 respectively in 1307, and most had probably more agricultural than non-agricultural tenants. With the possible exception of Cirencester, none was more than a small rural market town living off the local trade.

Use of Land after the Norman Conquest

In the century following the Norman Conquest the process of clearing woodland and extending the arable land continued. Several place-names are found for the first time in this period, indicating the creation of new settlements, and while these usually remained hamlets of existing parishes, some parishes also (for example, Nailsworth, Southrop and Chalford) appear for the first time by name during this time. Open field cultivation continued as the normal practice, with probably considerable regional variation in the number of fields and system of rotation. Generally most of the tenants of a manor were customary tenants, owing specified labour service for their land, and the lord's demesne was farmed largely by service they owed. In many of the Cotswold manors, particularly on the large monastic estates, the lord did not live on his estate, and the manors, sometimes highly organised in groups centred on one main manor, were run by the lord's bailiff. The manorial court, over which he presided and which the tenants of the manor attended as suitors, regulated the activities of the manor with regard to such things as the open fields and common pasture rights.

It has been estimated that in the fourteenth century the extent of arable land in the county of Gloucester had reached its highest level, and was already beginning to contract in the Cotswolds. One reason for this was that as farming became more efficient there was less incentive to cultivate the more exposed and barren parts of the uplands. Thus, for example, Eyford and the two hamlets of Naunton parish—Harford and Aylworth—all on the exposed uplands between Bourton and Stow, had gone out of cultivation by 1341, though in 1086 they had supported seven, four and five ploughs respectively. Another reason was the extension of sheep pastures in the most suitable areas, as wool became an increasingly important part of Cotswold trade. The large ecclesiastical landowners particularly were extending their sheep pastures and re-organising their estates to provide permanent summer pasture on the uplands and winter pasture in the more sheltered areas. Winchcombe Abbey derived a third of its profits from wool by the end of the twelfth century. Its estates were extended during the thirteenth century to form a chain of manors running across the Cotswolds towards Northleach. The large manor of Sherborne was the centre of the abbot's sheep farming, where the flocks were taken every year for washing in the Windrush and for shearing. Similarly Llantony Priory had extensive sheep pastures in Barrington, which was the centre for shearing and collecting the wool. In 1327 the two tenants in Barrington with the highest assessment for tax were called Shepherd. On the Bishop of Worcester's estates in Blockley, Upton had extensive pastures in the thirteenth century and Upper and Middle Ditchford were apparently depopulated for sheep pasture in the fifteenth. It was not only the monastic landowners who were re-organising their estates; in 1330 Thomas Lord Berkeley acquired the manor of Beverstone and bought out the freeholders' land in order to consolidate the demesne and stock it with sheep (see chapter 6).

Depopulation

The enclosure of former open arable land and its conversion to sheep runs has been blamed for the depopulation of villages, and undoubtedly it was a factor in the Cotswolds, in addition to the reasons mentioned above and the decline in population through plague in the fourteenth century, which meant that some small communities were no longer viable. A number of deserted village sites have come to light in the

Cotswolds, mainly in the more remote uplands, and in most instances depopulation seems to have taken place during the fourteenth or fifteenth centuries. Reference has been made above to Eyford, Harford and Aylworth, which were almost deserted by 1341; other small upland villages in mainly sheep-grazing areas were recorded in the poll tax assessment of 1381 as being uninhabited. Hullasey on the Wiltshire border had a chapel in the fourteenth century, but was deserted by the early fifteenth, and Roel similarly had its own church in the thirteenth century but was later absorbed into the parish of Hawling. It is possible that more evidence may emerge when these deserted sites have been fully excavated, but the existing information seems to indicate that there were several factors contributing to the disappearance of these upland villages, and that they do not necessarily represent depopulation for sheep runs or by plague, but may include elements of both.

Changes in Pattern of Land Tenure

The effects of the Black Death, with the changes in land uses and the greater fluidity of society towards the end of the Middle Ages, left their mark on the agriculture and the pattern of land tenure in parts of the Cotswolds. A rental of Winchcombe Abbey of about 1355 indicates a considerable disintegration in what seems to have been a neat division of land into customary holdings of a yardland, which was the usual unit of land division in open-field agriculture, being a quarter of a hide, though the acreage varied considerably in different areas. Of thirty yardland holdings at Winchcombe Abbey's manor of Bledington many had either lapsed to the lord or changed hands, and at Hawling twenty-eight virgates were then held by only fifteen tenants. There is evidence, too, on the Winchcombe estates and many others that, while the demesne was not contracting, labour services were becoming lighter and more irregular and evidently were being extensively replaced by wage labour. Some manors show a tendency towards consolidation of holdings and even piecemeal enclosure. The manorial demesne particularly was sometimes consolidated and enclosed in the fifteenth century, occasionally, as at Barrington, not without protest from the tenants. Thus towards the close of the medieval period, with the increase in wage labour, the ties between tenants and landowners were weakening, though the distinction between freeholders and customary tenants was to remain marked for some time, even where customary service was paid in money.

GLOUCESTERSHIRE COLLEGE
OF EDUCATION
LIBRARY

Ecclesiastical Influence

During the next few hundred years after 1086 ecclesiastical land-owners extended their influence, and continued to be among the largest landowners in the area until the Dissolution of the Monasteries. With the refoundation by Henry I of Cirencester Abbey, which from 1155 farmed the royal manor of Cirencester, and the foundation of the Cistercian houses of Bruern and Hailes, there were four abbeys, including Winch-combe, situated in the Cotswold area. The influence of monasteries out-side the area continued, notably Evesham, Gloucester, Tewkesbury and Westminster Abbeys, to which Llanthony Priory may be added after its foundation in the early twelfth century. Apart from the influence of these monasteries on the agriculture of the area, their influence was felt most strongly perhaps in the parish churches. By the end of the thirteenth century churches or chapels existed in most of the Cotswold villages, and on the monastic estates these were often controlled by the abbey, which would own a large part of the tithes and would be responsible for the presentation of the priest. Winchcombe Abbey, for example, had control of all but two of the churches in the parishes where it had land.

Foundation of Modern Characteristics

The early Cotswold villages were built largely of timber and thatch, which, in spite of the abundance of limestone in the area, were the cheapest and easiest building materials. Winchcombe Abbey is said to have been burnt down in the twelfth century and Wotton-under-Edge to have been devastated by fire in the early thirteenth, indicating an extensive use of timber. By the thirteenth and fourteenth centuries, how-ever, the local limestone was replacing timber for domestic and farm buildings, particularly for the larger farmhouses, which sometimes accommodated people and animals under one roof. Many of the churches, too, were built, or rebuilt to replace earlier timber structures, in stone at this time, and retain features of this period, though, particularly in the more prosperous wool towns such as Northleach and Chipping Campden, the fifteenth century often saw extensive rebuilding or enrich-ing of churches.

By 1500, then, the Cotswolds had acquired many of the physical features that are characteristic of them today; the villages with their stone farmhouses and cottages and parish churches formed compara-tively self-contained units, with usually a mill and a few rural crafts; but

Page 107 *Canals:* (above) *A Severn trow in the basin at Brimscombe Port above Stroud, about 1910;* (below) *the only major aqueduct on the Thames & Severn Canal, across the present A429 near Kemble. Smerril bridge was demolished about 1928, but the foot of the right-hand abutment can still be seen beside the road*

Smerril Bridge

Page 108 *Railways:* (above) *Great Western Railway pannier tank and train at Fairford;* (below) *Cheltenham to Paddington express climbing to Salperton tunnel, a 2–6–2 tank locomotive piloting a 'Castle', 11 May 1948*

they were not isolated. Roads ran throughout the area and parishes often shared the responsibility of repairing roads and bridges. The area was dotted with small towns and markets, forming centres of local trade and industry, but apart from the growing woollen industry the area was still predominantly an agricultural one.

Notes to this chapter are on pages 301–6.

4

Farming and Industry
Past and Present

Frank H. Garner and Michael W. Ingram

Farming
Frank H. Garner

THE COTSWOLDS are well known as an area of outstanding natural beauty. The farming here is of a very high order, for high yields and outputs have been obtained, often from conditions that have not been ideal. This area has produced several agricultural workers who have made their mark not only on British agriculture but also on the world. The late Sir George Stapledon, who made such an impact upon grassland farming, became interested in grassland when he was a lecturer at the Royal Agricultural College at Cirencester. It was the late Professor Robert Boutflour, one time Principal of the College, who did so much to further the modern ideas of feeding dairy cows; he gained much practical experience of feeding dairy cows while in the Cotswolds and working with the local farmers. He really revolutionised the feeding of dairy cows. The name of the late Mr Ivor Morris also comes to mind for his work on sheep, and as chairman of the Wool Board he was a pioneer in his day. The Cotswolds has produced many first-class farmers who have been pioneers in their day.

In some counties there is much waste land, but the official statistics show that 95 per cent of the area of Gloucestershire is agricultural land; 50 per cent is above sea level but below 300ft, and a small area is above 900ft. This latter area is not of great agricultural importance but it is of value, since it provides popular vantage points that are frequented by the general public, in suitable weather, as picnic areas, and it seems likely that these areas for picnicking will become more numerous and of greater importance in the future as the people of this country have more leisure time.

Climate

The climate on the Cotswolds is not very severe, but snow falls in most winters and frost often occurs, though not as frequently as in some other counties of the same latitude. The average rainfall of the county is below 30in, but in certain areas, namely west of the Severn, it usually exceeds 40in. Rainfall is very important in the county, for there are watersheds for no less than five rivers, namely the Thames, Severn, Wye, Bristol Avon and the Warwick Avon. With these watersheds and rainfall one would not expect to find water the problem that it is. All crops on the light lands will suffer at harvest if there is a prolonged or severe drought in May or June. Some may think that, since there is so much water about, irrigation would be widely adopted, but sad to relate there is not sufficient water for this to be practicable on many farms. The rainfall, especially in the wintertime, produces drainage problems on the low-lying heavy grassland, and particularly in the river valleys. It is on these soils that some land is irrigated in the spring but for a different reason, namely to produce early grass. This is done on what are known as water meadows, and the water is said to warm up the soil to give early spring grazing, followed by good cuts of hay or silage and finally by another grazing. These water meadows were first put down several hundreds of years ago and they are still used successfully, in selected areas, today. Springs are found in many parts of the county, and many outlying farms have depended upon such sources for drinking water. Now mains water supplies are available almost everywhere.

Soils

The soils of the county include the very heavy clays on the edges of the Cotswolds, from which good bricks can be made, and brick kilns are to be seen in many different areas. In general the clays are in the river valleys, though in some of these areas rich alluvium is present. At the other extreme, especially on the high land of the Cotswolds, the soil is very light and often contains a high proportion of stones (limestones). These stones can prove to be a serious embarrassment when growing potatoes and harvesting them by mechanical means, for machines cannot discriminate between stones and potatoes. Gravel deposits are to be found more or less scattered over the county, which is a great asset, since it reduces haulage costs when used for building purposes. After removing the gravel, water soon accumulates in the pits, and this is being used for irrigation, or for such amenities as sailing, water ski-ing and fishing.

The earliest records show that much of the land was used for grazing, the lower-lying being for cattle, while the poorer light land of the hills was for the sheep, though this was often shared with rabbits (which were present in very large numbers till the appearance of myxomatosis completely eradicated them from most of the county). It is with regret, from the farming aspect, that one has to admit that rabbits are returning to a limited extent in some areas. Formerly the higher and lighter land was arable (not the highest with the steep slopes) and was used in the main to provide food, all the year round, for the arable land sheep. For centuries sheep had been kept in these regions (as evidenced by the frequent references to sheep in the names of public houses and hotels) and the wool they produced resulted in the development of the woollen industry, including the making of the famous West of England Tweed in the Stroud Valley. Although there has been a reduction in this industry, the manufacture of some cloth still persists.

Agriculture before 1866

CROPS

Before complete statistics were kept, the early records for Gloucestershire show that the heavy land that was not grass, mainly found off the true Cotswolds, was cropped with beans followed by wheat, and then a fallow was taken; this rotation persisted for many years. The grassland was popular for summer grazing for cattle, and 150 years ago was let for this purpose at £5 to £8 per acre for fattening bullocks. Drainage has been a constant probem, despite various attempts to put matters right; it is true to say it is still a problem.

The alluvial soils in the river valleys have enabled the farmers to grow a very wide range of crops, and this range has been made even wider in the last few years. On the light arable land of most of the Cotswold uplands the cropping was very much controlled by the demands of sheep, for, in addition to the normal arable crops, vetches, turnips, swedes, sainfoin, and trefoil were all grown primarily for the sheep feed. The main cereals grown were oats and barley, but wheat was also grown on the heavier fields in the light soil areas.

It is interesting to record that oxen were preferred to horses for ploughing the light land, mainly because they were cheaper to feed. Oxen were from the Herefords and Gloucesters that had been bred pure, and also as crosses of these two breeds.

LIVESTOCK

On the heavy soils many cattle were found, but those from the Severn Valley were driven to London for sale as fat beasts. In 1813 the drovers' charges were 22s per head, which included all commission on sales. The older cattle did well on this grassland, but with the young cattle there was a constant problem of husk (a parasite that produces irritation in the bronchials, resulting in first a cough and sometimes death), and it is interesting to record that unless special precautions are taken today husk is still a major problem. It was customary to fatten veal calves for a period of up to 6 weeks in small boxes or cages, 18in wide, 48in long and 18in off the ground, and today similar arrangements are made for calf-rearing. Then it was usual for the calves to be born in early spring and to remain indoors if fattened for veal, but all others went outside on the grass in May.

For many years the dairy industry has planned spring calving, the heifers calving for the first time when 3 years old; this meant that all dairy cows and heifers were fed on grass when their greatest demands were being made for food. The milk produced was, in the main, used for cheese-making (it being considered that only milk from cows eating grass was suitable for this purpose); the output of cheese per cow was 350 to 400lb per annum. Some butter was also made. The cows that were kept for this dairying were Gloucesters and Herefords and the crosses between these breeds. These were also the breeds that provided the oxen— in other words the steers from the dairy herds provided the oxen for the farm work. Longhorns were introduced to improve milk production. It was many years before there was any appreciable sale of liquid milk.

The whey from the cheese-making was fed to pigs. It was necessary to have one pig to every two cows to dispose of the quantity of whey that was produced. The local breed of Gloucester Old Spot were kept, but they were never very highly regarded for converting whey into meat.

The breeds of sheep were rather mixed and nondescript, giving only a clip of 3lb of wool per annum (now local sheep will usually give double this). In an attempt to improve the wool production Leicesters were introduced to cross with the local sheep. The Cotswold sheep were never present in large numbers, otherwise the yield of wool would have been much higher. The winter feeding created a problem with sheep as with cattle, for it was difficult to maintain growth at a satisfactory rate through-out the year; this was most likely to be achieved by growing the special arable land crops, namely turnips and swedes, for winter food, while sainfoin, trefoil and vetches were mainly for spring and summer feed.

Other breeds of sheep were introduced to try to improve the local breed, and these included Ryelands, Dorsets, Wiltshires and Welsh. (It is interesting to note that the Welsh were mentioned, because more recently they have been brought into this county, not as a pure breed

but as a cross with the Border Leicester, and called Welsh Half-breed.)
Nearly 200 years ago one of the problems of the sheep breeder was mag-
gots, which must have taken a heavy toll of sheep (under hot humid conditions) in the summertime, and farmers still have to take precautions
against this pest.

The Last 100 Years

CROPS

Official statistics have been kept in this country since 1866. It is therefore possible to compare the changes that have taken place in Gloucestershire with those that have taken place in England and Wales and, where
possible, to try to account for the differences that may be observed. As
may be expected, the areas devoted to various crops have been subject
to seasonal fluctuations, sometimes due to weather, to wartime conditions
and, of course, due to the profitability of various aspects of British
farming.

Wheat. Nationally the acreage of wheat has varied considerably,
between 3,000,000 and 1,600,000 acres, reaching the lowest figures in
the times of depression. This has also been the general pattern in
Gloucestershire, though there has been, since 1938, a greater increase
in the county than in the country. It seems that the yields of wheat have
been doubled per acre in the last 100 years, but unfortunately the figures
for the county are not available.

Barley and Oats. On the national scale the acreage of barley has
increased some two and a half times in the last 100 years, but in this
county the rise has been of the order of three and a half times, with a
greater change in the postwar period. This is undoubtedly because a
vast area of the lighter Cotswold land has been brought under the
plough, due largely to the modern use of the combined drill, which sows
seed and artificial manures together. Thus by modern methods relatively good yields have been obtained from the poor Cotswold soils. The
increase in the acreage of barley has been at the expense of oats. Nationally
the acreage of oats has been quartered in 100 years but in this county
it has only been halved. This is no doubt due to the demand for oats
in the county for feeding to hunters. Over this period the yield of barley
has risen from around 15cwt per acre to the 30cwt level and it may be
assumed that Gloucestershire may be even better than the national figure.
On the other hand there has been a smaller rise in the average yield of
oats and this has accounted for the falling off of the acreage, the simple

fact being that it has paid the farmers better to change to barley. During the last few years the introduction of new varieties of oats has resulted in slightly higher yields being obtained, and there may be a slight swing back to oats as a consequence.

Peas and Beans. For many years the statistics have shown that peas and beans were grown for stockfeeding, but of recent years the area taken by these crops has been declining to such an extent that Government action has been needed to encourage the growing of beans. Yields are so uncertain, however, and other forms of protein feed are so readily available, that in the very near future both these stockfeeds may disappear, and the rate of decline seems faster in Gloucestershire than in other parts of the country.

Potatoes. The acreage devoted to the potato crop has fluctuated widely both nationally and also on the county basis. Owing to the presence of stones in the Cotswolds, potatoes have never been a very important crop, although the acreage grown now is double that just before World War II. A few farmers continue to grow them as earlies, though they cannot really compete with many areas.

Roots. Turnips and swedes have become less popular almost annually over the last 100 years, falling from nearly 2,000,000 to just over 100,000 acres, and in Gloucestershire the fall has been to only 2 per cent of that of 100 years ago. This fall to some extent has been met by an increase in the popularity of kale, mainly for cows, but also to a limited extent for other cattle and sheep. Kale is more popular in Gloucestershire than nationally, no doubt because it may not stand the lower temperature in some districts. The acreage of mangolds grown has experienced considerable changes, from being relatively unimportant some 100 years ago, becoming valuable during both World Wars, but markedly declining after World War II, owing, to some extent, to the adverse opinion expressed by the late Professor Boutflour, who advised farmers all over the country against the use of this crop for feeding to dairy cows. The same general pattern has been experienced in the county, but to an even greater extent, and the present acreage is now less than 10 per cent of the wartime acreage.

Bare Fallow. The acreage of bare fallow has been reduced in the county and also nationally as a result of the increased growing of some crops that themselves keep weeds in check, or provide an opportunity of their being checked either by cultivations or, more recently, by chemical weed control. Some may be surprised to find bare fallows are still made, but the weather may enforce it sometimes, and hence there is a big variation in the bare fallow acreage from one year to the next. This is especially so on the clay soils after a spell of weather that has been difficult for autumn drilling followed by a very wet spring.

Leys. Leys consist of grasses and/or clovers grown for grazing and/or cutting, and remain for 1 to about 4 years, depending upon the species selected and upon the farming policy. Another name given for leys in Government publications is temporary grass. Both nationally and also in Gloucestershire lucerne was most popular just after World War II, but ever since its popularity has declined everywhere. This is rather surprising, since one would have thought this drought-resisting crop would have been popular, and ideal, for the light soils of the Cotswolds. One can only assume that the problem of feeding the crop to stock, either in its natural state or preserved (as hay silage or dried), led to problems that are difficult to understand.

Nationally there has been a tendency to turn more and more to the production of fodder and hay from clover and grasses, but this has not been the case in Gloucestershire, where the permanent pasture is favoured. The nature of the leys has changed over the years : formerly sainfoin, trefoil and clover stock mixtures were grown for feeding to sheep and also for haymaking, since they are not needed by the sheep, but they have disappeared and their places have been taken mainly by various rye-grasses, to a lesser extent by fescues and by cocksfoot on the lighter soils, and by timothies on the heavier soils. These latter grasses have produced greater weights of food per acre than was obtained from the previous 'old fashioned' leys. There has been a general fall in the quantity of hay made from the permanent pastures because of the greater use that is being made of the leys, and also because there is a greater acreage being devoted to silage-making. Leys in Gloucestershire are on average more popular for grazing than for cutting, which is not quite in keeping with the national position. This is doubtless because the leys have been so productive in Gloucestershire.

LIVESTOCK

Cattle. In the last 100 years the total number of all cattle in this country has been more than doubled, and there has been an even greater increase in cattle numbers in Gloucestershire. One finds that everywhere the numbers of dairy cows have increased but the increase has been slightly more pronounced in Gloucestershire. To give merely numbers does not give the full story, for there have been dramatic changes in the breeds kept. Around 100 years ago the Dairy Shorthorn (and various crosses with that breed) were the dairy cows of the country and county, but today the British Friesian has superseded all other breeds nationally, and Gloucestershire is no exception to this general position. This breed was developed originally for milk production, but more recently it has been proved to be excellent for meat production whether the calves are killed for veal, reared and killed as 12 to 15 month young beef, or kept to 24 or 30 months and sold as mature beef. This applies to pure-bred stock and also to the crosses, often with Hereford. The Friesian cows, when culled from the dairy herds, also produce valuable meat.

It has been stated earlier that cattle were fattened on the grassland of the Severn valley and then walked to London, but of course this stopped with the advent of trains. More recently the fat cattle have been moved by road transport to London and the consuming areas. In addition many cattle leave the county as stores for fattening; some leave for rearing, others leave when they are around 3 months old, and others still are sold when ready for final fattening. Annually hundreds of cattle pass through Gloucester Market, which has a good reputation for the sale of good store stock, and buyers will attend from many parts of the country. A recent development in the county has resulted in the organising of rearer groups. In these groups calves are purchased when a few days old and reared till 3 months, when they are sold in batches of twenty to fifty to single purchasers. This is proving to be a sound financial scheme, providing the calves are healthy and the losses are at a minimum.

The original dairy industry of this county just supplied the milk for cheese-making and to a lesser extent butter, but with the advent of long-distance haulage more was sold as liquid milk and less as dairy produce; this was also the national policy. Here as elsewhere the sizes of the dairy herds have increased, although there are still many family dairy farms in the Severn valley. The bigger units usually have modernised buildings with cubicles to house the cows when being self-fed on silage. It would be true to say that the dairy farmers of Gloucestershire are very progressive with feeding grass, silage, hay with barley and protein additives that may contain minerals. An increasing number of cows are being milked through herringbone parlours.

Sheep. The national picture of sheep numbers has undergone considerable fluctuations owing to economic pressures and also to wartime conditions, but during the last few years it reached its postwar peak of 20,000,000 and it is again falling a little. In Gloucestershire the numbers were high till the beginning of this century, when they fell, and were up to the high level in 1966 but they are again falling away to a slight extent. In Gloucestershire the original sheep kept were the arable land sheep, but now they are essentially the grassland sheep that are bought in as lambs, or one year later from the hills of Wales, Scotland or the Border country. These mountain-bred sheep live largely on leys, where they are kept intensively. Some lambs are sold fat at weaning but a few will be sold as stores for fattening on roots on the arable land. The breeding ewes will have four or five crops of lambs before they are culled, or they may remain till the end of their breeding lives, when they are sold fat. The breeds have changed from the Cotswolds and Leicesters and their crosses to Half Bred from either Wales or Scotland, together with Cluns and Kerries from the Welsh borders. The rams used have been from the Oxford Downs (especially in wartime, when maximum weight was required) the Hampshire and and Wiltshires (when early fat lambs were wanted) and the Suffolk for good lamb production. More recently Dorset Horns and Dorset Downs have found more favour to produce fat lambs to be sold direct from the ewes. Store lamb sales are still held in the county, so the lambs may be moved away to fatten on the roots in the wintertime. Some of these store lambs may move right away from the county to the arable areas of the East and the North, for very few have remained for fattening in the county.

Pigs. Over the years the pig population has been subjected to more violent fluctuations than any other of the farm animals, with the lowest level just after World War II with just over 1 million, rising to over 6 million in 1965; the numbers have fallen away ever since. In Gloucestershire the numbers continue to rise and only show a falling-off in the rate of growth. These variations in the pig numbers are due to the big fluctuations in the profitability of pig-keeping and to the very rapid rate by which pig numbers can be modified. Originally the keeping of pigs was tied to the dairy industry, to use up the by-products, but more recently the by-products from the arable farms have played a part, namely cereals and potatoes. A limited quantity of swill has come from the larger towns. Now the pig industry is much more dependent upon the cereals than upon anything else. One of the local pig-breeders has made a name for his company by selling breeding pigs to many parts of the world; these pigs are the new hybrids that are now very popular. As on a national scale, so locally the pigs have moved into bigger herds, and also away from outdoor systems to indoors, with the pigs spending their entire lives on concrete.

Poultry. Since early records were taken the poultry numbers have increased from 10,000,000 in 1884 to over 100,000,000 in 1968, with of course, falls in the numbers kept in the two World Wars. These latest figures understate the real position, for with the broiler industry the birds are being killed at only 10 weeks old and many therefore never appear in the official returns taken on 4 June. Formerly the fat birds were over 6 months of age before they were killed. This national pattern has also appeared in Gloucestershire, where the latest figures give over 2,000,000 birds. Again everywhere the poultry are being kept in units that are ever increasing in size. In effect they are being kept on factory lines.

Horses. Before ending this discussion on stock some mention must be made of horses. The farm horse was an essential part of the livestock enterprise of the country 100 years ago, although in some areas, including Gloucestershire, bullocks were used for ploughing; now the whole of the farm work is done by mechanical devices for transport and cultivation. This change started first with the use of steam tackle, followed by the tractor, and today one has smaller equipment, such as self-propelled rotovators, used in market gardens. In Gloucestershire the horse has moved completely away from the farming scene after reaching its peak early in this century, with most rapid rate of decline after World War II. The introduction of the tractor enabled farmers to cultivate with much greater speed and so cover a greater acreage than was possible with horses. It also made it possible to cultivate some slopes that had hitherto been too steep for arable farming in the horse days; this has been very beneficial to the farmers of Gloucestershire. Modern equipment has made it easy to meet the shortage of labour by using sprays to kill weeds and big equipment to harvest corn and also roots. The yields have kept pace with those of the rest of the country and exceeded them except when there has been a drought in May, and that always has a serious effect upon corn yields in the Cotswolds.

Ponies and light horses for hunting and for hacking are increasing in popularity in the Cotswolds, and many are bred here. National riding events at Badminton, polo at Cirencester, and countless local pony clubs and horse shows encourage this.

Fruit, Flowers and Vegetables. The total acreage of land in orchards in England and Wales rose from 1870 to 1950 but during the past 20 years has fallen away. This has also been the general pattern in Gloucestershire, where fruit-growing is mainly off the Cotswolds proper. On closer examination one finds that both nationally and in Gloucestershire the acreage of Cox's Orange Pippins has been maintained, but the acreages of all other varieties has fallen, including Worcesters and Bramleys, while the acreage of cider apples has fallen away very much more rapidly, Gloucestershire being no exception to this general statement.

Pears for cider-making have also fallen in the same way. On the other hand Conference pears have been maintained both nationally and also in Gloucestershire. All kinds of plums have declined in popularity and the acreages of all kinds have fallen. If the situation is examined more closely, one finds there has been less fruit-planting in orchards in Gloucestershire than nationally, which means that the importance of fruit in this county must decline in the future.

Small Fruit. Nationally the acreage of small fruit has been falling over the last 40 years at the rate of at least 1 per cent per annum, but, contrary to this, the acreage in Gloucestershire has been increasing. On closer examination one finds that strawberries and raspberries have declined everywhere but it is in blackcurrants that Gloucestershire has differed from the national picture, for there has been a marked increase in this county, namely between two and three times since World War II. This development has taken place in the Newent and Dymock Areas and in fact quite extensively throughout the Severn valley, though the greater portion of blackcurrants would be just outside the Cotswolds. This crop was unpopular in the past because of the difficulty in obtaining pickers but with the new machines that are now being developed this problem has disappeared. This may lead to an even greater extension of growing of blackcurrants in this county, since both the soil and the climate are so suitable for obtaining good yields.

Glasshouses. In England and Wales the acreage of salads, fruits and flowers under glass has been almost static for the last few years, although it now shows some signs of rising slightly both in the case of fixed and also of mobile glasshouses. It would seem that the rise is greater than average in Gloucestershire, whether the survey is made in July or January. It is unfortunate that complete details are not obtainable from the national statistics, so one cannot be sure of the various crops grown in Gloucestershire.

One cannot help but wonder, with the United Kingdom joining the Common Market, whether those growing crops in glasshouses may have the most severe competition from the Continent, especially when one remembers that some of the countries that are at present in the Common Market can grow their crops out-of-doors without using any artificial heat.

Changing Pattern of Farming

The Cotswolds, in common with many other districts, have experienced changes in three main directions, namely :

(*a*) a fall in the number of farmworkers;

(*b*) partly from the fall in numbers of workers and partly from the very real rise in the cost of labour there has been an astonishing increase in mechanisation;

(*c*) in order to facilitate the greatest use of machinery, farms have been made larger.

Farmworkers have been falling in numbers ever since records began to be kept. Gloucestershire is no exception to this general rule, and one finds that because of this change a number of the farm cottages are no longer required for farmworkers—they are often sold off by the owners or let to workers from the towns, and also as weekend cottages. It is possible that this general trend may continue indefinitely, since fewer workers are required, and there is a growing tendency also for those farm workers to live in towns and villages and travel out to the farms to work.

Throughout this chapter references have been made to the mechanisation of various farming activities both with stock and also with crops, and this must continue wherever efficient machines are available. This is a sign of the times and must be accepted as inevitable, for farming in this country, including the Cotswolds.

The changing pattern of farming which has resulted in farms becoming larger, especially in the case of arable land, has been seen in Gloucestershire, for there have been many amalgamations on the lighter soils. This has made it easier for mechanisation to make the fullest use of modern farm equipment. Even some of the stone walls that are so characteristic of the county have disappeared with these amalgamations and with the increasing sizes of individual fields for the ever-enlarged farm equipment. Some farmers who have not made their farms bigger by increasing their acreages have made their enterprises bigger by co-operating with their neighbours, (*a*) in the use of machinery and equipment, (*b*) in the purchase of fertilisers, sprays and foods and various farm requisites, and (*c*) in the sale of crops and of livestock. There are all the signs that these various forms of cooperation will increase in the future.

Forestry

Some critics may claim that forestry and agriculture are quite separate and that trees should not be considered in an agricultural section, but of recent years trees have been playing such an increasing part in the development of the countryside that no real excuse need be made for their inclusion. The Cotswolds are famous for their beeches, indeed so famous that whenever foresters come into the district for a conference they invariably visit the Bathurst Estate at Cirencester where some of the very best beeches of the whole of the United Kingdom are to be found. Other trees are to be found and special mention must be made of the elms. These have been a feature of the countryside, but alas the dreaded elm disease has appeared and taken a very heavy toll of the trees. The area will be denuded unless there is a special planting programme in the near future. One might expect limes, chestnuts, conifers, and in selected areas some of the various oaks might find a place.

With the estate forestry there are also the estate timber yards for the conversion of timber both for use on the estates and also for sale. As in farming, also with forestry; the timber business is moving into the hands of the larger specialists who can make the greatest use of modern equipment and machinery.

Royal Agricultural College

No mention of farming in the Cotswolds is complete without some reference being made to the progressive, and far-seeing, farmers of the area who in 1845 played the leading part in the founding of the Royal Agricultural College outside Cirencester. This has very much influenced the farming not only of the Cotswolds and of the United Kingdom, but to some extent the whole world, since the college has attracted students from most countries and English students have gone from the college overseas. The RAC is independent. Its policy has been to teach sound commercial farming by having first a farm and later several farms of its own (which have been run on commercial lines for profit), and also of having the very willing cooperation of many of the Cotswold farmers, who have opened their farms, and sometimes their balance sheets, to students. This has been an invaluable asset to make the teaching really effective, so it is impossible to express adequately the help that farmers, estate owners, and their staffs have given over the past 125 years to some thousands of students.

Farm Life

The county of Gloucestershire has provided homes for a number of old farming families and, despite high taxation, many of these families have managed to retain their land. The farms on some of these estates are still let, though there is a growing tendency, at the end of a tenancy, for the landlord to retain the land to farm it himself (unless he sells it at an enhanced price with vacant possession) or to farm it in partnership with a new tenant. This is, of course, a recognised way of meeting the present taxation on unearned income.

For many years the price of land in this county has been high, largely on account of its amenity value and not because the soil itself is naturally very rich, for the light soil is naturally poor. It is a county in which a number of people wish to reside, first because of the natural beauty of the countryside and secondly because of the recreational facilities the county can offer, namely, hunting, shooting, and to a limited extent fishing. Thus a number of the smaller farms are not necessarily run on purely commercial lines but merely as country residences for those who commute to the towns and cities or for those who have retired. Some of these farms will provide summer grazing for hunters, while hay, oats and straw will be bought in from local farmers for use in the wintertime. This special demand will influence the farming policies of a limited number of farmers throughout the county.

Influence of Soil and Climate

To some it may seem unnecessary to say that farming is not influenced by county boundaries but by soil and climate. Thus it is not surprising to· find that the farming of Somerset, Wiltshire, Berkshire and Oxfordshire where it borders upon Gloucestershire, is mainly dairying, whether the land is the heavy clay (grass) or the light arable land, but on the latter of course cereals, especially barley, will be grown.

In the counties adjoining the north and west of Gloucestershire, namely Warwickshire, Worcestershire, Herefordshire and Monmouth, there will be a big variety of crops on the arable land. This will include various kinds of fruits and also vegetables (including potatoes) in addition to the usual cereals, and a limited acreage of sugar beet. Of the vegetables grown, brussels sprouts are of special interest, for they are often grown on contract. The farmer will be required to plough the field before handing it over to the hirer, who then applies the necessary artificials, does the cultivations and grows, harvests and ultimately sells the crop. It is usual to vacate the field by an agreed date to allow time for the preparations for the subsequent crop. The current rate for the hire of the arable field for the year is of the order of £20. From the owner's point of view that is good business, for it gives him a change of cropping without the need of purchasing any special equipment necessary to grow the crop or even any expertise in brussels sprouts production and marketing.

The outstanding change in the Cotswolds during the last few years has been the development of barley-growing on the lightest soils and also at the highest altitudes in the county. So satisfactory has been the yield of this crop that some farmers have grown it continuously on the same field for as many as a dozen years, without any loss of yield; this has been achieved by the liberal use of artificial manures. Some farmers are getting nervous of this continuous corn-growing and have been searching for other crops for a change. In this connection both peas on the lighter land and beans on the stronger lands have been tried with considerable success. Another of the new crops that has been grown is the ley of one or more years' duration. These leys have provided food for both sheep and cattle for intensive grazing in the summer and also for winter feed in the form of silage. On the heavier soils in the Severn valley the small grassland farms that are often family dairy farms present a problem, for they are not much wanted except for amalgamations, and so are often difficult to sell on the open market. Dairying has been developed on the lighter soils, where large herds are to be found on the large arable farms.

Sheep have undergone a major change, for whereas formerly they were fed on roots on arable land in the winter, the breeds that were suitable for such a system have disappeared, and in their places have come the hill and mountain breeds and crosses. These recently introduced sheep live on leys and grassland, often under intensive conditions with half a dozen ewes and their lambs on an acre. In this way as good returns can be obtained from the sheep industry as from the cereals.

Pig and poultry enterprises have followed the national pattern of moving from small units on many farms to big units on a few farms. In other words, factory farming has appeared in both pig and poultry keeping.

Common Market Prospects

Finally, in these days when so much is being said about the Common Market, it would seem that the farmers of Gloucestershire should, in general, be able to compete well with the Continental farmers. They will obtain good yields of cereals, and if the present prices prevailing on the Continent continue, this should prove satisfactory. The climate of Gloucestershire enables the farmers to grow grass from permanent pasture and leys, which enables them to provide good food both in the summer and winter for cattle (dairy and beef) and also for sheep. Provided they can use the maximum quantity of grass and the minimum of cereals, the farmers should compete very favourably with those in the Common Market countries.

Industry
Michael W. Ingram

The Cotswolds never have been and probably never will be an industrial area. The countryside is very sparsely provided with mineral

Page 125 *The wool and cloth trade:* (above) *Dunkirk mill, Nailsworth;* (below) *Lodge-moor mill, Stroud*

Page 126 *The wool and cloth trade:* (left) *circular stove-house at Woodchester;* (below) *a mill wheel at Painswick*

resources, and the nature of the landfall has ensured that towns would not grow to any great size and that the uplands would only support small villages. As the area is now designated one of natural beauty, it is very unlikely that this situation will be reversed.

Changes in Last 100 Years

Industry in the area has historically depended upon the natural produce of the hills, with very few exceptions. The cloth and wool trade (see Chapter 6) provided virtually all the means of employment, apart from farming and its ancillary services, for many hundreds of years. It is only in the last century that the decline in the woollen trade has slowly drawn other industries to the district to fill the vacant mills and to employ those who are left without their traditional work. More recently still, small companies have been attracted to the district, often largely because their owners and founders thought that the Cotswolds were agreeably situated both from the transport and community point of view. But the population continues to grow more slowly than in many other parts of Britain, and unemployment has been lower in the area than almost anywhere else outside the immediate neighbourhood of London and the South-east. This has prevented companies growing beyond a relatively small size, and it is now the policy of all the local authorities involved to continue this state of affairs. The development of motorways and the railway system has restored the splendid transport system which the Romans gave the Cotswolds, and now the area is extremely well situated to distribute goods throughout England.

The development of business has still largely followed the natural progression from industries ancillary to the cloth trade and farming, although in some cases companies have developed widely away from their original purpose and have exported with success throughout the world. Indeed, this has often been a necessity, as the local home market has been limited by the sparsity of population.

Former Trades apart from Wool

The earliest industry, apart from wool and cloth, which came to the Cotswolds seems to have been glassmaking, and Mr J. S. Daniels has written about the establishment of the Woodchester Glass House in the latter half of the sixteenth century. This was established by a small body

H

of Huguenots, who began making more common glass vessels in this country than those provided through the Venetian monopoly. They originally started in Kent and moved through Surrey, Sussex and Hampshire, where they established a Glass House between Winchester and Salisbury, and moved across the country from there to Woodchester. They had to move fairly quickly from place to place because of the enormous quantity of timber they needed to fell to feed their furnaces. A Glass House could use 400,000 billets of wood in one year's working. Their stay in Woodchester appears to have been no longer than 25 years, and the group of glassmakers moved on about 1615 to the Forest of Dean.

Since that time the Cotswolds have had comparatively few foreign workers, until some Poles and Italians settled in the district after World War II.

At Cirencester the woollen trade declined earlier than it did in the Stroud valley, in consequence of which a number of attempts were made to provide employment for the inhabitants of the town in other ways. This led, for instance, to the establishment in the seventeenth century of the Cirencester Society in London, whose members comprised prominent citizens of the town and businessmen living in London who still maintained connections with Cirencester. The Society had as its purpose the apprenticing of boys from the town to London Merchants and Manufacturers, who could give them far better opportunities than were available at home. This Society still provides from its charitable funds assistance to young people learning a trade.

Rebecca Powell, in the establishment of one of her schools in the town, decreed that the girls should be taught the art of framework knitting, and some kind of industry was established in the town, although it proved to be short-lived.

In the latter part of the eighteenth century, Cirencester was also famous for the production of curriers' knives. These long wedge-shaped implements, which were used for stripping the hair from the hide, were made with considerable success in Cirencester and later in Gloucester, but in the 1820s Birmingham took over the supremacy in this field, although four edge toolmakers in Cirencester are still recorded in the *Gloucestershire Directory* of 1820.

POSTLIP MILL

One of the most interesting continuing industries in the district has been papermaking. On the edge of the Cotswolds there must have been a very large number of corn mills which were just as under-used as that at Postlip, near Winchcombe, but few if any others took the logical step of using the same water power that drove the corn mills after harvest to make paper at other times in the year.

The mills at Postlip were mentioned in Domesday Book, but it was only in the early eighteenth century that one of them, at the junction of two streams that join at the point where the Mill is to form the River Isbourne, came to be used for the manufacture of paper. In 1752, John Burnham of Postlip, Paper Maker, gave evidence in a lawsuit about various means of making scale board from beech wood, and in 1789 Simon Moreau, writing in his *Tour of the Royal Spa at Cheltenham* says that 'at Postlip is one of the most considerable Paper manufacturers in the Kingdom belonging to Messrs. Durham and Stevens. Writing paper is made at Postlip'. The name Durham is one of the earliest recorded watermarks (1764) of an English firm.

The mill changed hands a number of times until the present firm of Evans Adlard was established in 1849. At this time the prosperity of the mill fluctuated with the annual rainfall; there was no shortage of demand for printing paper but if water power was cut off in a dry summer, losses could easily be made. In 1854 the first steam engine was installed and production doubled! Dependence on a wet English summer had been broken.

The company has always made specialist papers, and early made the self blue paper still used for the pack of Seidlitz Powders and corrosion-free paper for packaging of needles. Since 1869 filtering paper has been made and between the world wars production was concentrated on various types of specialised filtration media. Now the emphasis which anti-pollution imposes on clean air must give an added importance to this type of production, although the motor car industry, as so often is the case, is the largest customer. Petrol, oil and air filters in the modern car use paper to keep foreign bodies from circulating in the engine.

A new development is glass-fibre-loaded filter paper to protect the atmosphere from radioactive particles discharging from nuclear power stations. A laboratory employing three graduates and a liaison with Hollingsworth & Vose of Massachusetts enable the company to progress into similar new fields.

The managing director and works director are still descendants of the original Adlard family, but ownership has passed to the Imperial Tobacco Company through its papermaking subsidiary, Robert Fletcher & Son Ltd. In company with other Cotswold family concerns, fast expansion and independence have been irreconcilable. But Postlip Mill still nestles in the valley by the river, to the side of which its owners could walk and catch a trout. Evans Adlard is typical in many ways of the Cotswold valley industries that had their roots in farming of the land but moved with the passage of time in completely new directions.

Stroud Valley from Mid-nineteenth Century

The prospectus inviting subscription to the Cheltenham & Great Western Union Railway Company, which was engineered by I. K. Brunel, was authorised by Act of Parliament in 1836 and refers to the manufacturing districts of Chalford, Stroud, etc; and although at this time the valley was almost wholly dependent on the cloth and woollen trade, the beautiful mills that were emptied as the trade declined provided both the buildings and the source of power that made it a thriving industrial community.

Originally, any metalworking was established so as to provide machinery and equipment for weaving and carding, and one large Dursley firm, Mawdsley's, think that the first metal product produced in their factory was the common pin, used in carding before the headed pin was invented. But as the woollen industry gradually declined and migrated to Yorkshire and greater availability of power, the mills became empty and business which had been dependent on the industry was compelled to move into other fields. Four of the largest of the companies—Daniels' of Stroud, Lister's and Mawdsley's of Dursley, and Critchley's at Brimscombe, all fell into this category, and most of the principal employers in the area have their roots in the middle of the nineteenth century.

World War I brought about considerable expansion, and some of the firms were entirely occupied in the manufacture of armaments, which caused them to expand at a rate that was difficult to sustain in the 1920s and 1930s. But World War II in its turn brought new industries to the district and stimulated the growth of existing firms still further. The result has been that in the Stroud valley at present there is a great variety of light industry, with the consequence that the valley has never been dependent recently on one sector of the national economy for its prosperity, and employment has been maintained at a very high level, even when the rest of the country has had its difficulties. Now, growth is restricted, not so much because of lack of opportunity, but from the geographical nature of the country, the steep hills and availability of land making it difficult to provide any flat industrial land.

The history of firms like Daniels' and Lister's are typical of the way in which the Stroud valley and Dursley have developed.

DANIELS'

The Daniels family moved into the valley from Nympsfield about 1840 as blacksmiths. The smith was then the maintenance engineer to the woollen industry, repairing its plant, making up fixtures and providing a certain amount of the engineering background, and the firm, which was officially started in 1840, continued in this capacity and acted as millwrights generally in the neighbourhood for as long as 40 years, before they opened their first Grey Iron Foundry, which itself continued in being until 1969. To serve the foundry, a small pattern-making shop and a small machine shop were established. These were followed by a fabricating shop, and by gas-producing plants, which drove the gas engines that were then popular throughout industry for providing power. As a firm with its roots in the country, it also made corn-milling machinery and textile machines for the remaining cloth industry in the valley. It is typical of the way in which industry developed here, with both local interests and the wider interests of industry throughout the country being served at the same time. Between 1905 and 1914 'Trusty' oil engines, which were the forerunners of the modern diesel engine, were made and the Excelsior Pump Company, which had a valid licence from the German firm Gütermuth for high speed pumps was taken over, and Daniels' began to export pumps (another Cotswold speciality) all over the world for mines and railways. They also made the first 'still' engine, which was a combined steam and oil engine used for propelling ships.

Its first move into the plastics industry, now the mainstay of the business, took place when it began to make extruders for a local rubber company which at that time operated at Thrupp Lane, and it made rubber vulcanising equipment for the repair of early type car tyres. Domestic gas-producing plants were also very popular and were used extensively for producing electric lighting before this was produced on any wide scale. Derry & Toms, for instance, installed a 170hp gas engine in 1907 to light their London store.

During World War I armaments were made and portable water treatment plants to provide drinking water for the troops, and in 1916 the first hydraulic presses and twin-screw extruders were made for Erinoid at Lightpill, one of the pioneer companies in the manufacture of plastics for the production of casein, which was at that time widely needed for military purposes. Pumps, presses and other equipment for the plastics industry have since then been the mainstay of Daniels' production, although again in the 1939–45 war the company was of necessity compelled to produce, among other things, bombs for use by aircraft, rocket-launching units and hydraulic equipment for aircraft. Chain saws were also made, bringing Daniels' back again into the agricultural field, and the name Danarm is widely associated with these saws.

In 1961 the company obtained a quotation on the Stock Exchange and has since that time gradually lost its intimate connection with the Daniels' family. More recently, having been taken over by the Unochrome International Group, the name was changed to Daniels of Stroud Ltd, and then upon acquiring the two Hamilton Machinery Companies to Daniels Hamilton Ltd. The progression from small family-owned company to one of national stature has now been completed, with the company being a sizeable subsidiary of an International Group.

LISTER'S

The history of Lister's, who employ approximately 3,000 people in and around Dursley, is in many ways similar, both in the nature of their beginning and their involvement with the production of power units. But now the businesses have turned in very different directions from one another.

The first Lister in the company, Robert Ashton Lister, came down from Yorkshire in the 1860s to open a modest foundry, with three men and a boy on his payroll, once again serving the woollen industry in the neighbourhood. But very soon the company's product range had moved into the agricultural field, and the well known Beaufort Hunt Corn Crusher and the Lister Chain Harrow were introduced. Both are still made to this day, together with sheep shearers and elevators for bales, but the company was very early to recognise the importance of electricity, and countless houses, farms and factories throughout the world have generated their first power with Lister engines. In 1909 they secured the exclusive licence for a patented fully automatic electric generating plant, powered by Lister petrol engines. These now largely use diesel as fuel and are sent all over the world.

From the 1890s the company has exported, and the many sons of the family must have travelled miles and miles in obtaining millions of pounds worth of export business. Lister's was one of the earliest Cotswold firms to have subsidiaries elsewhere in the county and the country, and has had from time to time branches at Cinderford, Wroughton and Manchester. Like Daniels', it was for many years a company wholly run by the family, and it still has members of the family on the board, but it was taken over by the Hawker-Siddeley Group after the company celebrated its centenary year in 1967, and the older generation of Listers has now retired.

MAWDSLEY'S

One of the early factories owned by the Lister family was the Rivers Mill, which is probably the earliest building still to be occupied by a manufacturing company in the district. The earliest product there was the simple pin; leather was widely used for driving the machinery of that time and the building had a tannery. The Rivers Mill was taken over in 1907 by Mr Mawdsley, who already had a considerable reputation as a designer of electrical machines, and he renamed the Mill 'Zone Works' to commemorate his 'Zone' patents. Generators supplied to government departments, electric light and other companies were generally of a large and specialised nature, which did not compete with the products manufactured by Lister's. Mr Mawdsley retired in 1934 and the company was taken over by a small group, Southern Areas Electric Corporation Ltd, and the range of products began to broaden. The company went extensively into producing for the Admiralty, the business expanding very fast during World War II. Now, as so often seems to happen in Gloucestershire, the company has been acquired by an outsider to the district, the Adwest Group, but as at Lister's, the family atmosphere still continues.

Nailsworth and Area

NEWMAN HENDER

The Newman Hender Group in Nailsworth started in rather a different way. A Mr Brice, who was in a Bristol firm of Founders which was crippled by a strike lasting upwards of a year, moved to Nailsworth in 1879 so that he could carry on business in partnership with Mr Newman, the grandfather of Mr Noel Newman, who was until a very short time ago chairman of the company. A brass foundry was established in a disused dye house. This was beside the newly cut railway line running up the valley. Throughout its history, the company has been brass founders, and from very early days made valves and other fittings in general for the power industry for whatever source of power was employed at the time. As at Mawdsley's, water was early used to generate their power, but the success of the company, which now employs approximately 2,000 people in the valley, has been based on the capacity to produce very high quality brass parts of a large size. Specialisation has been the key to the company's success, and although diverted by war from its customary products (over 40 million fuses and primers were produced during World War II), it continued throughout as specialists in the valve field. In

1948 Newman Hender was perhaps the first Cotswold company to go public, and in the next 12 years it took over a number of other companies in the same field, outside the district. Despite its preoccupation with industrial valves, the company has branched out into agriculture with Ben Nevis Egg Equipment Ltd, which manufactures (now at Trowbridge) and sells all types of egg-grading machinery and automatic packing equipment. The family connection is now on the wane, however, and Newman Hender itself has been taken over by Hattersley Pegler with the intention of rationalising the manufacture of valves throughout the country. A very large proportion of its output of valves is exported and very little, of course, used locally. The oil industry has compelled members of the company to spend much of their time abroad and to visit countrysides very different from the Nailsworth valley in which the company started. There is indeed a Canadian company among other foreign subsidiaries.

CHAMBERLAIN'S

Also in the Nailsworth valley and close to Newman Hender's is Chamberlain's, the largest remaining family company in the Stroud area. The family interest has been continuous since 1879, when Mr E. A. Chamberlain, the sole representative of the British Board Mills, bought them out, the company having been established in buildings formerly belonging to a cloth manufacturer. First cardboard and then fibreboard have been the principal products of the firm, which now operates the second largest mill of its kind in Europe. Many thousands of tons of board are sold annually, and moulded board from Nailsworth is extensively used in cars and suitcases all over the world. The original staple product of the company was the insole reinforcer made from board, which forms part of nearly all shoes of conventional make. There are probably few people today in the country who have not trodden on Chamberlain's fibreboard!

Stroud Valley Manufacturers

The Stroud valley has a large variety of manufacturers, one of which continues an old tradition. Pins have been made in Gloucestershire since the seventeenth century, and Gloucester was at one time the centre of the industry, but solid headed pins were made in very large quantities by Critchley Bros, whose principal business is now electrical cable and wiring accessories, such as markers and ducting. Indeed in 1906 when they employed 300 hands they must have been one of the largest employers in the valley. They still make knitting needles, and pins are made at Painswick (see Chapter 6).

Brimscombe also has Benson's International Systems Ltd, another public company, which is the largest maker of rings for loose-leaf books in the world.

Bentley Pianos remain one of the few flourishing English piano manufacturers, having moved from Woodchester to another mill in 1911. They now export two-thirds of their output, and have supplied pianos to the Emperor of Nepal and Prince Rainier of Monaco. They are not the first maker of musical instruments to have inhabited the Stroud valley. Richard Clutterbuck, a blind man living in Rodborough in the seventeenth century, is recorded as having 'made violins, bass viols, and citterns, and virginals with double jacks, and other improvements of his own invention. He also taught music according to a scale of his own forming and cut his notes upon pieces of wood'. Perhaps he thus invented an early form of braille.

Export has always been a strong element in the prosperity of Cotswold firms and has contributed much to their continued survival in a district which would seem to be ill adapted from its geographical situation to support flourishing manufacturing units. The necessity to look beyond local markets has perhaps led them to look abroad for their sales.

Cirencester and Tetbury

Cirencester and Tetbury provide the only genuine industrial sites in the district, and as these have only been established since World War II, it is natural that the enterprises on them are comparative newcomers. Only the maltsters, Hugh Baird, were in Cirencester before that time, when food-processing was virtually the only industry. Now plastic moulding, as in the Stroud valley, is carried on by a number of firms, including one operating from a former bacon factory. There are also three companies making precision equipment of various types: one in the office machinery field, a subsidiary of a Swedish company Addo, whose headquarters are in Malmo; another, Ticket Equipment Ltd, making mechanical and electronic equipment for the issue of tickets in the transport industry; and a third, GIB Precision, whose products are used generally in engineering firms.

The Mycalex Group, which came to Cirencester from London in 1940, also manufactures electrical insulating materials composed of glass and mica, and small electric motors which are extensively used in the domestic appliance industry.

There are also toolmaking companies, as there are in the Stroud valley.

The industrial site is being extended and another site on the land formerly occupied by the railway yard will be available for light industry.

Tetbury was formerly one of the centres of the building trade, and a firm there at one time employed 300 men; now its industrial site is occupied by, among others, a subsidiary of LRC International, which makes vending machines and diecastings, and REEMA, the manufacturers of prefabricated houses.

Pumps, Beer and Food-processing

The only manufacturing company of any size which is situated on the Cotswold hills is Godwin's, whose pumps have been made for more than 50 years in the village of Quenington. Serving initially the farms of the area and providing much needed water, its products have since spread over England and many parts of the world. Now no longer family-owned, its founder still lives beside the factory he established.

The Cotswolds lying between Herefordshire and Somerset have never been cider country, although the hills overlooking the Berkeley Vale were reputed to have been the best wine-growing area in England, but there were many flourishing breweries. Cirencester had three, Burford one and Stroud several, but now the only beer brewed on the Cotswolds comes from Donnington, the smallest brewery in the country, with only seventeen houses, and the delightful tradition of good beer and a truly local flavour. It is sad that so many small breweries have disappeared, but the area is not large enough to support a large modern brewery.

Food-processing has also declined, and now Hillier's at Nailsworth remains the only bacon curer on the Cotswolds, two having shut down in Cirencester in the last 15 years. But there is a large NAAFI Bakery at Cirencester which serves many of the military establishments in the South of England.

Crafts and Furniture

The beauty of the district has always attracted craft industries, and there are a large number of weavers, potters, and stonemasons in the area—their wares are exhibited annually at Painswick—but two of these have grown into sizeable undertakings. On the north-west escarpment the monks of Prinknash Abbey have built up a thriving business in their highly individual black ware, which has done much to support the rebuilding of their Abbey.

At Broadway, modern furniture designed by Sir Gordon Russell and his successors has been made for many of our churches and cathedrals, as well as offices and schools all over England. This company had its origins in Sir Gordon Russell's concern for the furnishing of the Lygon Arms at Broadway, which he owned. The antique furniture required for the house frequently needed repair and restoration, and a number of cabinetmakers were got together at Chipping Campden for this purpose.

Raw Materials

WATER

The only basic raw materials that the Cotswolds provide for industry are stone and water. Water now has little importance as a source of power, but the great majority of people who dwell in the Cotswolds are fortunate to have a pure and wholesome supply of water which requires the minimum of chemical treatment, and in spite of the sparsity of population of the area, there is now only one small and somewhat remote parish (pop 138) in which a mains supply is not available. It is estimated that in England and Wales 97 per cent of the population now has a mains supply and the authorities in the Cotswolds have not lagged behind in the national effort to secure that the most essential of one's daily needs is literally on tap.

Consumers in a small area of the Western Cotswolds receive water abstracted from the Severn at Tewkesbury, and this water, because of the trade effluent content originating where the river flows through highly industrialised areas, is the subject of extensive purification treatment at the Mythe works. The supply to other consumers comes entirely from wells and boreholes in the Cotswold Limestones and it has been claimed that much of this water could safely be consumed without further treatment. Even so, no responsible authority would place its consumers at risk in this matter, and the obvious minimum precaution of chlorination is taken without exception.

The average rainfall in the Cotswolds is below the national average but it is, nevertheless, sufficient to keep a constant flow percolating through the hills and escarpment to the underground sources, and it has been only in times of extreme drought that restrictions on supplies have had to be imposed. This is not to say that the rain which falls in the Cotswolds is of itself sufficient to meet the demand for water and, as far as the deepest of boreholes are concerned (ie, the Bibury source at 190ft depth), it has, indeed, been a matter of some conjecture as to whence some of the water at that source originated. It is conceivable that it comes from as far away as South or Mid-Wales.

Much of the water used by its residents discharges eventually into the Thames and is used several times again before it gets to the sea.

STONE

Stone has always been available for building. Cotswold stone has been used outside the immediate area. The quarries at Taynton and Burford provided much of the material for Blenheim, for instance. Now far less quarrying goes on and Cotswold stone as quarried is mostly used for stone-walling beside the roads maintained by the Gloucestershire County Council, but reconstructed Cotswold stone is now widely used both in the Cotswolds and elsewhere, and Bradstone has become a well known name. Bradstone is made by E. H. Bradley & Sons Ltd, whose gravel pits at South Cerney, just off the edge of the hills, form part of the Cotswold Water Park. The massive programme of extraction which has taken place to allow the motorways to be built has formed an almost continuous stretch of water from Poole Keynes at the south of Cirencester to Whelford, west of Fairford. The County Councils of Gloucestershire and Wiltshire have planned jointly a Water Park in these disused gravel pits which will provide sailing and many other aquatic pastimes for people in the centre of England unable easily to reach the sea. Access roads have already been built and many keen sailors and water skiers are already using the Park.

The industry of the Cotswolds is then stable, outward-looking but not able greatly to expand; it conforms to the needs of the countryside, where there has been little unemployment for many years. It has been largely owned by its founders but this is a declining trend, and such giants as BP and Hawker Siddeley now have some interests here. But if the planners have their way, it is to be expected that units will remain small by modern standards and as far as possible specialised.

Notes to this chapter are on page 307.

5

Transport

Christopher Cox, Charles Hadfield and David Bick

Roads
Christopher Cox

ROUTES ALTER, roads decay or are enlarged; some roads vanish from use, new ones are built. The road pattern is a good deal more subject to change and variation than that of railway or of canal, and to the enquirer offers a kind of peregrinatory palimpsest, striking his attention not only by the frequent and often considerable alteration of route, but also by the paradoxical persistence of roads through the centuries. Thus to attempt a definitive account of roads over the Cotswolds for the last four centuries would be somewhat presumptuous, but at least samples may be taken and examples examined.

Roads have three functions. First is that of the throughway, a road enabling people and goods to pass through the region in question. The second is fulfilled by those roads which bring people and goods into, or take them out of, the region. Third come those routes, whether road, track or path, which are of local concern, from the catchment area of a market town to the individual needs of the inhabitants of a single parish.

Throughways

ROMAN

The first planned throughways over the Cotswolds were those of the Romans, designed and built to serve military requirements. Conspicuously they kept to the interfluvial ridge-tops, traversing the high ground, serving the need for rapid—and obvious—transit through the land. In many places their alignments persist to this day. The line of the Foss Way is a spinal route, from Moreton-in-Marsh, through Stow-on-the-Wold past Northleach to Cirencester. Much of the alignment south of Ciren-cester, however, is no longer in use, mainly one may assume because traffic was attracted off the road towards Tetbury and Malmesbury. Cirencester, of course, was a centre of Roman roads, and one may still follow the radial Ermin Street to the scarp edge at Birdlip for Gloucester (though the Roman route down the hill is no longer used), or go north along the White Way, north-east along Akeman Street towards Quening-ton (though towards Coln St Aldwyn the alignment has been diverted by the great park), or south-east towards Cricklade. These were the main military roads, and undoubtedly other 'Roman' roads existed in the Cotswolds for the use of local traffic to villa and settlement, not subject to the military need for speed and observation. As these routes have persisted over such a length of time, they must have been kept in regular use over centuries in order to receive maintenance.

BUCKLE STREET

One which seems to have lost its function as a primary route is Buckle Street, which, heading nearly due south on to the Cotswolds from Bidford-on-Avon, may be seen, for example, on either side of Condicote as barely a rough track. We must not think, of course, that travellers in the past hurried along such routes without a pause : they would have dropped off the upland track for refreshment for themselves, or for water for their animals, as mail coaches did at Burford; or halted at the infrequent wayside inn that catered for their needs. But these roads, especially in the northern part of the Cotswolds, known to and travelled by Shakespeare, justify the comment he gives to Richard II that

> These high wild hills and rough uneven ways
> draw out our miles and make them wearisome.

SALTWAYS AND OTHER THROUGHWAYS

Other routes, later than the Romans, may have lost their function and declined into local lanes or mere tracks. Thus we may follow the great Saltway which, coming from Droitwich, crosses the Cotswolds from Hailes to Lechlade past Hawling, Hazleton and Quenington. Lechlade was the head of navigation on the Thames, and of course many local 'salt-ways' branched off this main track for villages and towns in the region. Such ways may still echo their past with names like Salters Lane, Saltway Farm, Saltridge, Saltbox; but their former purpose has now quite gone. Yet other similar routes have maintained themselves. Thus Ogilby in the late seventeenth century numbers among his roads that from Salisbury to Chipping Campden, which must have been one of the great medieval routes for the export of wool. His map lists towns as follows : Campden–Stow–Burford–Filkins–Lechlade–Inglesham–High-worth, for Marlborough and Salisbury. While the Cotswolds no longer send great wool trains to London, Bristol or Southampton, this general route is still a busy one, with industrial Swindon now providing much

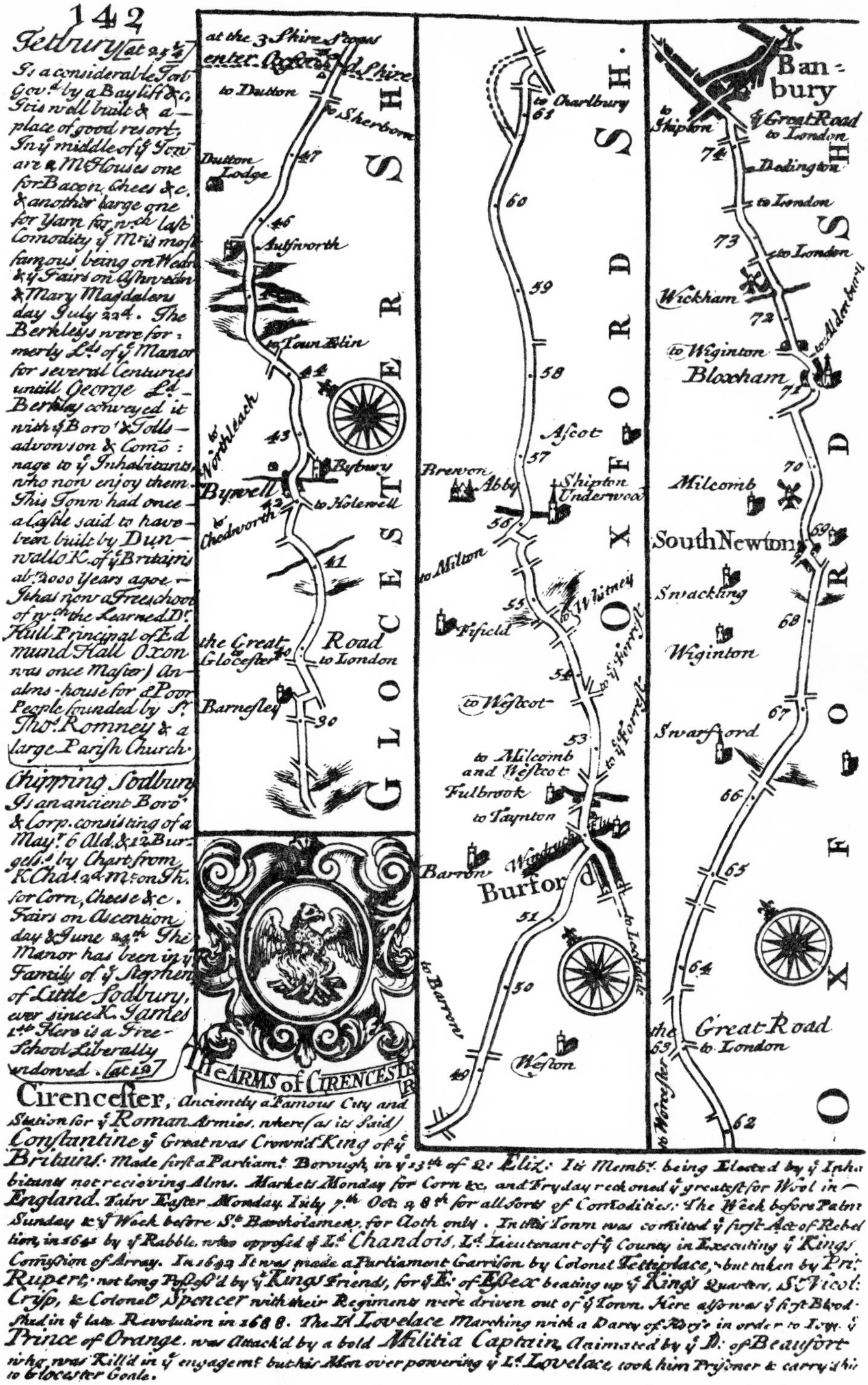

142

Fig 20. Road from Cirencester to Banbury in the late seventeenth-century. A plate from Ogilby's *Britannia*, by courtesy of the Gloucester City Library.

GLOUCESTERSHIRE COLLEGE OF EDUCATION LIBRARY

of the attraction for cross-traffic. Burford is still a road-crossing, the importance of which is brought home to us by the memory that it was here that Cromwell in 1649 had the army demonstrators shot for mutiny, while we may note that in our own century the GWR ran a longish bus service from Banbury, through Chipping Norton, Burford and Lechlade to Swindon.

A century before the armies of Parliament and King marched and countermarched over the Cotswolds, Leland followed the road—still taken today by travellers—from Faringdon, through Lechlade, Fairford and Poulton to Cirencester. Another such is that from Oxford through Witney and Northleach to Gloucester, for so long a cause of complaint for the badness of its surface. Arthur Young said it was the worst turnpike he had ever travelled on, a scandal to the country; he had a very low opinion of all the counties and places it led to on account of their 'barbarous' method of mending this main road. Two hundred years after Young's complaint, this road is now being doubled to ease the heavy traffic it still carries. For while roads have persisted, equally persistent has been the grumbling of travellers about their state, from Shakespeare's Richard to Anna Freeman, who wrote in 1717, 'I thank God I gott to Oxford, very safe, where I found the Dear Children Mr Willson and Mr Seale waiting for us, almost in despair, the roads being so bad . . .'; and from Anna Freeman to Samuel Rudder in the 1770s writing that the Gloucester to Birdlip turnpike was one of the first, '. . . I wish it might be said to be one of the best'; and from Samuel Rudder to a correspondent of the *Stroud Free Press* who exclaimed in 1851 : 'The roads around and about Stroud are a disgrace to a civilised community'.

Road Books—Ogilby, Paterson

Nevertheless people travelled the roads—because they had to. Ogilby selects and charts, on our first usable road book, a number of through routes. He does not chart the London–Gloucester road beyond Cirencester, though it is mentioned. Other parts of his routes are now less used, or used not at all. Thus the Ebrington–Campden–Willersey route is now not the one generally favoured, nor would one now choose to go from Cheltenham or Winchcombe to Chipping Campden through Snowshill. Thus there has been some rerouting and improvement, especially to cut out awkward gradients, but generally speaking the throughways have remained fairly constant. This may well be seen in a comparison of Ogilby's roads with those given in Paterson's road book of the end of the eighteenth century.

Page 143 *Small towns:* (above) *Wotton-under-Edge from the old London road, Wotton Hill;* (below) *a distant view of Painswick*

Page 144 *Villages:* (above) *Edge;* (below) *Duntisbourne Rous*

Paterson's book and other editions or similar publications point to change. Thus Paterson's Bath–Birmingham–Derby route tells of the growing importance of the industrial Midlands, while social Bath is assuming a new importance for travellers going south. Traffic increased considerably during the eighteenth century, and some of it changed direction.

Turnpike or Toll Roads

In 1555 Parliament passed an Act which laid on each parish the duties of repairing and maintaining the roads in that parish. This might have been adequate for local needs, but soon proved most inadequate where traffic was heavy and especially where there were throughways which did not directly benefit the local inhabitants on whom the duty had been laid to keep the highways in good repair. The great difficulty was the cost, and where administration was local, and the financing of such administration also local, some different method had to be tried. The answer was the turnpike or toll road, whereby the repair was (in theory) paid by the road user, not merely by the local inhabitant. In fact, parishes were still rated for turnpike roads in their areas: the first turnpike Act was 1663, and the system of parish responsibility lasted at least till 1835, while in the Cotswolds toll roads lasted till the late 1870s or 1880s.

The first toll road in our region is that from Gloucester City to the tops of Birdlip and Crickley Hills, from an Act passed in the Parliamentary session of 1697–8. Then for the next 40 years, other stretches of main road were brought under toll—as we have seen from the caustic remarks of travellers, not always with the intended good result. Up to the 1740s the roads turnpiked were marginal to the area of the Cotswold plateau, as may be seen in Fig 21. In the session of 1725–6 the road from Gloucester to Stone (the present A38) was turnpiked, and with it various roads from the Severn to the hills, namely those to Stroud, to Frocester Hill (for the road to Bath), to Dursley, Wotton-under-Edge and to Sodbury. At the same time the road from St John's Bridge near Lechlade to Cirencester was brought under toll, and also that from 'Chappel on the Heath to the Quarry above Bourton-on-the-Hill', part of the 'Great Road' from London and Oxford to Worcester, for a distance of 8 miles, which 'by reason of the Deepness of the Soil thereof, and the many heavy Carriages passing through the same, are become so ruinous and bad, that in the Winter Season many parts thereof are impassable for Waggons and Carriages, and also for Horses laden'. Thus we see that the roads over the clay were amended, while those on the limestone plateau had to wait till later.

I

GREAT ROADS

The plateau roads—the Great Roads or throughways—were brought under toll mainly in the 1740s and 1750s. One reason may have been the spread of enclosure on the Cotswolds. Marshall, for example, says in *The Rural Economy of Glocestershire* (1796) that until the middle of the eighteenth century the Cotswolds 'lay almost entirely in an open state'. Enclosure of the 'champaign' land would confine traffic, both wheeled and hoof, strictly between the new stone walls. Rudge in his *History of the County of Gloucester* (1803) has this to say: 'Within the last hundred years a total change has taken place on these hills. Furze

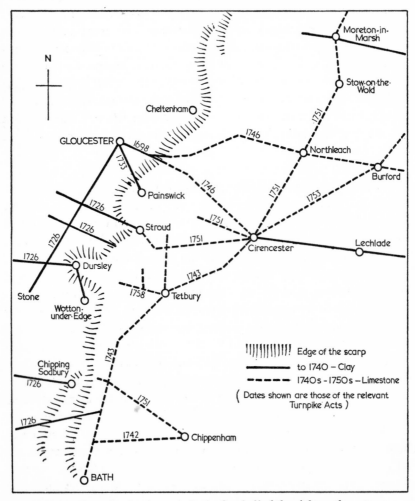

Fig 21. Turnpike development in the first half of the eighteenth century.

and some dry and scanty blades of grass were all their produce, but now with few exceptions, the downs are converted into arable enclosed fields, and an easy communication is made with the different villages, through a county formerly almost inaccessible to the stranger, and sometimes travelled with difficulty even by the natives'. Shaw, in his *Tour to the West of England in 1788*, writing of the road near Minchinhampton, says 'the road is flat and unpleasant and instead of the verdant bloom of hedge-rows the eye is continually disgusted with the unsightly objects of loose stones heaped in strait lines and angles.' Fig 21 shows the roads turnpiked by the mid-eighteenth century, and this makes clear what were considered to be the Great Roads—the main or primary routes through the Cotswolds. North from Cirencester, the Foss Way is still important, though south of Cirencester it is followed only to Jackaments Bottom, and thence heads through Tetbury for the watershed route near the western scarp, for Bath. In the north the Oxford—Worcester road goes through Morteton-in-Marsh; the A40 route to Gloucester went past Burford and Northleach (though then not through Andoversford); another road to Gloucester kept to the old route from Lechlade to Cirencester, whence routes radiated out like spokes from a wheel-hub; and two roads west from Chippenham were turnpiked towards Bristol. Burford then, as now, was an important road junction for cross-traffic.

CONTROL AND IMPROVEMENT OF TURNPIKE ROADS

Turnpike roads were at first under the direct control of the county JPs, but before long special Trusts were set up, with the affairs of the Trust being managed by a small committee of local gentlemen. Turnpike Acts were originally for a stated period of years, usually 21, as it was thought the roads, once put back into repair, could then revert to parish control. It is to be doubted whether any reversion was in fact done.

Improvements in alignment were made, often at the instigation of local gentlemen for their own convenience. But traffic, besides increasing, tended to concentrate on certain routes. Thus the earlier route through Ebrington to Chipping Campden and down the scarp at Willersey (given by Ogilby) would decline in favour of the road down to Broadway—'a well formed serpentine road', as Shaw remarked. With the improvement of the road west from Cirencester to Minchinhampton and Stroud, the much older road through Cirencester Park, down 'Gulph Hill' near Park Corner to Bisley, and from Bisley over the Slad valley to Painswick, fell into decline, though it was being given as an alternative route to Gloucester in bad weather as late as 1800—heaven alone knows what the other possible routes must then have been like! But perhaps the most notable improvement was that on the Northleach–Gloucester road. Earlier travellers had continued on the ridge-top between Hazleton and Compton Abdale, descending to the Coln valley near Shipton Solers. At the Frog-mill Inn they would turn left and climb up to Kilkenny, where they would turn left for the Seven Springs and Crickley Hill for Gloucester, or if bound for Cheltenham, take the narrow and sharp descent past Dowdeswell to Charlton Kings. Various schemes were put forward for improvements, including a road east of Cheltenham through Northfield, north of Whittington, to join the main existing road east of 'Shipton Olive' (ie Shipton Oliffe). The present road through Andoversford is thus 'new', one later consequence of which has been to isolate the Frogmill Inn in a cut-off, no longer easy of access to the passing traveller.

This present descent of the A40 to the vale down the Chelt valley brings out the point that while the Romans led their roads down the steep scarp to the Severn vale by nicely zigzagged alignments, medieval and later roads just went straight up and down, not only on the ridge-ends where Cotswolds face the vale, but in the steep western valleys also. These old roads are now often abandoned, and streams wander down their silted-up holloways.

IMPROVED ROUTES

So far turnpiking had been 'improvement' of existing roads. A different direction was given in 1780 with the formation of the Nailsworth–Dud-bridge Turnpike Trust. This offered a new conception, the avowed purpose of which was to provide a better link between Bath and the north of the county. Earlier travellers from Gloucester to Bath seem to have gone to Bristol and then changed coaches for the journey from Bristol to Bath. By the mid-eighteenth century, however, the accepted route was south from Gloucester (along the A38) to Claypits near Eastington, then turn-ing left to climb the scarp at Frocester Hill and proceeding through Nympsfield, past Kingscote towards Lasborough, then turning right for Bath. An alternative route from Cheltenham was along the scarp edge from Birdlip, above Cranham and Painswick; or through Bisley, Chal-ford, Hyde (east of Minchinhampton) and Avening to Tetbury; or from Minchinhampton down the precipitous slope to the valley below and thence up again close to Nailsworth to join the plateau road at or near Tiltups Inn.

In place of these awkward and precipitous gradients, the Nailsworth Valley Trust offered a new and improved route : the ascent of the hill out of Nailsworth was by a series of well designed curves, far gentler for coaches than the straight and steep earlier roads. This new road seems to have stimulated the management of the Old Bath Road into improving *their* route to avoid loss of income. Paterson dates the present alignment up Frocester Hill to 1784 : the older, steeper route was abandoned, except for the use of farm carts and quarry sledges. This was the track which saw the escape of Governor Massey of Gloucester from the escort of Commonwealth soldiers, on a summer's night of violent wind and rain in 1659 (Massey like many others had changed sides). Nympsfield was now bypassed, thus avoiding the dip down to that upland village, and new milestones were set up. In the *Glocester Journal* of 4 September 1780 we read that Christopher Coleman, of the George Inn, Frocester, begged leave 'to acquaint the Nobility, Gentry and others' that the Bath Road through Frocester was now repaired and good, the road up the hill in complete order and quite commodious, which 'renders the former Trouble and Expence of putting on additional Horses to the Carriages going up that Hill unnecessary'.

But the other, and probably the main, reason for building the new Nailsworth Trust road was the growth of industry. Towards the end of the eighteenth century processes in the cloth industry were beginning to be concentrated on water-power sites, and in any case trade was increasing in the western valleys. The promoters and committee of the Nailsworth Trust were all local people, almost entirely closely connected with the cloth trade, and quite obviously in desperate need of better communications with the outside world, both for the despatch of their cloth, and also for the bringing in of coal and corn for the numerous poor. What is new and interesting is that their alignment from Nailsworth to Dudbridge near Stroud was routed close to the valley bottom, whereas older routes kept to the valley slopes, joining up the spring-line settlements, and needing to descend the hillside to cross each side tributary valley.

ENGINEERING OF TURNPIKE ROADS

At least 30 years before Macadam took over the Bristol roads, this local group advertised for a qualified road engineer. The specification called for a road 30ft wide, with the centre at least 12in higher than the sides before 'stoning', that is surfacing with broken stone. No ascent or descent on the valley section was to be more than 2in to 1yd; cuttings were to be made, bridges and culverts built, ditches dug. The sides of the road were to be at least 14in higher than the ground surface in certain low-lying areas liable to waterlogging. With such roads, of course, only the centre half was surfaced, the verges being left for the easier passage of carriages meeting each other, but orders were given that the stones were to be 'well and sufficiently broken to the satisfaction of the

Trustees', and where gravel was to be laid, there had first to be a bed of stone, and the gravel was to be put on this to a maximum depth of 3in. Such specifications anticipate much of the better known work of Macadam and Telford by nearly a generation. The engineer who built the road, and within the stipulated time, was one Dennis Edson from Chester, who later was to be connected with the Gloucester & Berkeley Canal.

In the Stroudwater district it was to be another 20 years before any 'new' roads were again built, but then for 25 years roads were built in every valley round Stroud, just above the valley floor, climbing the valley sides to the pateau top by curves and gradients much gentler than those of the earlier tracks. One result here was to enhance the importance of Stroud, by making it a minor route-centre, whereas the focus earlier had been at Cainscross.

We see then that a new, though local, pattern was now superimposed on to the older pattern of 'main' roads. Elsewhere turnpiking was extended out from important local centres, as we have already seen at Ciren-

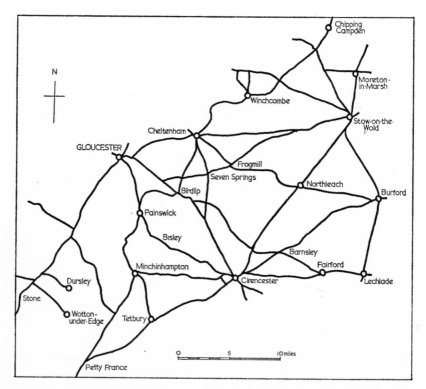

Fig 22.   The 'Great Roads' of north and mid-Cotswolds in the 1780s, after Tunnicliffe. Lechlade-Burford-Stow road inserted.

cester, which increased the number of radial routes, and especially at
Stow in the north, sitting in the centre of its spider's web of market roads.
In the narrow belt of the south Cotswolds, the great commercial and
industrial lodestone of Bristol drew all routes towards that city.

Road Maps, 1780 and 1819

Road maps and road books proliferated towards the end of the
eighteenth century, and 'mail', coach or 'turnpike' roads do not always
coincide from map to map. But we may take as our example the Great
Roads of Gloucestershire as given by Tunnicliffe in the 1780s (Fig 22).

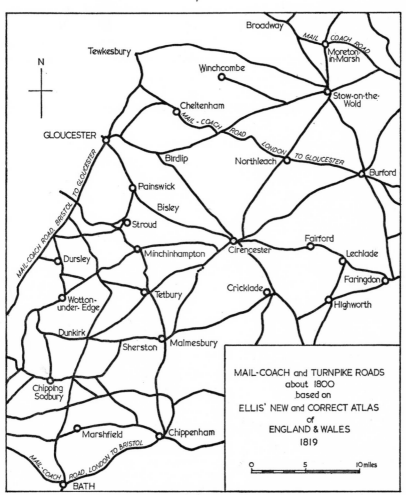

Fig 23.

The pattern is growing more complex even at this date both east and south of Gloucester, while both Stow and Cirencester stand out as route centres, both for local marketing, and for cross-journeys. The emerging pattern of somewhat isolated through routes across the Cotswolds from Cirencester to Moreton in the north, the tangle of shorter industrial roads in the valleys of the mid-Cotswolds, and the centering of routes in the south on Bristol, is brought out more clearly in Fig 23 which is based on *A New and Correct Atlas of England and Wales*, published by Ellis in 1819.

Upkeep and Costs, early Nineteenth Century

With the coming of the railways, the traffic on, and the importance of, the main or primary roads died away, though local roads continued in use, and probably increased in use, as feeders to railway stations. But as turnpike routes lost traffic and revenue, the burden on the local rate-payer still remained. Hence the continued complaints on the state of the roads. 'Viator' writes in the *Stroud Free Press* of 17 February 1854 that the Nailsworth road was 'bad, very bad, wretchedly bad, almost dangerous. We are very tired of waiting for them to make it better'. This problem was not to be solved until the creation in the 1880s of county road authorities. Even the turnpike system did not exempt the parishioner from paying a road rate, and this was resented the more when it appeared the tolls merely went to pay the interest on the subscribers' shares, the interest of the mortgagor, or—in the nineteenth century—the newly created business of 'toll farmer'. Indeed, this latter imposition incensed the younger David Ricardo so much that he was the centre of an unfortunate test case at Stroud in the early 1850s when he was fined for not only refusing to pay toll at Chalford, but forcing his way past one of what he called 'the little ragged boys at every corner' whose job it was to collect tolls for someone possibly living in Birmingham. The original Stroud turnpike of 1725–6 had immediately been mortgaged, and such arrangements were usually made, with an annual auction of the toll gates, such as that for the Chipping Norton toll gates in 1794, and that for the Lower Slaughter gate in 1827. Leases of the Burford Roads Trust gates in 1833 were as follows :

Wykham Gate	£371	and in 1836	£423
Chapel Heath	233		242
Burford	269		240
Chipping Norton	162		not let

In 1841, the Trustees holding the auction at the White Hart Inn, Chipping Norton, were receiving bids only in the £120 range for Burford gate, and the taker had to provide tickets, lamps and oil. Some idea of costs in the same Trust may be seen in the 3 year contract of 1810 for road repair for £540 a year, the contractors being entitled to a proportion of the parish road rate in addition to the tolls collected. And with all this, carriage by road could be expensive. Charles Stephens, described as a clothier of Stroud, giving evidence before the Committee of the House of Lords in the matter of the Cheltenham & Great Western Union Railway Bill in 1836, said that his cloth was sent by land carriage to London at £10 a ton (the return freight charge was £5), and that he spent £1,200 a year in this way; water carriage was cheaper, but less convenient, and on this he spent only £10 a year. Edward Barnard of Nailsworth sent his cloth by coach, not waggon, at £14 a ton—waggons were cheaper at £5 or £6 a ton, but very slow—and he also said that goods from London in winter might be 4 months on the journey.

Saltways, Droving Roads, Ridgeways, Bridle-paths

Perhaps we pay too much attention to the roads which were turnpiked for the benefit of the wealthy traveller or for the royal mail. Ogilby's routes will remind us that other roads existed and were in considerable use. The Salt Way has already been mentioned. Quite apart from the numerous 'coach roads' (usually local roads bypassing the much disliked toll gates), until the coming of the railways the heavy traffic in animals had to walk the roads, not only to local markets, whether Stow, Tetbury, Gloucester or any other, but also to the great metropolitan market of London. For such purposes Cirencester (to take but one example) was completely bypassed. Travellers going west would generally turn north at Fairford, or even earlier at Lechlade, pass through Barnsley and the then important road junction at Ready Token. This route is still marked on Ordnance maps as 'Welsh Way' and from Barnsley, as Ogilby shows, it headed through Bagendon for Ermin Street (well north of Cirencester), or travellers might even go past the now isolated village of Elkstone to High Cross before heading for Birdlip. Between Cirencester and Birdlip, where now are minor roads, dead-end lanes or no road at all, numerous tracks formerly took goods from the Bisley area to the east. Ogilby's route north of Cirencester is heavily marked with crossroads, often with directions such as 'To Stroud, To Tetbury', etc. Below Edgworth Church there stands a three-slab stone clapper bridge. The stream itself can be crossed at a jump, but the passage of uncountable pony-hoofs would have torn the adjacent banks into an impassable morass unless some dry water-crossing had been provided. Ridge-tops, too, would provide drove ways for sheep and cattle, and the traffic in animals may explain why the verges of the turnpiked roads eastwards from Minchinhampton are considerably wider than the common dimensions of turnpike roads. Parish roads continued, of course, as they had always done, in use. Improved or new turnpike roads frequently have straight stretches reminiscent of Roman days, with wide verges useful for widening in the days of the motor car; parish roads are usually much narrower (though many are now being widened in the interests of motor traffic), wind about from settlement to settlement and round property, and usually are confined between wall or hedge with no perceptible verge or margin. Nor must one forget bridle-path, track and footpath, far more important to the local community than the turnpike road used by those on their way through. The valleys of the central and north Cotswolds show well the distinction between main or turnpike road, and local or parish road. The A40 takes its isolated and windswept course along the top of the interfluvial ridge. In the valleys below, the villages are strung along the local road; the separation is almost as complete as that between motorway and country roads today.

Local Coach Enterprises

There seems to have been a growth of local enterprise towards the end of the eighteenth century, with small towns and villages producing their own coaches. Thus in 1780 the 'original' Hampton and Cirencester Machine set out from the Salutation Inn, Minchinhampton, at 4am on 3 days a week, taking 16 hours to reach the Bell Savage Inn, in the summer months travelling through the night. Fisher, in *Notes and Recollections of Stroud*, records that in 1770 a stagecoach left twice a week for London, and also that from the 1790s to about 1807 the only coach between Stroud and London was run by the Masters family of Cirencester; but that in 1807 a company of local subscribers was formed to set up a new London service. It failed within 2 years. The Gloucester and Bath Diligence left the Bell Inn thrice weekly at 7am, travelling via Stroud and Tetbury: travellers in 1780 made the journey for 12s 6d (62½p) and were allowed 12lb of luggage. From London to Gloucester about the same date the fare was £1 12s (£1·60) with 10lb of luggage, travelling from 5pm to noon the next day, and with a guard from Oxford to London.

There seems in fact to have been a development very like that of the motor-bus and motor-coach organisations of the present century, starting often with local, often one-man, services, with eventual amalgamation with, or absorption by, larger groups, and a concentration on fewer centres. Such centres as Cheltenham or Gloucester must have presented a scene not unlike that of a busy long-distance coach station today. Hibbs' *History of British Bus Services* gives an account of the growth of bus services, both local and long-distance, in this region, with a complex interchange of services in the Stroud area at the start of the 1950s, and the concentration of long-distance coach routes at Cheltenham in the early 1930s, based on the Black & White company. In this connection it may be interesting to look at the coach office lists of two hotels in Cheltenham in the 1820s, just about 100 years earlier.

From Haines Coach Office and Royal Hotel there left :

5.30 am	daily to Oxford and London
7 am	daily to Bristol
7.45 am	daily to Malvern
8 am	thrice weekly to Oxford and London
	daily to Birmingham
	daily to Worcester
8.45 am	thrice weekly to Shrewsbury and Holyhead
	thrice weekly to Birmingham
	thrice weekly to Leamington
10 am	daily, a 2-day coach to Oxford and London for invalids
10.30 am	thrice weekly to Bristol
11 am	thrice weekly to Hereford
11.30 am	thrice weekly to Leamington and Coventry
	(alternating days with the other Leamington coach)
1.30 pm	thrice weekly to Bristol
5 pm	daily to Gloucester
6 pm	daily to Gloucester
	daily to Carmarthen
	thrice weekly to Swansea

as well as a daily morning coach to Liverpool and Manchester.

From the Royal Mail Coach Office at the George Hotel :

5.30 am	'Defiance' coach to London
6 am	Birmingham, Liverpool and Manchester
	Shrewsbury and Holyhead
	Worcester
7.30 am	Gloucester and South Wales
	Bristol
8 am	*Sovereign* coach to Oxford and London
	Malvern
	Leamington (thrice weekly)
9 am	Oxford and London (invalid coach)
	Bath

	Southampton, Weymouth, Portsmouth and Gosport (thrice weekly)
	Gloucester and South Wales
10.30 am	Bath
	Gloucester and South Wales
3 pm	Worcester
4 pm	*Telegraph* coach to Oxford and London
5 pm	Gloucester and South Wales
	Gloucester Mail
	Bristol Mail
	Birmingham Mail
6 pm	Worcester

CARRIERS

These earlier long-distance coaches generally kept, as do the express motor-coach services today, to the main ridge-top routes, though branching off for the valley towns as at Burford. But the 'main' routes were, of course, fed by carriers. In the Stroud area, for example, goods were taken up the steep hillside tracks to collecting points at such depots as the Bear Inn, Rodborough, or the Road House, on the narrow neck of land between Rodborough and Minchinhampton Commons. Mountain's stage waggon, we read in the *Glocester Journal* for May 1777, left the Horse and Groom at Gloucester at noon on Saturdays, and arrived at the George, Snow Hill, London, on Thursday morning, via Painswick, Stroud and Minchinampton; Hyde, east of Minchinhampton, was a collecting point on the Sunday night, Upper Hyde near the Ragged Cot, being a cross-ways for east-west and north-south traffic. Gell & Bradshaw's 1820s *Directory* gives useful detail. Dawes' fly waggons went to London via Northleach, Witney and Oxford three times a week, with a guard; and also to Stow, Chipping Norton and London, from Gloucester and Cheltenham. Tanner & Bayliss were another important firm of carriers, especially for the Stroudwater district, with their London depot at 35 White Cross Street, Cripplegate, and in Gloucestershire at Cheltenham, Gloucester and Bristol. T. Arkell carried goods to Cirencester, Stroud and Tewkesbury, S. Best to Winchcombe, J. Page to Cirencester and so on.

An interesting earlier example of a special delivery is given in the *Glocester Journal* for April 1725. The distributors of this newly founded paper are given as follows :

John Butler—Stroud water, Tetbury, Malmesbury, Chippenham etc.
Walter Nelms—Frampton-on-Severn, Cambridge Inn, Eastington, Frocester, Cowley, Cam, Dursley and on for Thornbury etc.

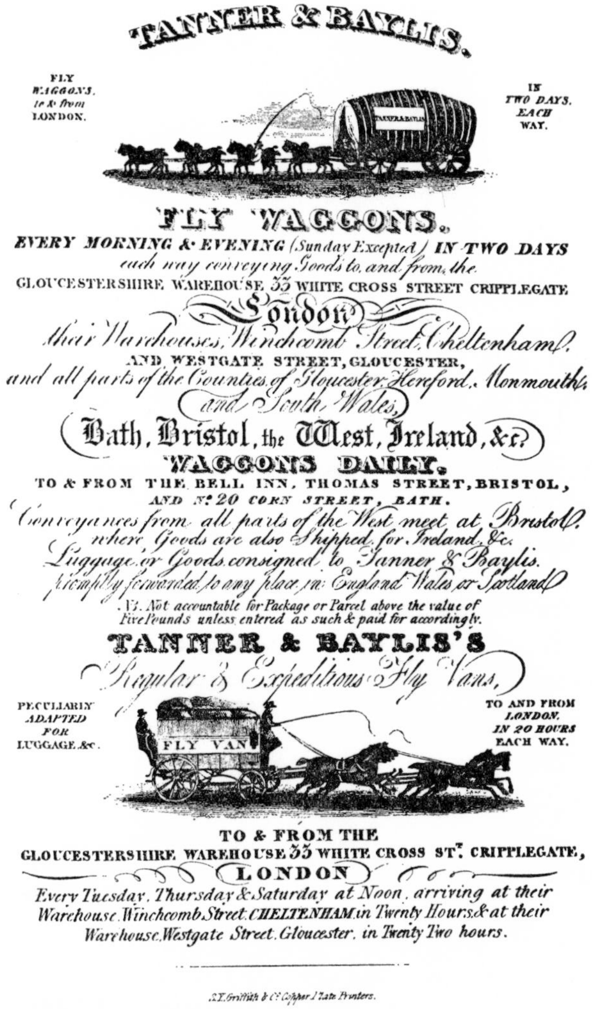

Fig 24.   A road-haulier's advertisement, early nineteenth century, from S. Y. Griffith's
History of Cheltenham 1826.

James Pewteris—Painswick, Bisley, Cirencester, Fairford, Lechlade, High-
worth, for Wiltshire.
James Warwick—Birdlip, Withington, Northleach etc.

This shows the use of older roads, notably that through Painswick and
Bisley to Cirencester.

Lists of markets and fairs show that local traffic was focused on such
towns, as enumerated, for example, in a *Topographical Description of
Gloucestershire* by J. & S. Lewis in 1712, N. Spencer's 1771 *Complete
English Traveller*, or Gell & Bradshaw's *Directory*; and these demonstrate
continuance with the list given by Leland in the sixteenth century. Nor
must we forget letters, diaries and itineraries of private travellers. The
Clutterbuck Journal of a Journey to King Stanley in 1773 tells us that
the old track across Rodborough Common, descending to the left of
Rodborough Fort, was then still in use. A record in the Gloucestershire
Records Office of a journey from Dyrham to Derbyshire and back in
1726 gives not only the route across the county, but also the distance
travelled each day, and the inn at which the travellers stayed each night.
This reads: 'Thursday 14 July through Petty France, Dead Martin [*sic*]
Tedbury to Cirencester (20 miles), on Friday 15th through Fostbridge,
Northlech to Stow' (where they stayed at the Kings Arms); and on the
next day via Mickleton to Stratford, the White Lyon, and so on. The
grand total for this return journey was estimated at 237 miles. Petty
France, we may remember, was where Catherine Morland and Henry
Tilney made a prolonged stop in their (fictional) journey from Bath to
Northanger Abbey.

Coming of the Motor Car

The ubiquitous motor car has replaced private coach or horse, and
the automobile engine has in fact had a double effect. Firstly many
former tracks and roads have been abandoned, with a concentration
often on fewer roads; secondly the motor car has increased the use of
roads, has led to their widening, to the cutting of awkward corners, and
has very considerably eased access to places previously difficult of
approach. This has perhaps been most noticeable in the growth between
the two world wars of the country bus service. While the express coach
routes follow the trail of the older stagecoaches, the local bus map in
certain places resembles, not the single long strand of the through route,
but a complex interwoven tracery more like the entanglement of a wet
fishing net. Attempts at local mechanical transport had been made a

century before. J. Hibbs records that in 1831 Sir Charles Dance ran a service from Gloucester to Cheltenham three times a day, with an average speed between 10 and 12 miles an hour—little or no improvement on the horse-drawn stagecoach. The still-existing (though restored) toll-charge board at Butterow Pike near Stroud announces a toll of 1s 'For every Carriage, drawn or propelled by mechanical machinery or Power other than Animal Power'. And in 1902 there was a proposal for a light railway up through the Painswick valley by a Mr Nevins, which pro-duced the following outburst, reminiscent of earlier protests against the new turnpike roads : 'the agent of a mammoth American trust that is attempting to control, for main-road railway and electric traction pur-poses, all the ready-made highways of Great Britain that have been nursed by local enterprise till they promise and invite profitable exploitation by external capital' (Letter [H] F2 24 in the Gloucestershire Collection).

The demands of motor traffic today, whether public transport, lorry or private car, are indeed having a very pronounced effect on roads. But this is not entirely new. Not only were new alignments constructed through untouched field and common in the turnpike age, but buildings were removed to ease traffic. Thus in 1821 a turnpike house outside Tetbury was demolished in order to widen the road; then as now the convenient proximity of the toll house to the road has often caused its removal.

Traces of Old Roads

Roman roads are perhaps those which most compel recognition long after they have gone out of use. In places a boundary, a hedgerow or line of trees, or the depressions left alongside an amended road may reveal the existence of a former route. St Clair Baddeley in the *Bristol and Gloucester Archaeological Society Transactions* for 1929 referred to the 'irregularly-pitted east side of the road' (past Lypiatt Park) which 'represents the Stroud–Bisley road before it was widened for coaches . . . in the post-Waterloo years'. These depressions have now been filled in.

Turnpike roads specially built may be recognised by the remains of former wide verges and by milestones. Toll houses, too, may be the mark of the past, with their typical three-faced frontage, but this is slightly misleading, as many early pike houses were merely ordinary cottages, with-out special feature except perhaps a ticket hatch like a small window. Occasionally this, usually now bricked in, will tell of the former use, as we may see in the wall of a cottage near the Ragged Cot, Minchin-hampton, on the road leading down to Hyde and Chalford, formerly a minor cross-country route from Tetbury to Birdlip and Cheltenham. A good example of the 'typical' toll house shape can be seen at Butterow, Stroud, with the charges board still over the entrance.

Continuing Change

These are indications of past changes, reflecting the changing function and use of roads. Change still continues. The growth of private-car ownership causes a decline in local bus services, and it is not impossible there may be a reversion to the situation of the early eighteenth century, when those with means of transport could move about and away, but those without could not; and many lived all their lives within walking distance of their native villages. Another force of change, the effect in the 1970s only beginning, is that long-distance or through traffic may leave the Cotswolds and concentrate in the motorways. For example, traffic for South Wales uses the M4, and the new Severn bridge, which after so many hundreds of years replaces Gloucester Bridge as the lowest river crossing. On the other hand, the greater ease of access to the Cotswolds from places much further off, and the likely industrial growth in the basin of the lower Severn, may—who knows?—lead to intensified settlement in the Cotswolds themselves, and consequently an increase in local traffic. Roads change with changing function.

Comparisons with the Past

But much remains the same. We can still complain (perhaps unfairly) of dilatory postal services. In the 1820s post was conveyed from Moreton-in-Marsh to Winchcombe three days a week, on Sunday, Wednesday and Friday, with in winter perhaps no delivery at all owing to the state of the roads. This delivery took $4\frac{1}{2}$ hours for 13 miles; the official reply to the complaint was—that the matter would be looked into. We can find entertainment in our companions on a coach journey : Mr Jackson writing in 1745 to his brother said the journey to Gloucester had been tolerable, the company pretty fair, but 'an impertinent Quaker woman gave us a great deal of diversion; she was very angry with the Methodists and made us laugh with her reflexions'. We may still be fined for infringement of road regulations—ignoring 'stop' signals (as at turnpike gates), using illegal tyres (whether as now with too little tread, or as in the eighteenth century with too much—rose-headed nails tended to tear up the surface), or riding to the public danger, as did Thomas Chaple of Cowley in 1781 : he had to insert a public apology in the press—'which I

Page 161 *Cotswold village architecture:* (above) *the old village of Stanton;* (below) *new buildings at Naunton*

Page 162 *Fine Cotswold building:* (above) *barns at Ablington, near Bibury;* (below) *Nether Lypiatt Manor*

hereby publicly do, and do desire that this may be inserted in the *Glocester Journal*, in order to prevent others from indiscretly galloping upon the Roads, and committing the like Offence'. It is to be hoped, of course, that we do not meet the same misadventure as befell Mr Rayer of Cutsdean and Mr Smith of Ford, who, returning in 1816 from market at Stow, were 'overtaken by a genteel man, well mounted, who presented a pistol at Mr Rayer's head and demanded his money; observing that he had been an officer in the Army and fought at Waterloo; but was driven to this desperate measure by distress, and having seen death in many shapes was careless of the consequences'. Mr Smith escaped without paying; the highwayman returned to Mr Rayer and asked his address, alleging that 'should fortune smile on him, he should probably return him his money'. Nor are notes to current road books likely to read (as Paterson has it of the Stroudwater district): 'The steep acclivities and continued unevenness of the ground, render travelling through this district rather troublesome, but the great diversity of picturesque landscape which on every turn is presented to view, and the various dyes of the cloth as it is stretched on the tenters, . . . afford a succession of objects pleasing to the eye, and more especially grateful to the contemplating mind of the politician, who beholds with exulting pride the increasing riches of his countrymen, the effects of unrivalled ingenuity and perseverance'.

If we travel the Cotswold roads today we are unlikely to commit some past faults, such as killing, singeing or cutting up cattle on the highway, making bonfires or letting off fireworks, or even playing football or allowing the light from any blacksmith's shop to shine on the road. But this list of prohibitions of 1821 also included the instruction to keep to the left on meeting other travellers, failure for which might bring a penalty of £5. But all roads come to an end somewhere, and it is time to bring this journey into the past to a halt.

Canals
Charles Hadfield

From 1697 onwards there were schemes to make the Stroudwater navigable from the tidal Severn to Stroud, to bring coal and the other wants of the valley, and to take away its products. It is difficult, however, to reconcile the needs of navigation and of water-powered mills on a single river, and though Acts to make a navigation were passed in 1730 and 1759, nothing was achieved against millowning opposition until 1774.

In the end, a canal not a river navigation was authorised in 1776. The

K

Stroudwater Navigation was completed in 1779 from the Severn at Framilode to Wallbridge, Stroud, just under 8 miles long with twelve wide locks able to take craft carrying some 60 tons. It was modestly successful, paying its first dividend in 1786.

Even before its building, men had envisaged its junction with the Thames. Such a canal, they saw, would not only open a wide market for Stroud valley products, but serve also as a through route to the Thames towns and London for Staffordshire coal, Coalbrookdale iron, Birmingham manufactures and, from the south, the trade of Bristol. A route also to bring back London-imported goods.

So in 1783 the Thames & Severn Canal was begun, and finished in November 1789. With forty-two (later forty-four) locks, it rises up the Golden Valley from Stroud past Brimscombe Port, a notable inland harbour, and Chalford to Daneway. It was then cut through the edge of the Cotswold escarpment in Sapperton Tunnel, to emerge at Coates. The tunnel, some $2\frac{3}{8}$ miles long and big enough to take broad barges, was a remarkable engineering achievement in spite of the vicissitudes of

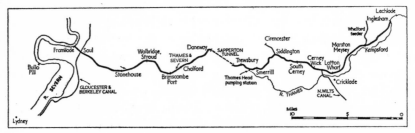

Fig 25.   The Stroudwater and Thames & Severn Canals.

its construction : at that time the longest in Britain, it had taken half the construction time of Brindley's shorter bore at Harecastle in the Potteries. Thence the canal ran over the single-arched Smerril aqueduct over the Malmesbury–Cirencester road to Siddington, with a $1\frac{1}{2}$ mile branch to Cirencester, and on by South Cerney, Cricklade and Kempsford to the Thames at Lechlade, $28\frac{3}{4}$ miles long. Bristol, Birmingham and London had been linked by inland waterway.

But not for long. A few months later a shorter route between London and the Midlands was opened by way of Oxford and Rugby, and in 1810 others opened from Bristol more directly to the Thames. Thus the Stroudwater and the Thames & Severn lost any major role in through transport about as soon as they had gained it, but they kept a minor one.

One of the 1810 canal lines between Bristol and the Thames was the Wilts & Berks, a narrow canal running via Melksham, Wootton Bassett and Swindon to Abingdon. In 1819 a short branch, the North Wilts, was opened to connect the Wilts & Berks at Swindon with the Thames & Severn at Latton near Cricklade, so enabling the variable and awkward navigation of the Thames between Lechlade and Oxford to be bypassed. Almost at the same time, in 1820, the Gloucester & Berkeley ship canal reached its junction with the Stroudwater Navigation at Saul on its way from Gloucester to Sharpness. Thenceforward a narrow-boat trade sprang up between Gloucester, London and intermediate places via the ship canal, the Stroudwater, Thames & Severn, North Wilts and the Wilts & Berks.

The main traffic was, however, fairly local—most notably in coal, to the Stroud valley towns and the mills, now turned over from water-power to steam, and higher to Cirencester and the upper Thames valley. In April 1821–2, for instance, the Stroudwater carried 62,101 tons of coal (of which 39,572 tons was going through to the Thames & Severn for points above Wallbridge), as well as 17,257 tons of general goods. This coal came mostly from the Forest of Dean, but substantial amounts came also from Staffordshire, Shropshire and South Wales.

Before railways the Stroudwater company was prosperous, in the 1830s paying dividends that sometimes exceeded 20 per cent and always 15 per cent. The Thames & Severn was not. Soon after opening, its capital had had to be written down, and even then it could only pay $1\frac{1}{2}$ per cent in the same period. Among its troubles that of water supply was the greatest. Much of its summit level, from Sapperton to Siddington, ran through ground which could not be made to hold water: the result was excessive leakage, and high costs of supplying water by pumping from the great well at Thames Head near the Foss Way crossing, and from the Churn, the latter supply involving compensation payments to local millers.

The railway threat to the Thames & Severn was made actual when the Great Western line from Swindon via the Golden Valley to Gloucester was opened in May 1845. Toll receipts, which had averaged £8,368 pa for the years 1839–41, were £5,443 in 1848–50 and £2,220 in 1863–5. The Stroudwater, its coal trade far less affected by the railway, fared better: comparable figures are £6,731, £5,948 and £4,796. In these last years of 1863–5 its dividend was still in double figures, whereas 1864 was the Thames & Severn's last dividend year. The much smaller Stone-house & Nailsworth Railway, authorised in 1863, and the Midland's branch to Stroud, hit the Stroudwater more severely, bringing receipts down to an average £2,974 for 1869–71. Thereafter the Thames & Severn ceased to have importance as a through transport route, and the Stroud-water became a local carrier only. In this role, supplying the mills and towns with coal and materials, to a lesser extent taking away what they made or grew, the little navigation showed extraordinary staying power. Though it paid its last 5 per cent dividend for the year 1879–80, and dividend of any kind for 1922, the Saul–Wallbridge section continued to carry commercial traffic until 1941, when it finally became disused. The part from Saul to Framilode had hardly been used since 1900. It was abandoned in 1954, though the newly formed Stroudwater Canal Society was considering restoration in 1973.

By 1865 the Thames & Severn Canal committee had decided if possible to turn their line into a standard-gauge railway which could use the existing tunnel at Sapperton. Their line, probably backed by the Midland Railway, planned in conjunction with others as part of a through route from south Wales and the Forest of Dean to the trunk railway lines at Oxford, was to run from Stonehouse to Fairford. The Bill failed in 1866. In 1875 the canal, now in a thoroughly bad state, was taken in hand by a group headed by Richard Potter, former chairman of the Great Western Railway.

Potter first tried to restore the canal's trade; then, realising it could not be done, he once more proposed a railway conversion from a rail junction with the Midland at Stroud to the Cheltenham–Andover line at Siddington. Opposed by other canal companies, he dropped his Bill and sold his controlling shares to the Great Western Railway at a comfortable profit.

Some 10 years later the management proposed to close the canal east of Chalford. Opposition was mounted, and the canal taken over by a Trust compounded of navigation companies and local authorities. Having failed to reopen it fully, they in turn passed it in 1900 to the Gloucestershire County Council. By 1904 the canal was open again, but little traffic followed. The last commercial craft passed the summit in 1911; in 1927 the canal was abandoned, except for the still used Chalford–Wallbridge section, and 6 years later the rest followed.

Today, most of the Thames & Severn can be traced from Inglesham above Lechlade to Chalford. Below, some has gone for road-widening or factory building. The Stroudwater line is still to be seen, except at the M5 crossing. The curious will be particularly interested in Sapperton tunnel, especially the ornate eastern portal, and in its two canal public houses, Tunnel House at Coates and the Daneway Inn below the western portal. All five of the canal's circular lengthsmen's houses are still standing, at Inglesham, Marston Meysey, Cerney Wick, Coates and Chalford, as also are three unique wharf structures at Cirencester, Cricklade and Kempsford. These combined a wharfinger's house and warehouse under one roof, and have no counterpart elsewhere. The long flight of locks down the Golden Valley can be seen by following a path from the Daneway Inn down to Chalford—much of the old towpath is a public right of way, and makes one of the best country walks you can find. On the Stroudwater, the ship canal crossing at Saul and the old Severn entrance at Framilode can easily be visited.

Railways
David Bick

Hilly, thinly populated and practically devoid of mineral or industrial wealth, the Cotswolds have never held much attraction for railway promoters, and therefore, with few exceptions, those lines which eventually came arose simply because the hills had to be crossed. Indigenous traffic was encouraged but it was not a consideration of first importance.

The railways, of course, benefited the area, particularly in the case of the later lines, which were also the poorest and most vulnerable. But with the inevitable closures of recent years, the routes are barely equal in extent to those of the 1850s, and the services are in some respects worse because many stations have closed. Nevertheless, the trains that remain are fast, punctual and well patronised. One must hope that stability has at last been achieved.

First Railways

Rail transport in the Cotswolds dates from the last decade of the eighteenth century. At the time railways were primitive affairs with wooden waggons pulled by horses. Because speed and power were limited, few amounted to more than 10 or 15 miles in length, and they were mainly confined to industrial regions for moving coal, stone and iron.

In spite of the drawbacks, tramroads had certain advantages over canals. There was a lower initial cost, especially in rugged terrain, and none of the perpetual problem of water supply. Hence it is not very surprising to find that the first Cotswold railway (also the first in Gloucestershire) was laid down in one of the highest parts of the range to carry stone.

This innovation occured inconspicuously near Cheltenham about the year 1798, shortly after Charles Brandon Trye had inherited the parish of Leckhampton with its hilltop quarries of building stone. A gravity worked inclined plane was constructed, enabling the laden trucks to descend to the main road, and at the same time pulling up empties to the top. (An incidental consequence of the construction was the forma-

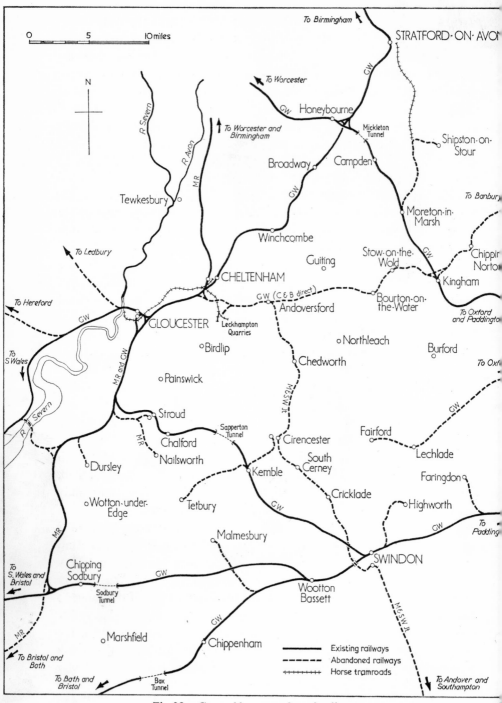

——————	Existing railways
- - - - - -	Abandoned railways
+++++++	Horse tramroads

Fig 26.   Cotswold tramroads and railways.

tion of the well known landmark the 'Devil's Chimney'.) The system apparently worked well and was instrumental in encouraging a much greater development, this being the Gloucester & Cheltenham Railway. The line, usually called the Gloucester & Cheltenham Tramroad, was largely inspired and financed by Lord Sherborne, and was primarily to carry coal to the expanding spa, of which he was Lord of the Manor. Although strictly outside our area, the line is nevertheless of relevance because a 2 mile branch was constructed from it to connect with Trye's tramroads at Leckhampton. Two additional inclines were needed to make up the difference in levels.

After the main line opened in 1811, Leckhampton stone could go the entire way to Gloucester by rail. The branch handled upwards of 20,000 tons of stone annually for many years, and various extensions and inclines were added as the quarries developed.

By the 1850s, demand for building stone was falling and in 1861 the Gloucester & Cheltenham tramroad closed due to competition from modern railways. The branch also closed, and only the quarry lines and inclines remained in operation, now merely bringing stone to the foot of the hill. However, in this contracted form, these ancient tramroads continued until 1924, when a newly re-formed quarry company abandoned them in favour of a full sized railway from the GWR line at Charlton Kings. Within 3 years this extravagant venture failed and with it ended centuries of quarrying at Leckhampton. The hill was afterwards acquired by the borough council and dedicated as an open space for public enjoyment; it has proved to be extremely popular.

There is always a fascination in railways that might have been. The Cotswolds had a good share, of which the earliest most deserves a mention because of a remarkable origin.

Projected in 1812, it was to have extended from the tramroad at Cheltenham to a newly erected works at Fox Hill near Guiting, some 11 miles to the east in a remote part of the hills. Here, at the Stone Pipe Company's headquarters, a Boulton & Watt rotative steam engine drove machinery to cut water pipes of various sizes from solid stone by a process patented (No 2837) by one Sir George Wright in 1805. Huge quantities were sold, mainly to Manchester Water Works, the directors of which were also largely those of the Stone Pipe Co. The parliamentary bill for the proposed Cheltenham & Cotswold Hills Railway was, however, defeated and soon afterwards the company itself collapsed, the directors no longer being able to conceal that their products would literally not hold water.

Evidence for this remarkable fraud is still there, in the shape of broken pipes and cores in field walls that now surround the tree-covered works by the little road that descends westwards from the Fox Hill Inn. (For further details see *Cotswold Life*, December 1970.)

The only horse railway outside the Cheltenham area with claim to Cotswold soil commenced at Moreton-in-Marsh and ran 16 miles northwards to the navigable River Avon at Stratford. William James inspired this line as part of his proposed Central Junction Railway from London to Stratford. The line was standard gauge with fish belly rails upon stone blocks, opening on 5 September 1826. A branch to Shipston on Stour was completed in February 1836. Much later, the portion from the latter town to Moreton was converted to a modern railway (in 1889). The old remnant to Stratford fell out of use about 1904; during its best days some 15,000 tons of coal were hauled up to the two towns annually.

An early plan for a 2 mile branch from Moreton to quarries at Bourton-on-the-Hill came to nothing; this was another of James's many projects, of which only the Stratford–Moreton ever came to fruition.

Steam Era

The Great Western Railway aimed at Bath and Bristol, and intended to cut through the southern Cotswolds by means of a 'monstrous and extraordinary, most dangerous and impractical' tunnel at Box. Farther north, ideas of easy communication with the metropolis attracted Gloucester and the rapidly growing Cheltenham Spa, then at a height of popularity.

But in the latter vicinities the Cotswold escarpment is formidable. Several routes were therefore considered and in 1835 Cheltenham's newspapers were reflecting the local 'railway madness'. Heated discussions weighed the pros and cons of the more direct Oxford and Tring Line (to meet the London & Birmingham), and the circuitous broad-gauge Cheltenham & Great Western Union, to connect with Brunel's projected Great Western Railway at Swindon, via Gloucester, Stroud and the Golden Valley.

Much argument centred around unavoidably expensive earthworks and operating problems. At a time when locomotive climbing power was considered to be very limited, heavy gradients confronted both routes, more especially in the case of the Oxford line, which would have had a positively saw-tooth profile. Robert Stephenson, however, with London & Birmingham interests at heart, dismissed the geography as 'no difficulty . . . of the least importance' and Captain Moorsom, the surveyor, claimed gradients of only 1 in 330 from Andoversford to Tring. Brunel said that such a route was next to impossible, but it was really no worse than much of the c & gwu, to which he was engineer. Opinions rather depended on who was paying your salary. In 1836 the matter was effectively settled when the c & gwu got its Act of Parliament for building the line, but the Tring scheme died hard; its ghost was to appear several times in the future.

The Great Western opened in 1841 from London to Chippenham, with the c & gwu line operating from Swindon to Kemble and thence to Cirencester by means of a branch some four miles long, that ran for part of its length over a high embankment. The rest of the c & gwu (which was eventually absorbed by the gwr) did not reach Cheltenham until October 1847. The delays were due to chronic shortage of cash and difficulties with the long tunnel at Sapperton. This was the sole line to cross the high Cotswold backbone until the Cheltenham–Banbury line opened in 1881 via Andoversford.

The most northerly line was the Oxford, Worcester & Wolverhampton Railway, which ran via Moreton-in-Marsh. Apart from the company's treacherous dealings with the gwr, the line's early days are best remembered for the 'Battle of Mickleton tunnel', which arose when a failing contractor refused to allow possession. The line opened in June 1853.

Later Developments

Insofar as the Cotswolds are concerned, a lull in railway construction followed the Oxford–Worcester line. Pressing demands had been met and later developments mainly arose from companies competitive to those established, and therefore in a potentially weak position. The East Gloucestershire Railway was the first of these to reach construction stage.

The project, proposed in 1861 to run from Cheltenham to the gwr at Faringdon, was never completed in its original form, although earthworks were begun. The only part to be finally opened (in January 1873) took the form of a branch from Oxford to Fairford—one which has been delightfully described by Paul Jennings in *Just a Few Lines*.

South of Gloucester, to serve the industrialised valleys near Stroud, the Midland Railway built a 6 mile branch from Stonehouse to Nailsworth, which opened in 1867.

Bravest of the later railways was the Midland & Southern Western Junction, which took the difficult but direct route from Cheltenham to Swindon and beyond. It began as the Swindon, Marlborough & Andover in 1873, but money shortage delayed even this portion opening for a decade. From the start the venture was quite oppressed by the GWR, and hopes of gaining independence and more traffic rested in extending northwards across the worst of the Cotswolds to meet the Midland at Cheltenham. Such a link would provide a route from Manchester and the West Midlands to Southampton, and indeed had been an 1840s' aspiration of Robert Stephenson, as the Manchester & Southampton Railway, via Cheltenham, Seven Springs and Cirencester.

To this end, an Act was obtained in 1881 for the Swindon & Cheltenham Extension Railway, via Cirencester and Andoversford, where it was to meet the Banbury & Cheltenham (then opening) about 6 miles from the latter town. The new company's funds were equally short, and although Cirencester was reached in December 1883, heavy earthworks and a desperate financial position delayed the final link-up until 1891. Before then, the two Swindon lines were amalgamated as the M & SWJR, with a receiver in control from the start.

Early in 1892 fortunes took a turn for the better. Sam Fay (later Sir Sam Fay of the Great Central) relinquished his duties on the London & South Western Railway to become secretary and general manager of the M & SWJ. Sweeping changes in senior staff were made and within a few years his determination and efficiency had elevated the company from bankruptcy to a dividend-paying condition.

In 1898, to avoid restrictions imposed by the single line from Cheltenham to Andoversford, the M & SWJ projected a northward extension via Winchcombe—the Andoversford & Stratford-upon-Avon Railway. The first portion of this route had been envisaged as long ago as 1835, being part of the so-called 'Giles line' from Cheltenham to Tring. However, the scheme was rejected by Parliament when the GWR agreed to build the Cheltenham–Winchcombe–Honeybourne connection.

The Cheltenham–Banbury line has already been mentioned. Opening in 1881 as the Cheltenham & Banbury Direct, this was the final expression of a desire which went back to the 1820s for a Cheltenham–London railway via the Chelt valley. By changing at Kingham Junction on to the main line from Worcester to Oxford, the metropolis could certainly be reached, though severe gradients and curves across the Cotswold backbone prevented anything much better than bicycling speeds. This route held an easy record for a standard gauge summit level in Gloucestershire, being some 800ft above OD at Notgrove. The company was absorbed by the GWR in 1897.

Further south, there was another development before the close of the nineteenth century—the Kemble to Tetbury branch, which opened on 2 December 1889.

During the Edwardian period the Great Western entered a final phase of expansion in which two important new routes were constructed through Gloucestershire. These were South Wales–Swindon via the Severn tunnel, Chipping Sodbury and Wootton Bassett (opened 1903), and the Cheltenham–Honeybourne, thence to Stratford & Birmingham (opened 1906). The former involved construction of a $2\frac{1}{2}$ mile tunnel near Chipping Sodbury, and stations were built at Brinkworth, Little Somerford, Hullavington, Badminton and Chipping Sodbury. The new line shortened the South Wales–London route by 10 miles and carried heavy coal traffic. The Honeybourne line skirted the foot of the Cotswold escarpment, and was of benefit to its north-western fringes, in particular to Broadway and Winchcombe.

In a region where quarries are everywhere in evidence, it might have been expected that much stone traffic would have arisen; but by and large, Cotswold oolite is too soft for roads. As far as I can discover, only two quarries had standard-gauge rail access—at Foss Cross, and at Leckhampton where a mile long branch ran up an incline from Charlton Kings station. Both had limekilns, but only the former connections lasted any length of time.

Services

A glance at a relief map shows how isolated the Cotswolds were before the railways came. Canals helped in the southern parts but above Cirencester, where the land is highest, there were no means of moving coal and other heavy materials except by badly surfaced and steep roads that gave rise to an almost ruinous expense. The railways were therefore a blessing, and they eventually spread until only two areas—Elkstone and Barrington—were more than 6 or 7 miles from a station. Most villagers, however, made infrequent use of the trains; there was little time or money to spare for towns. The latter rather tended to reach out for business in the shape of coal wharves and other amenities that grew around most country stations.

To give an idea of facilities offered for travelling 60 years ago, there were four trains each weekday from Kingham Junction to Cheltenham St James, stopping at all seven intermediate stations. The journey of $24\frac{1}{2}$ miles took exactly 1 hour. On the M & SWJR line, the 7 miles from Chedworth to Cirencester required 20 minutes. For those wishing to get from Tetbury to Stroud, there was an 8 minute wait at Kemble for the connection, the whole distance ($18\frac{1}{2}$ miles) taking 46 minutes.

Sunday trains ran infrequently, if at all. I have been told a reliable story of how at Cheltenham late one Saturday evening, a sailor alighted from an express with a large portmanteau which required urgent delivery to Stow-on-the-Wold. For a guinea a man with a handcart volunteered to help him push it there. The offer was promptly accepted, notwithstanding the prospect of 18 miles of Cotswold roads.

Certain through trains, stopping only at major stations, managed to put up presentable performances. Before World War I, the best time from Southampton to Cheltenham was 2hr 27min—creditable enough for 95 difficult miles. Another through route was from Cardiff to Newcastle, which from 1906 until 1939 took an improbable course via Cheltenham, Andoversford, Banbury and the Great Central. This needed a loop at Hatherley near Cheltenham, and a flyover at Kingham to avoid the Oxford–Worcester line. Unfortunately for Cheltonians the potential of the Banbury route as a quick way to London was never really exploited, although it was much shorter than the old Gloucester–Stroud–Swindon circuit. The line did, however, carry a great tonnage of iron ore destined for South Wales from Oxfordshire and beyond. Churchward 2–8–0 locomotives, slow but very strong, usually worked these trains, which amounted at one time to sixteen daily. A driver told me 'they would pull a row of houses down'. But the hilly routes were never a very sound proposition. After World War II, with economies being everywhere sought, services worsened, with inexorable trends that could only lead to closure.

Sometimes withdrawal of trains seemed brutal and unnecessary, especially in cases where the line was retained for other services. An example was the Chalford–Stroud–Gloucester run, which had its origins in October 1903 when the GWR introduced their new rail motors between Chalford and Stonehouse. Later, the service was extended to Gloucester; trains ran every 45 minutes or thereabouts in peak periods and stopped at ten intermediate stations and halts. But in spite of being well patronised by commuters and shoppers it was abruptly terminated and stations demolished in 1964, leaving a deficiency which no road service could hope to fill.

Ironically, as late as 1947, serious proposals came forth for rail extensions from Cirencester to Fairford, and from Tetbury to the South Wales line near Acton Turville. Even then, wholesale abandonment for most of the Cotswold lines within the next 20 years would have been a thought too ludicrous to contemplate. However, with the declining convenience of motoring, trade is returning to the lines that first penetrated these hills well over a century ago. The old Cheltenham & Great Western Union line, though singled in parts, carries the popular Cheltenham Spa Express, which has recently accelerated its time to 2hr 10 min, or only 1hr 25min from Kemble to Paddington.

There have been rumours of closure for the Oxford–Worcester service, but at present it can still offer times of under 1½hr for the 92 mile journey from Moreton-in-Marsh to London.

Unexpectedly, the last railway to be built (Honeybourne–Cheltenham) has had a last-minute reprieve. After a period of virtual abandonment it now relieves the main Cheltenham–Birmingham line and carries substantial freight traffic. Its future seems safe for the time being, and we must hope that an economic system has at last been achieved. *– CLOSED AUG '76 BETWEEN STRATFORD & CHELTENHAM.*

Railway Engineering

Brunel's tunnels at Box and Sapperton are amongst the best known works associated with Cotswold railways, and as both display certain unusual features, together with an interesting history, it is worth saying a little about them.

When projected in 1835, the tunnel under Box hill, nearly 2 miles in length, was much more ambitious than any yet constructed for railways, although at the time there were many longer tunnels for mining purposes; nearer home, the Thames & Severn Canal 50 years previously had penetrated over 2 miles beneath the Cotswolds. The scheme's feasibility was therefore never really in doubt, in spite of various alarming prognostications.

The tunnel took a falling gradient of 1 in 100, with the deepest part 300ft below surface. Construction involved the labour of 300 horses and 4,000 men, and 100 of the latter were said to have been killed during the 5 year period. A valuable consequence of excavation was the discovery of large deposits of Bath building stone. These deposits were afterwards exploited, and one of the tunnel air shafts actually passes through the subterranean workings. Both ends of the tunnel were made very high for the sake of appearance; the splendid western portal is readily seen from the Box–Corsham road.

Though less famous, Sapperton tunnel has a more complicated history. Originally it was proposed at a low level to minimise the climb from Stroud and was to be constructed entirely on a gradual curve just over 1½ miles long. It was soon realised, however, that the curve was better avoided. Brunel revised the plans, substituting an almost straight boring of 2,730yd, upon which, in May 1838, work was being executed separately from five shafts. By October 1841 nine shafts had been sunk and a good part of the task was completed.

The c & gwu was very short of funds at this period, and after it had been absorbed by the gwr in June 1843, Brunel embarked upon a further revision, presumably for reasons of economy. The well advanced tunnel was altogether abandoned in favour of two new borings at a higher level, one long and the other short, with a short distance of daylight in between.

This meant increasing the already steep grade from Stroud to about 1 in 60, but the existing shafts could be employed for construction. Once the decision had been made, work proceeded rapidly and both tunnels were finished by February 1845, their combined length being 1,908yd. However, considering the amount of expenditure to be written off, it is difficult to understand how Brunel justified the new start.

The open section between the tunnels is close beside the Stroud-Cirencester road and easy to find. Perhaps less well known is the western end, where the line begins a sinuous descent through the lovely Golden Valley and the 'little Switzerland' of Chalford. There was no more pleasant spot than here for those who found enjoyment in watching steam locomotives at work.

A few miles to the east is Kemble station, where branches used to leave for Cirencester and Tetbury. Near the end of the down platform was a pumping station, dating from 1872, for providing Swindon works with water. A two-cylinder horizontal steam engine was employed until October 1971, being housed in a building below ground level. When a new well with electric pumps was installed nearby, the old plant was scrapped and the site levelled, only a slight hollow remaining to mark the spot. A massive overhead water tank is still a conspicuous feature, especially with its smaller tank above, now demolished, which once supplied the village.

Remnants

In the country, railways have a value that is often forgotten long after the metals have gone—not in any commercial form, but as a perpetual source of pleasure for the walker, the botanist and the industrial archaeologist. The old Cotswold lines are certainly fruitful in this respect and, being shown on most maps of the area, their routes are easily found. However, such is not the case with the earliest lines. Near Cheltenham, Trye's quarry tramroads and inclines are worth a visit and have been described in my recent booklet *Old Leckhampton*.

Several fine bridges and earthworks survive on the northern section of the Stratford & Moreton Tramroad, and there is also a preserved tram waggon at the Stratford end of the line.

From the 1860s period, remains of the East Gloucestershire Railway are to be seen 1½ miles west of Andoversford just north of the A38 at the foot of Tunnel Hill, where a long embankment parallel to the road is the clearest relic of this uncompleted project.

Most bridges associated with the closed lines have been demolished and it is a pity that so few of the wayside stations and dwellings survive. In common with turnpike houses, they might have found new uses and provided objects of interest and curiosity for future generations. Still, many people will remember them, like Adlestrop, if only by name.

Notes to this chapter are on pages 307–9.

GLOUCESTERSHIRE COLLEGE
OF EDUCATION
LIBRARY

6

Wool, Woolmen and Weavers

Lionel F. J. Walrond

THE STORY of wool and woollen cloth, like the yarn itself, weaves its way into every aspect of Cotswold life. Not only has history revolved around its fortunes, but it has profoundly influenced the landscape, the villages and towns, the churches and the mills, and the people themselves.

Pre-Roman to Medieval Times

Evidence of spinning and weaving in pre-Roman and Roman times can be found in almost every museum in the area. From Cleeve Hill and Salmonsbury Hill have come the large triangular weights of baked clay used to tighten the threads of vertical looms. The prehistoric weave was beaten into place, using bone combs and awls, which were also found at Salmonsbury. Spindle whorls for the preparation of the yarn have been found on sites too numerous to mention, with little or no development over a period of centuries.

At Cirencester, a century of excavation has revealed almost every aspect of domestic life, with little evidence of an organised industry. Spindle whorls were not numerous, and the presence of two delicate bronze objects, almost certainly spindle shanks, implies the spinning of very fine embroidery thread, in keeping with the obvious grace of Roman town life. Several small pairs of iron shears may well have belonged to dressmakers or simply represent a part of the work-basket of any well-to-do home. Heavy cloth for winter cloaks must have been produced in the villas around.

The excavation of a Saxon weaver's hut at Bourton-on-the-Water causes one to speculate whether the weaver worked to supply the needs of his family alone, or whether the craft had become more highly organised. By early medieval times the emphasis lay not on cloth, but on the production of wool for export.

The characteristics of medieval Cotswold wool remain a mystery. Some writers regarded it as long and others as short. It was certainly fine,

Page 179 *Chipping Campden:* (above) *street scene;* (left) *detail*

Page 180 *Detail in stone:*
(left) *a doorway in Gloucester
Street, Cirencester, showing
Gothic and Renaissance
detail together, 1695; (below)
a fourteenth-century tomb
recess in Meysey Hampton
church*

but this seems not wholly constant. The quality may well have been influenced by the practice of cotting—keeping the sheep in partially roofed pens during the winter months—and there is a distinct possibility that cross-breeding may have changed the appearance of both sheep and fleece not once but several times. Certainly in the medieval period Cotswold wool was known to be among the finest in Britain, and British wool the finest in Europe.

Medieval Sheep Farmers

By this time the bulk of the land was owned by the great abbeys. We know a lot about sheep-keeping at Blockley and Sherborne from monastic documents, and probably these conditions were general in villages owned by other religious houses (see chapter 3, p 104).

About 1279 the parish of Blockley, near Chipping Campden, then the property of the Bishop of Worcester, was assessed as having enough pasture to feed 800 sheep. Twenty years later the number had been increased to 1,612 and by 1383 to 2,065. This could represent increased pasture following the depopulation of the Black Death, but far more likely there was a growing tendency by the Bishop to move his flocks from manor to manor. In this year his entire flock was taken to Blockley for shearing, and in 1384 William Grevel of Chipping Campden bought 14½ sacks of wool from him for £133, this being made up from the wool of 1,100 sheep grazed in Blockley and 2,014 from other manors owned by the Bishop. In the same year he spent £14 on a stone sheep cote eight bays long, and bought in an extra 319 lambs for £29.

Only a few miles away in the little village of Sherborne near Northleach fifteen of the parish's ninety-one tenants owed a day's service to their Lord, the Abbot of Winchcombe, helping wash and shear his sheep. This type of service was not repeated elsewhere in any of the abbey's holdings, which were among the largest in Britain. Earlier in the fourteenth century the Florentine Peglotti estimated the abbey as one of England's twelve greatest wool producers, yielding forty sacks and implying a flock of at least 8,000 sheep. In 1485 it took 4 days to shear 2,900 of the Abbot's sheep, filling fourteen sacks with wool. As at Blockley, the Abbot purchased the wool grown by his tenants and sold it with his own. In both places the operation, though recorded only in certain years, was clearly a regular event, implying permanent sheep washes, shearing sheds, wool stores, and pens and shelters for the sheep.

For almost a century, till the end of the 1360s, Britain was exporting no less than 32,000 sacks of wool annually (about 5,200 tons) to be spun

L

and woven in the great European centres of Bruges, Ghent and Ypres. The decline after this was in no way due to a diminution in sheep-farming, but to the growth of home production of cloth for sale overseas at an even greater profit. It is little wonder then that there grew up a group of wealthy clothier-merchants. John Tame kept flocks of sheep and ran weaving sheds at Cirencester. Northleach was the home of Thomas Fortey and of William Midwinter, both of whom were graziers and wool buyers, whilst the Cely family of Chipping Campden were famous as wool exporters. William Grevel, who died in 1401, was the greatest of the local wool merchants. We know of several others who lived at Cirencester, Chipping Campden and Northleach, such as Robert Page, Reginald Spicer, William Welley, John Townsend and John Bennett, to name but a few. They either owned ships to carry their produce to the Continent, or had business arrangements with ships' captains who would. If they were at all like the merchants of Devon, they would have traded not only in wool and cloth, but in wine, honey, salt, metals, dyes and fine draperies, in fact anything that would produce a profit.

The known factor common to many who lived before 1540 was the money spent on their local churches. William Grevel rebuilt Chipping Campden church, the Forteys partly rebuilt the church at Northleach, John Twinyhoe added a chantry at Lechlade, and the Tames take credit for almost everything at Fairford. Cirencester church contains the marks and symbols of many wealthy persons, some still unidentified. These marks were the signs used by the woolmen and merchants to indicate ownership of goods. They appear on tombs, monumental brasses, roof corbels, ceiling beams, stained glass, in fact anywhere. Most have been recorded, but some, like the mark in the nave roof at Stow-on-the-Wold, get no mention in any of the standard histories.

The most famous Cotswold merchant of all, 'Dick' Whittington, was born at Pauntley in the mid-fourteenth century, and exported the finest cloths. He was thrice made Mayor of London, and in 1395 he appears to have acquired a large part of Stroud and the valley up to Brimscombe. Perhaps it was through him that the Stroud cloths first gained their high reputation on the Continent. He, too, gave lavishly to the church, to Gloucester Cathedral and numerous institutions in London.

Middle Ages to Nineteenth Century—Wool Production

With the passing of the great merchants, wool production did not cease. The merchant guilds which had dominated the larger towns became unpopular as their authority declined. Itinerant bands of shearers moved from estate to estate, and we read of William Walker and John Short who, c 1628, were paid 6d per score for wrapping 1,272 fleeces at Sezincote. Instead of monastic sheep ranges, every yeoman now had his little flock. Tyndale's comment that 'God gave the earth to men to inhabit and not unto sheep' was apt, for soon after this there were half a million sheep in Gloucestershire alone. Early in the eighteenth century 20,000 were changing hands at Stow-on-the-Wold's annual fair. Northleach had declined by this time, but Sir Robert Atkyns, writing in 1712, described the wool market held every Friday in the Booth-hall at Cirencester as the largest in England. Open-sided market-houses sprang up in almost every town, not only for the sale of wool, but for all forms of merchandise. Gradually farmers began to sell their wool direct to the clothiers, who came mainly from the south Cotswolds and the Trowbridge area. This reduced the importance of the market. By 1800 Samuel Rudder found that the Cirencester streets, so thronged with wool waggons 40 years before, were now empty, and the famous market was reduced to a mere nullity.

Whether wool was sold in markets or on the farms, a means of weighing had to be perfected. The units of weight commonly used were the tod of 28lb, the pocket containing 12 tods and the sack of 13 tods. The purchaser would carry the exact weight of 3, 4 and 7lb. These would be enough to check the accuracy of any beam scale, and most farms had one or more stone blocks carefully cut down to serve as 14lb weights. This was no doubt the origin of the term 'stone' given to this unit of weight. Most have perished, but there is in Stroud Museum a block weighing 2 stones. The official weights were never numerous, but there is a fine series for wool-weighing in Cheltenham Museum, ranging from the reign of King James II to that of George III.

All the while, the character of the wool was changing, if not the breed of sheep itself. The theories of Robert Bakewell (1725–95) on selective breeding and improved feeding systems certainly produced heavier wool yields, though probably at the expense of quality. The enclosure movement contributed likewise in that it separated the improved from the less healthy flocks. There was moreover a national trend towards larger sheep, better suited to meat production regardless of a coarsening of the fleece.

Wool is not a simple commodity, uniform in length and texture. It varies with the breed of sheep, its diet and environment, and the part of the body from which it is taken. Short wool was the best suited for the traditional local broadcloth, and the loosening of the short fibres before spinning was called carding. Very long wool could not be carded and had to be combed. In between there was a medium length that could be treated either way. Cirencester seems to have had a specialist interest in the preparation of long wool. When John Cripps the younger died in 1695, he had in his garret 121 tods (3,388lb) of long wool worth £157 6s, and wool that may well have been long worth over £25. The rest of his yarn and wool, short or of unspecified length, was worth over £450. By comparison, his horse, and all his household possessions, including his silver spoons and tankard, were worth only £52 5s. Much of the long wool would have been used for warp, lists and what we might describe as a form of worsted. In 1830 wool of this type was being prepared at Tetbury and Cirencester.

Not even the vast output of the Cirencester market was enough to meet the requirements of the rapidly expanding cloth industry. As long ago as 1567 Britain was importing 12,550lb of wool from Spain, though its use in mills at Kingswood and Uley does not appear till a century later. By that time Spanish wool was considered by some to be finer than that produced at home. By 1820 wool was coming in from Saxony, and it became so popular that by 1830 it comprised 65 per cent of our imported wool. This in turn was superseded by Australian wool. In spite of the popularity this was soon to enjoy, it had been tried at both Stanley Mill and Eastington by 1824 and found unsuitable for the type of cloth then being made.

Cloth-making Processes

The history of the wool trade is simple by comparison with that of the cloth industry. Under the medieval guild system each urban craftsman was responsible for one process only, the product changing ownership repeatedly in its progress from fleece to cloth. The rural clothier on the other hand bought the wool and supervised every process up to the marketing of the cloth.

The raw wool was first sorted according to length and quality, and washed. Stoving (sulphur-bleaching) could be done at this stage, after spinning or on completion between scouring and fulling; and some wool was dyed blue, using the fermented leaves of the woad plant. After drying, the wool was oiled, sometimes with butter or goose grease, but more often Seville or Gallipoli oil. Thorough mixing was achieved by scribbling, a tearing operation which also loosened the denser parts of the fleece.

Until the installation of spinning machinery in the mills, the next part of the operation was done in the cottages, in that it did not require either water or power. First the raw wool was combed or more commonly

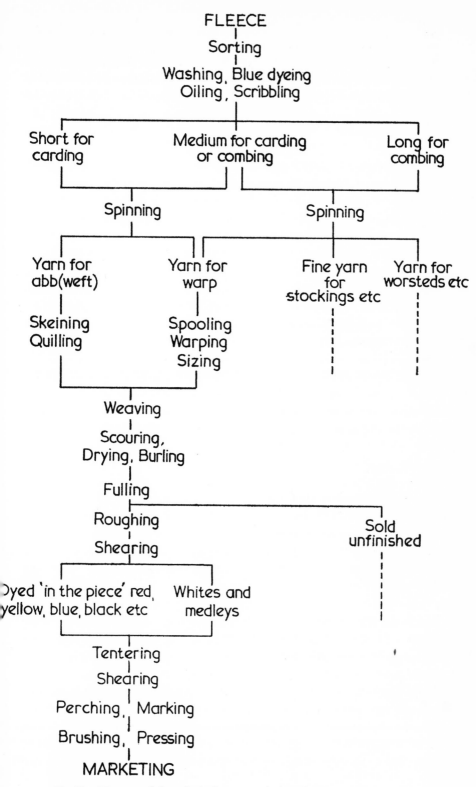

FLEECE
|
Sorting
|
Washing, Blue dyeing
Oiling, Scribbling
|

Short for carding　　Medium for carding　　Long for combing
　　　　　　　　　　or combing

Spinning　　　　　　　　　　Spinning

Yarn for abb(weft)　　Yarn for warp　　Fine yarn for stockings etc　　Yarn for worsteds etc

Skeining Quilling　　Spooling Warping Sizing

Weaving
|
Scouring,
Drying, Burling
|
Fulling
|
Roughing　　　　　　　　　Sold unfinished
|
Shearing

Dyed 'in the piece' red, yellow, blue, black etc　　Whites and medleys

Tentering
|
Shearing
|
Perching, Marking
|
Brushing, Pressing
|
MARKETING

Fig 27.　Diagram of the principal processes in broadcloth manufacturing.

carded to open the fibres still more. In this state it was hand-spun using wheels of the type more commonly seen in nineteenth-century Welsh rural scenes. These were slower in use but far cheaper to make than the 'Saxony' wheel now commonly seen. After being reeled into skeins, the yarn was collected by the clothier or his agent for reissue to the cottage weavers.

Looms varied in width and in detail, according to the type of cloth to be produced. Usually they were set up in the attics of the older houses, but were often on the ground floor in the cottages erected c 1800–20. The yarn for the warp was spooled and measured by passing it around a series of pegs in a frame. Every strand, now of equal length, had to be sized to improve its strength and reduce friction on the shuttle, and then threaded into the loom. This was no simple task, with up to 4,000 to be wound on without tangles or variation in tension. The weft, or abb as it was locally known, was the weaker of the two, and was wound on to quills which fitted inside the loom shuttles. With the help of his family a good weaver could produce 10–12ft of cloth in a day.

On its return to the mill the cloth was scoured, usually in stale urine to remove the oil and size. After partial drying on large wooden adjustable racks, it was examined for knots, flaws and foreign bodies before being fulled. The cloth was soaped, carefully folded and placed in the trough of the fulling stocks with a little warm water. Heavy wooden mallets, operated from the water-wheel or beam engine, fell alternately, slowly turning the cloth to produce an even felting process. Fullers' earth, a yellow clay once dug at Minchinhampton, was at one time used for fulling. From time to time the cloth was removed and inspected. Rotary fullers had come into general use by the 1880s and the older form was last used in the Stroud area in the mid-1930s.

After fulling, the length of each piece had shrunk from 54yd to 40yd. It was also narrower but much thicker. At one time the cloth was hung over a beam or 'perch' and stroked with teasel heads set in a 'handle' to raise the nap. Upon mechanisation it was passed over a drum around which the teasels were fastened in metal frames. This method is in use today, no better method having been discovered. The machine was called a gig and the operation was described as roughing. Before dyeing, the raised woolly surface had to be shorn down. At one time this was done with large hand-shears over a curved pad, but the operation was speeded considerably after 1815 with the invention of the rotary cutter. Until the sixteenth century a large amount of undyed cloth was exported directly after fulling, and after 1820 many of the lesser clothiers must have sold at this stage because they had not the facilities for dyeing and high-class finishing. Apart from the whites and medleys, all cloth was dyed 'in the piece' before being taken into the fields to be stretched on the tenter racks for drying. It was perched in order to touch up any dye flaws, using a goose quill rather than a metal point, and to remove any imperfections, however small, and then repeatedly shorn and brushed. Finally it was given its glossy or damp-resistant quality by hot pressing, or one of the other highly specialised patent processes before marketing.

Early Mills

The industry was tied to the stream courses only because water was needed to wash the wool, to dye and rinse cloth and, once mechanisation had begun, to turn the water-wheels. The earliest references to mills are in 1086, in Domesday Book. The majority clearly operated corn mills, but along the River Frome there were twenty-eight mills in seven parishes. Apart from this abnormal density, the area had a low population and was ill suited to growing corn. One might suggest that some at least were fulling mills, though the terms does not appear in documents till a century later.

We know all too little about our very early mills. Probably timber-framed, they were little larger than a garage, of one or two storeys, with an external water-wheel at the gable end. The streams and small rivers upon which they were built were often the boundaries of parishes and these in turn the boundaries between manors. Technically, the machinery of a corn mill would have been the more complex in that the power had to be transmitted through 90° to the stones above. In a fulling mill the stocks could have been operated by cams on the axle shaft with no such problems. A very early date could therefore be expected.

Although large numbers of corn mills were built immediately following the Norman conquest, the first documentary reference to a fulling mill appears in 1185, when the Knights Templar held two at Barton, in the parish of Temple Guiting, on sites where mills of some kind were known to have existed 10 years earlier. A few years later John Blundell had a fulling mill at Winchcombe, the water supply to which was diverted by the monks from the abbey.

By the end of the thirteenth century there were others at Cerney near Cirencester, Fairford, Chedworth and Hawkesbury, whilst the famous Minchinhampton Custumal mentions a further four. The industry was important enough by 1321 for Cirencester to be levying a tax on fleeces, wool, many types of cloth and embroideries, and various dyes and chemicals. In 1377 Winchcombe had a tax on wool, woad, alum and teasels. From the time of its inception the cloth industry has undergone a great surge of progress at regular intervals of about 200 years.

Records of the sixteenth century frequently refer to cloth mills, as at Munday's Mill, North Nibley—'a fullinge mill and a grist mill under one roofe'. This combination of uses could have been achieved from one wooden water-wheel provided it was larger and operated by a greater head of water. But more often the mill would have had two wheels operated from the same pond or, as at Egypt Mill and Day's Mill, both of Nailsworth, by twin ponds placed side by side. Improved power was often achieved by rebuilding the mills a few yards from the river bank on slightly higher ground, thus permitting a millpond to one side of the parish boundary, and using the old stream bed as an overflow channel. The increased head of water necessitated rack and pinion sluices to control the water flowing on to the wheel, and for draining the millpond for repairs, etc. There was also a fixed overflow weir to prevent damage in the event of thunderstorms. Wyatt's Mill at Slad was washed away when the mill dam burst, probably due to inadequate flood controls; and many others burst, causing less severe damage.

Mill leats also appear about this time. These were narrow open conduits conducting water from a spring or stream to feed a pond it would otherwise miss, or to enable water to flow without loss over porous sand beds. A good example, now dry, can be found opposite the Star Inn, Slad, where a spring was once diverted to serve a pond higher up the valley. An enormous leat can still be seen behind Dunkirk Mill, Nailsworth (p 125). Some 15ft wide, this was successively widened from 1798 to 1855 and served as many as five water-wheels.

The close of the eighteenth century saw further changes. Iron began to replace wood in the making of parts of water-wheels, which as a result became larger and more powerful. Ponds were further adapted to supply more water. One of the new mills, c 1800–20, at Ebley had five water-wheels running side by side. The extra power was needed to drive the newly invented machinery housed in large multi-storeyed mills, of which many still survive in the Stroud valleys. When more power was needed, this usually came from Boulton & Watt beam engines, often coupled to the water-wheel shafting. By 1815 there were already four such machines in Gloucestershire, the one at Longfords Mill having cost £970. The last beam engine at Ebley Mills was broken up during World War II, but engine houses survive at Dunkirk Mill and in the larger mills on the Severn plain, usually plastered with an ornamental cornice, a splendour reserved only for the king of all machines.

The last working water-wheel in any of the Cotswold cloth mills, by
this time manufacturing hairpins, was at Brookhouse Mills, Painswick
(p 126). This stopped in 1962 and was broken up 2 years later. Strangely,
its end was in no way due to the wear of nearly a century and a half
of action. Sediment and land reclamation had reduced the size of the
pond, necessitating an auxiliary source of power in the form of a gas
engine, and it was the total failure of this that finally led to the abandonment of both in favour of electricity.

The Age of Prosperity, c 1600–1800

The cloth industry, by this time dead over much of the north and east
Cotswolds, was expanding in the valleys around Dursley and Wotton-
under-Edge, and in particular around Stroud, Chalford, Woodchester
and Painswick. Here the visible evidence of the changes of the late
sixteenth and seventeenth centuries is best preserved in the houses of the
clothiers, which were set alongside their mills. One of the best examples,
Ebley Court, built 1587, was demolished in the summer of 1971, but
good examples still survive at Salmon Springs, Stroud, 1607; Egypt Mill,
Nailsworth, 1698; St Mary's, Chalford; and Southfield, Woodchester.
Others were remodelled or rebuilt in the eighteenth or nineteenth centuries.
At least two, Salmon Springs and Haregrove, Cranham, contain fifteenth-
century details, the former having been originally timber-framed.

Away from the mills, the better-class seventeenth-century houses were
often built either by lesser clothiers or broad weavers. Three storeys high,
their attics formerly housed broad looms. At Leonard Stanley a fifteenth-
century timber-framed weaving shop stands at the rear of a mercer's
house. Above it a wool and cloth store was approached only from the
master's bedroom. In the same parish the attic of one farmhouse still
retains a shaft up which the bales of wool and cloth were hoisted. The
clothier at Lodgemoor, Stroud, lived in but a part of what appears to be
an early eighteenth-century mansion, the attic and rooms at either end
being really warehouses or for non-mechanised cloth processes (see p 125).
Less than a century ago some of the garrets at Cirencester retained doorways from the time they were wool combers' warehouses.

Perhaps the most remarkable building of all, bearing the date of its
erection in 1687, was the centre part of Wallbridge Mill. Culverts
passed beneath it from the former millpond, which was abandoned when
a nineteenth-century wing was added. The walls stood four storeys high,
but the roof was a replacement. Far too large for a clothier's house, it
had, nevertheless, a number of carved Gothic style fireplaces and a

lateral chimneystack incorporating a spiral stair. At first floor level opposite the fireplace was an original loading doorway—probably the oldest authenticated example in all Britain. A modern factory now stands on the site.

Unlike the medieval wool merchants, these clothiers of the post-Reformation period could not express their piety by adorning the local churches. Their charity was bestowed instead upon the setting-up of almshouses, hospitals and grammar schools. Many names remain familiar —Lady Dorothy Chandos of Winchcombe, Sir Baptist Hicks of Chipping Campden, Thomas Dutton of Northleach, Elizabeth Bridges of Ciren-cester and Sir William Romney of Tetbury. Less well remembered are Thomas Hughes and Henry Windowe of Stroud, John Taylor of Bisley, Hugh Perry and Thomas Dawes of Wotton-under-Edge, Edward Webb of Horsley, and many more besides. Their schools had distinctive uniforms, both yellow and blue at Cirencester, red at Stroud, and blue at Bisley and Wotton-under-Edge. The clothiers would no doubt have sold or given the cloth that was damaged in production for clothing the pupils.

Cloth output was increasing all the time, and clothiers built their reputations upon the quality of their individual products. Since the majority of the people were illiterate, a form of trademark was used to denote each man's product, just as the wool merchants had done in the north and east Cotswolds. In 1634 Thomas Webb of Painswick was in trouble for not having woven his mark in the correct place on two pieces of red cloth. These marks were closely guarded, and Jasper Estcourt of Lightpill willed his to his son Richard in 1661. When Richard Clutter-buck built The Grange at Leonard Stanley, the decorative stone labels on either side of the main entrance bore his mark on one side and the date 1580 on the other. Thomas Bennett of Ebley Court did the same over one of his windows. Door lintels were the commonest place for marks, and some may be seen at Kings Stanley, Dudbridge, The Hill, Salmon Springs and Church Street, Stroud, as well as on many of the finer houses around Stroud.

Throughout the Elizabethan period much of the cloth was exported undyed and in an unfinished state, though an ever-increasing amount was dyed locally. Records are strangely silent on what dyes were used until comparatively recent times. Traditionally the success of making Stroud-water scarlets and Uley blues lay in the softness of the water. This is in no way borne out by the analysis of the spring water of the west Cots-wolds. The story was a complete hoax to outwit any who would come from 'foreign parts' to learn the mysteries of the art. The real secret lay in the preparation and blending of the raw wool and yarn, and in the dyes themselves. Temperatures and strengths of solutions were not measured by instruments but by consistency, and, most important of all, by tasting. At Lodgemoor and Brimscombe Lower Mills there were large ponds in which water could lose some of its temporary hardness and permit impurities to settle before being used in the dye houses. Tall trees were planted along the south bank to keep the water cool during the summertime. A painting in Stroud Museum shows white, red, yellow and blue cloth drying in the field alongside Wallbridge Mill. Blues and blacks were most commonly seen around Uley and in the southern part of the escarpment, whereas the Stroud–Gloucester area was famed for its reds and scarlets. Some dyes were obtained from plants grown locally, such as woad. Weld and madder were in great demand and were also grown in this country. Once trade was established with more distant lands, cochineal and indigo became popular, and numerous shades could be achieved by crushing the wood fibre of exotic trees. Brazil wood, old fustic, young fustic, log wood, sanderswood, bar wood and camwood would no doubt have been imported into Bristol, and the essential mordants for use with the dyes were produced locally. Synthetic dyes were not available until the second half of the nineteenth century. Colours used in any one dye vat were rarely changed. Except for medleys, which contained a mixture of wools of different colours, most cloth was dyed after fulling. Blues and blacks were an exception, for they were 'woaded in the wool' in addition to their final dyeing.

The eighteenth century was an age of characters, of spectacular fortunes and equally rapid collapses. Both Samuel Sheppard in 1730 and William Dallaway, the 'eminent clothier' of Brimscombe, in 1766 rose to the rank of High Sheriff of the county; yet James, the heir and younger brother of the latter, had lost everything before his death in 1787. George Hawker built Rodborough Fort, 1761–5, a vast sham castle with no water supply. Samuel Sheppard's son, Edward, built Gatcombe Park, but his son Philip had to flee to Dunkirk in the early nineteenth century to escape his creditors, having spent £100,000 in 13 years. Onesiphorus Paul entertained the Prince of Wales at Southfield Mill in 1750, and became a baronet in 1762. Two years later, when he and his lady visited Bath, they were described as 'the finest couple that has ever been seen here since Bath was built'! His son in 1788 demonstrated the processes of cloth manufacture to King George III during a visit to Woodchester Mill.

The lesser clothier was opulent at times, and poor at others, for he had not the capital to maintain himself over the lean periods. How much more perplexing for the weaver who knew not how he was faring from one week to the next! Among the poor, petty theft was not only rife, but was treated as a right and a necessity. Punishment was severe—varying from imprisonment for theft of a little wool to death for stealing cloth from the tenters upon which it was stretched to dry. The *Gloucester Journal* published many notices of theft or conviction between 1722 and the end of the century. A sad entry in the Minchinhampton burial register is typical of the period: '1800 August 17th Joseph Stephens. Executed at Gloster on the 16th for cutting cloth in the tenters of Messrs. Wathens of Woodchester'.

The Great Rebuild 1800–25

Practically every cloth mill along the west escarpment of the Cotswolds was rebuilt in the 20 years after 1800. How far this led to the spate of bankruptcies and how far it was dictated by a need to keep abreast with the times is not clear. But these are the buildings with their unique character that survive to attract students and tourists alike into the valleys of the Rivers Frome, Ewelme and Little Avon. Elsewhere the cloth industry had virtually died. Tetbury had turned its attention to wool combing and spinning. Cirencester was producing yarn for hosiery, and both cloth and carpet making there were to end within the next 40 years.

The origin of these mills, four or five storeys high and stone-built, can be seen in Wallbridge Mill, already described; in Clayfield's Mill, Chalford, overlooking the Thames & Severn Canal; and Egypt Mill, Nailsworth. Their stone-mullioned windows were inspired by the domestic architecture of the late Gothic period, and were more plainly domestic than in the later mills. Some nineteenth-century structures went up on the footings of their predecessors. Churches Mill, Woodchester, and Monks Mill, Alderley retained much of the old work, but quite often it is only the tooling of the rough stones of the dam, visible in the mill basement, that tells us of an earlier structure.

Externally, the larger mills fall into three categories: those of a simple rectangular plan, purely functional with no undue elaborations; secondly those of rectangular plan but with the central part of the side walls thickened to support a large pediment in the classical style; and thirdly an aggregation of separate mill blocks. The second plan development could occur on one side only, as at Day's Mill, Nailsworth, or on both sides. Probably the finest example, now but a sad remnant of its former glory, is Millbottom Mill, Nailsworth, where the doorways were centrally placed, with rusticated jambs or ornamental fan-lights, the flanking ranges producing a harmoniously balanced façade of eleven bays in all.* This type of building was often quite large. Woodchester Mill, until its destruction by fire in 1938, was one of several that comprised ten bays, and Brimscombe Lower Mill formerly had twenty-two bays.

Of the third category, Egypt and Dunkirk Mills in the Nailsworth Valley are good examples of two and four units set in line. The latter is unique in that every phase of the building's elongation bears a date. Seen from the hillside opposite, the dates run 1855, 1798, 1818 and 1827, and although the walls between were common, the floor levels were not made continuous, and doorways linking the blocks were few. At Ebley Mill there were four large multi-storeyed buildings, one of which was demolished in 1966. The oldest of the remaining blocks is eighteen bays long and may well be considered the largest of its type in the Cotswolds. Some of the blocks were linked by a series of single or two-storeyed ranges. Although every mill had its cluster of smaller buildings, used as stores, stables and repair shops, more than one large block would only have been found on the largest sites.

One of the most important mills of all was built in 1813—Stanley Mill near Kings Stanley church. This was of brick incorporating a unique decorative iron frame and brick vaulted ceilings in an attempt to cut down the risk of fire. There were also many fine cloth mills near Easting-ton, Cam and Kingswood, some of which exist still. All these however, are on the Severn plain and therefore cannot here be discussed in any detail. Cloth mills are also to be found at Chipping Norton, Witney and Trowbridge, all of them very near the east flank of the Cotswold hills which feature prominently in their history. Since river valleys divide them from the Cotswold plateau they too must remain beyond the scope of this account.

The majority of mill windows of the period 1800–20 have either wooden frames or are flat lintelled with stone mullions. At Ebley Mill and St Mary's Mill, Chalford, the lights are paired, each with a flattened three-centre head. Woodchester Mill includes a building with a long window on the upper floor, and many have a narrow elongated range of lights along the length of the roof on one or both sides of the building. These long windows were not for weavers, and are not found in any of the cottages where weaving was carried out. More likely they lit the

* For convenience of comparison, the number of bays here quoted is the same as the number of windows (or areas of equal proportion) along the frontage. In practice the distance between the windows is greater on either side of the base of the pediment, where the roof trusses are closer and unrelated to the ceiling beams in the floors below. Thus Millbottom Mill has eleven window bays but thirteen roof bays. How far this applies to other mills of this type is a little uncertain in that many of the finest examples have long since been demolished.

rooms in which the cloth was perched—hung over beams and examined for minute flaws. Circular windows occur in pediments and gables, and were often emphasised by the use of large rusticated stones. Several of the most sophisticated mills had cupolas upon their roofs, but none of these now survive. Metal-framed windows appear at this time, sometimes rectangular, but often with a radial head. These closely resemble their successors of the mid-nineteenth century, but the panes were rather smaller, owing to the problems of glass production.

Most mills had 'stove houses' set a short distance from the rest of the buildings. Many of these were put up in the eighteenth century. The circular ones, of which at least nine are known, could well be the latest form. Wool was placed on racks around the walls and bleached, using burning sulphur, a process which was declining by 1820.* The example at Woodchester was later used for storing the teasels required for nap raising. It has been suggested that stoved wool was only sold white or dyed blue. But stove houses were formerly so common along the River Frome, where red was the predominant colour, one can but assume that the mystery of dyeing red after stoving had been overcome. It could well have been one of the secrets of our high quality scarlets, so closely guarded that it died with the end of the practice of stoving (p 126).

All the buildings were wonderfully functional. The mill blocks, for instance, usually had a stair at one end, leaving each floor as a huge working area often with a loading door at the opposite end. The span, combined with the weight of the equipment, often necessitated the use of columns in either a single or double row, sometimes of wood, sometimes iron. Floor and roof timbers were green at the time of erection, their size alone preventing major warping. St Mary's Mill, Chalford, has a series of braces in the ceiling of one room, almost certainly to overcome any such tendency.

Water-wheels, fulling stocks and gigs would have been in the basement and ground floor rooms. Above some of these rooms would have been stores, but the bulk of the space would have been for manual processes, mainly oiling, spinning, perching, and shearing. With the change in fashion from heavily fulled broadcloths towards cassimeres, efforts were made to attract weavers to work in the mills rather than in their own homes. The men preferred what they were used to, and for a time at least these large galleries may have been little more than prestigial

---

* There is a tradition, supported by contemporary evidence, that some stove houses were for wool drying and not bleaching. Conversely some of the round houses near large mills appear too small to dry the quantity of wool that would be required. Since the stove houses vary in size and shape, it becomes increasingly likely that the larger ones were for drying whilst the small ones could have been used for drying or bleaching.

monuments of opulence and optimism. Hope Mill, Brimscombe, had a loom factory of only twelve narrow looms in 1802, yet 4 years later Timothy Larten of New Mills, Alderley, had twenty and Brown's Mill at Bridgend, Stonehouse, had twenty-three. Power looms came in 1836, and 101 had been installed by 1838, some clearly as an experiment. By this time mills fell into three groups, those with 50–100 hand looms, those with under thirty looms and those relying solely on cottage weaving.

Before 1800 most of the mills stood on sites in use since early medieval times, many of the remainder being of the seventeenth century. The master clothier owned the wool and supervised both mill and cottage processes from the fleece to the finished product. Subcontracting did occur, but more as a private arrangement between friends than as an essential part of the manufacturing system.

Prosperity bred complacency, and after 1800 new mills sprang up on every available stretch of water, often to the detriment of the neighbours above and below. When trade was good, the water-wheels turned incessantly, water flowed and the size of the millpond was of little importance. Small springs from the hillsides were harnessed, often with the greatest ingenuity, by making small pounds in series and wheels of irregular form. Little mills so constructed could not cater for every power process, and we see the rise of specialists. Some did nothing but dyeing, whilst others prepared the raw dyes. Buildings for dyeing could be recognised by their round wall vents and long roof louvres to permit the escape of steam.

Mills were built so small that they could not be recognised as such. Two, at Painswick and Nailsworth, looked like cottages, and small ones at that. A very small stream of water passed through, turning an internal wheel above which were two living rooms for the owner. Whether these buildings were used for scribbling or for gigs is unknown, but both must have been uncomfortable to live in. Both were subsequently converted, and dozens more no doubt demolished.

Mechanisation came very slowly at first, followed by an outburst of activity after 1815. Scouring, fulling and nap raising had been powered by water from a very early date. Scribbling machines to open the wool appear at the close of the eighteenth century, only a few years after the spinning jennies had replaced the slow process of hand spinning. The equally slow process of shearing the surface of the cloth with heavy hand-shears had been automated but with no improvement in the finished product. A Gloucester man, Isaac Sandford, was producing equipment of this type from 1801 till his death in 1809. The makers of these machines called themselves millwrights, but were in fact basically carpenters. Wood was the principal material used even in heavy machinery like water-wheels. Comparison of the sale inventories of Stephen Price, 1820, and John Price, 1848, both millwrights of the same premises in Acre Street, Stroud, shows how sudden was the change over from carpentry to engineering.

All at once every process had to be faster. Scribbling became more efficient. During the decade 1828–38 Crompton's mules replaced the spinning jennies. In quick succession Wm Lewis of Brimscombe, Alfred Flint of Uley and William Bayliss of Painswick took out patents for rotary scouring. Steam-heated fulling stocks were designed by James Dutton of Hillsley, John Price of Stroud and Stephen Clissold of Ebley, and disputes arose over the use of each other's ideas. So, too, with the rotary shearing machine. After many abortive attempts, the idea was perfected by John Lewis of Brimscombe, followed a few years later by Gardner & Herbert's model made at Leonard Stanley in 1824 and others by George Oldland of Hillsley in 1830 and 1832. In 1831 the idea was used in the patent by Edwin Budding of the first lawnmower. Later patents represent improvements upon these basic principles or the production of such time-saving devices as adjustable spanners. New names appear—the Ferrabees of Thrupp, James Apperley and William Clissold of Dudbridge, Richard Clyburn of Uley, P. C. Evans and T. Sampson of Brimscombe, H. J. H. King of Nailsworth—each making their further contribution to this modern age.

Such feverish activity had an effect far wider than the profit and loss of the cloth industry alone. The erection of about 200 new mills or allied structures between 1800 and 1825 led to the opening of quarries and limekilns. Huge unplanned settlements grew up to house the cottage weavers and spinners. Good examples of these can be seen to this day at Chalford Hill, Bussage, Eastcombe and around Nailsworth. All are on hill slopes, formerly common land, totally unsuited for agriculture. Instead of the cottages being built along well defined, more or less straight roads, they remain sprinkled in a haphazard manner with narrow lanes meandering around and between the garden plots. Often the cottager built his own house, mining the stone from a narrow shaft in his garden. Jonathan Cole of Horsley saved £100 in 20 years to buy land and in 1824 built a house large enough to contain four looms. In some places landlords indulged in speculative building. At Cam, Reuben Hill built sixty cottages in terraces, each housing two looms, and let by him at £6 to £9 per annum.

A cottage weaver's life was hard. Joseph White, Regius Professor of Arabic at Oxford, the son of a Randwick weaver, was as a boy roused

Page 197 *Cotswold events:* (above) *Crowning of the May Queen procession, Scuttlebrook Wake, Chipping Campden;* (below) *Stow-on-the-Wold Horse Fair*

Page 198 *Two places to visit:* (above) *the Gimson room at Arlington Mill, Bibury. The Gimson brothers, Cotswold craftsmen and furniture makers, worked at Sapperton early in the twentieth century;* (below) *early summer beauty at Upper Slaughter*

at 4 am and had to weave till 9 or 10 at night. A 15 hour day was common, and life itself revolved around the loom. In spite of this, every cottage weaver dreaded the thought of losing his independence and having to work in a factory; and every mill worker felt that progress was a direct threat to his security. Such was the fear that in 1802 mill-owner Paul Wathen had a letter from the local shearmen :

> Wee Hear in Formed that you got Shear in mee sheens and if you Dont Pull them Down in a Forght Nights Time Wee will pull them Down for you Wee will you Damd infernold Dog. And Bee four Almighty God we will pull down all the Mills that heave Heany Shearing me Shens in We will cut out Hall your Damd Hearts as Do Keep them and We will meock the rest Heat them or else We will Searve them the Seam.

The cottage weaver had to carry his finished piece to the mill. Distances like Oakridge to Cirencester, Chalford to Ebley or Horsley to Chalford were common. When factory weaving became accepted, such long walks became a daily event, and since most of the journeys were before dawn or after sunset, stones were laid to mark the paths that crossed open common land. These were probably limewashed rocks rather than permanent dressed columns.

In spite of the enthusiasm shown by the clothiers towards the Stroud-water Canal and Thames & Severn Canal, which together formed a water-way from the Severn across to London, interest was waning before this was opened in 1789. The canal was, however, extensively used by the clothiers for handling chemicals, wood and, most important of all, coal from the Forest of Dean. This was needed to heat water for a number of the processes in cloth manufacture, not to mention raising steam for the beam engines which augmented water power after about 1815.

Most of the wool, yarn and finished cloth was moved by road, using either pack-donkeys or horse-drawn waggons. Apart from prehistoric and Roman roads, which remain in use to this day, there was a pattern of early medieval roads part way up the steep hillsides linking the houses that existed a few yards above the natural springline. From these, steep tracks ran down to serve the individual mills. Quite a number of these tracks survive either as footpaths or as lanes along which the visiting motorist would be ill advised to travel. Many of the turnpike roads which succeeded them were in the valley bottoms, either cutting through meadows and orchards or linking a series of short existing pieces of trackway. For the first time it was possible to travel from one mill to the next without a steep climb followed by an equally steep descent. No longer had each mill to be a self-sufficient unit. The new roads

M

opened the way to cooperation and specialisation, particularly in dyeing. No longer was the journey to London a major hazard. Firms like Tanner & Bayliss ran a regular service, leaving Rodborough daily at 7am and 7 pm (see pp 156, 157).

Depression and Poverty

Although the eighteenth century and early nineteenth was a period of prosperity, it had its sadder moments. There were riots, strikes, petitions and bankruptcies. But by and large these were of short duration and frequently localised. If they had any impact at all on the local scene, it was trivial compared with what was to follow. Long before 1825 the shrewder clothiers knew something was wrong. Already enough trouble had come from the practice of getting credit on their wool against ultimate sale of the cloth through the factors of Blackwell Hall, the principal London cloth market. Too often the factors had said, as they did to William Phelps of Dursley, 'The Scarlets prove such bad Colours that we cannot sell them' or 'the imperfections render'd them unsaleable'. Later the cloths were simply kept until a customer made an offer, often little more than the cost of manufacture. In this way profits were minimal and capital was tied up, with threats of bankruptcy to follow. Any clothier who decided to retire whilst still wealthy found selling his mill increasingly difficult.

Writers have given other reasons for the decline—the sinking of too much money into new building schemes, buying new machinery that had not been fully tried out, or the drunken habits of the weavers. No doubt these reasons were valid, but another major cause was the proximity of each mill to its neighbour after the building of so many mills on new sites. Any mill not operating for even a few days would cause the level of its pond to rise and interfere with the working of the next mill upstream. Downstream its neighbour was deprived of water. Jealousy and ill-will arose, and often the out-of-work clothier would release his entire pond at dead of night, so wasting thousands of gallons of water. Admittedly this filled the next pond, but no more would be available once that was used. Such actions led to the holding up of work in hand. Contracts could not be fulfilled on time and yet another clothier might face a financial crisis.

When in 1833 the Factory Commissioners visited Wotton-under-Edge, Uley and Dursley they found that twelve out of nineteen manufacturers had ceased production within a period of 3 years. The county as a whole suffered eighty-five bankruptcies, and to this one should add

at least an equal number of clothiers who retired or came to a settlement
with their creditors. Out of forty-one mills at Chalford, only fifteen were
producing cloth in 1838, fifteen were empty and four had been demolished.
Money could be borrowed by clothiers in trouble, but all too often the
moneylender himself had to foreclose to save his own skin. At least one
was using the situation to reduce competition to his own family's cloth
business and to acquire property cheaply for later development.

It was the cottage weavers who suffered most as their profit margin
was reduced, for they had no capital to fall back on. Chalford and Uley
were the worst hit. There, many weavers had to abstain from religious
worship for want of decent clothing. Breakfast was usually warm water
with a little salt or pepper in it, and a crust of bread, whilst dinner was
simply bread and cheese or potatoes with a little hot fat over them.
Meat and tea were out of the question. The entire family might sleep
on loose straw with but a torn quilt to cover them. James Lewellyn of
Horsley and Benjamin Burford of Avening were poorer still, for they
had been obliged to sell or pawn every piece of furniture as well as much
of their clothing.

At Uley 1,000 persons lost their work when Edward Shepherd's mill
closed in 1837. Built at a cost of £50,000 it was sold for £2,300. With
no hope of other employment over 100 able-bodied workers emigrated
from Uley to America and Australia, plus another 100 from the parishes
adjoining. Families at Bisley did the same. How many went in all we
shall never know. The sites of their cottages can occasionally be found.
In some places entire communities vanished, leaving only a hazy tradition, a heap of mossy stones and a mark on an early map.

Poor relief was inadequate, for there were too many poor and no
prospering mills. Parish workhouses were inadequate until new legislation
was put forward in 1835 for grouping into Unions, each with a large
building to house up to 500 inmates. Life inside was bleak, but the
cottage weaver knew at least that he would be better fed and clothed
than hitherto. Yet in spite of closures and poverty a contemporary writer
observed that as much cloth was being made as hitherto.

After 1840 the situation improved. Mill closures continued partly as
a result of trade fluctuations and partly due to difficulties arising over
private mortgages. Weavers now realised that the demand for broadcloth had declined in favour of tweeds, and later shawls. It was clear
that mechanisation had come to stay and that the same work could be
done by fewer people. By 1861 the number of Gloucestershire people
employed in the woollen industry had fallen to 6,716, and it was only
3,898 in 1891.

Modern Times

Over the past century a pattern has steadily emerged. Throughout the area as a whole, there has been a steady drift away from the steep-sided valleys in favour of broader valley bottoms nearer the Severn plain. Except for one mill at Cam, the cloth industry died in the Dursley and Wotton-under-Edge area, where main-line rail services were available only with some inconvenience. In the Stroud area all the mills now lie below Stroud, with one exception. This is Longfords Mill, where the construction in 1806 of their 15 acre millpond gave them an independence unique in the county. The water is used even now, but not for its original purposes.

The gloomy picture of declining employment figures is misleading. The empty mills and surplus labour were taken up by expanding variations on two existing trades, both vital to the cloth industry, producing a tripartite pattern that survived well into the 1930s and is still very visible today. First there was cloth, not only the cloth mills, but all the subsidiaries and allied concerns like silk weaving, stocking knitting, tailoring, flock and shoddy making, carpet making, worsted spinning, dye works (both dyeing and making the dyes), chemicals and paper and fibreboard making. Waste products of textiles were the ideal raw materials for papermaking. The second group, derived from the eighteenth-century woodworking millwrights, have developed into firms making office furniture, pianos, carpenter's planes, dairy equipment, walking sticks, buttons, general wood turnery and wooden knitting needles (see Chapter 4). The third group originated with the blacksmiths, who developed, via millwrighting, into engineers, so many of whom invented equipment later used throughout Britain. Their range includes iron and brass founding, tinplate working, wire drawing, pin making, boatbuilding, aircraft parts and almost every aspect of general engineering.

Successive Gloucestershire firms have tended to occupy the same site with no sudden change of use. Dudbridge, for instance, began as a group of cloth mills beside an early river crossing. In the nineteenth century one millowner patented new machinery, and was one of the first people to consider production-line methods. A part of his works was devoted to making textile machinery, and later motor cars. Cloth is no longer produced there, and the various occupants have built a reputation for both heavy and light engineering.

Excluding the few hand loom weavers who make cloth as a craft rather than an industry, woollen cloth is now made only by two firms who between them occupy five mills. Winterbotham, Strachan & Playne Ltd of Cam, Lodgemore and Longfords Mills still produce scarlets (the traditional colour, and famous still as the uniform of the Guards), military, RAF and naval officers' uniform cloth, flannels, coatings and industrial cloths. Their products are exported to almost every country in the world, and the firm is directly linked with the Yorkshire combine of Illingworth Morris & Co Ltd. Marling & Evans Ltd, now part of the Marling Industries Group with related properties in Staffordshire, occupy Ebley and Stanley Mills. In addition to men's suitings and ladies' costumings the firm also produces man-made fabrics for filtration and protective clothing. Woollen products, however, make up 70 per cent of the firm's output.

A century and a half ago the cloth output from Gloucestershire was 1,769,762yd annually, and even at the close of the great depression in 1841, the figure was 1,151,280yd. This is only fractionally above today's annual output, even though the number of mills has fallen from well over 200 down to five. The Cotswold woollen industry has played a major part in the national economy, and it is clear that in spite of many changes its history is far from ended.

Notes to this chapter are on pages 309–10.

7

Towns and Villages

Alice Mary Hadfield

THE COTSWOLD LANDSCAPE is made more beautiful by its towns and villages. They are built of the stone of their own wolds, grey, cream or pale gold limestone, and, perhaps due to the great age of the settlements here, they are sited with close adaptation to their position, whether high, exposed and using every dip in the contours, or sheltering under the escarpment edge, or compact on a stream in a combe of the wolds. So far, through planning control, they are mostly unspoilt, a distinct pattern in the beauty of England.

The Cotswold region as defined in this book is roughly 40 miles long and 16 wide, 640 square miles, of which 575 are in Gloucestershire, with extensions into Warwickshire and Oxfordshire. It contains no big towns in the modern industrial sense. Gloucester and Cheltenham are not on the Cotswolds but in the vales at their feet. The area is largely rural and agricultural, and contains roughly 145 villages. Under the present local government system these come under various Rural District Councils and their own parish councils, with Urban District Councils for the few towns. Much will be changed when the revised local government system comes into action in 1974. Good roads mostly run lengthwise from south-west to north-east. The M4 and M5 motorways keep clear of the Cotswolds and run on each side on lower ground.

The highest stretches of the wolds are in the north, though high beacons and table-tops rise up throughout the region. The land climbs from the eastern dip-slope to the western escarpment over the vale of Evesham. Here are Chipping Campden, Winchcombe, Moreton-in-Marsh and Stow-on-the-Wold, small towns. The villages are open, often tilted on the slope, built round an old road crossing or a stream ford, the streets spreading out in natural growth towards farms or along the road.

The central region slowly subsides in great rolling wolds down to the head of the Stroud valley, where the land splits into a different Cotswold of rough clefts and peaks, little jumbled fields, dense woods, fast streams. One half of this central region has open weathered villages, with Cirencester as the central town on gentle land where essential roads naturally pass. The other half, west of Cirencester, approaching the escarpment, has steep broken country, often timbered, with villages hidden from the traveller, mills and houses perched above or below the twisting road as steep land will allow.

The south Cotswolds slope into the big limestone hills north of Bath, showing their smaller and wilder characteristics in the little known areas of Badminton and Sodbury. The villages have long been remote, and keep that simplicity and the look of primitive careful country life among woods and fields.

Basic Characteristics

All Cotswold towns and villages are old, being based on very ancient occupations such as farming and wool, including the Stroud valley area, which developed more recently. Water was always precious on the lime-stone soil, and springs or streams influenced the growth of settlements. Along the Roman Foss Way the settlements have Roman remains to show, in Cirencester, Chedworth, Bourton-on-the-Water, Stow. Elsewhere they are likely to date from the first Saxon farmers who settled there in the seventh or eighth century, laid out their bits of land and put up a stone or cross. Most have something medieval to show, and much seventeenth- and eighteenth-century building in mill, bridge, barn, farm, cottage, house or church. Most of them reflect the character of their Cotswold environment in past centuries, remarked on from Shakespeare to Cobbett, of remote, exposed, rough wolds, poor soil, few roads, little cover for 30 or more miles, and hard winter weather along the escarp-ment and on high levels. The houses keep close for shelter and company, cluster round a church and manor house, ford or crossroads. Inns are seldom for more than local custom. Straggling for miles along lanes or across fields is not a Cotswold village characteristic.

Isolation and close company has produced common characteristics and a sense of harmony. All one village may be built from one quarry, fencing stones for gardens and pigsties all from one other; the design of all cottages and cowsheds will be companionable; a local firm probably made all the porches, a local man cut the tombstone inscriptions. These necessities have faded, but the villages keep a calm timeless look from the similarity of stone and design. You could call the look remote, cool, certainly unconcerned with fashions or with passers-by.

Architecture is dealt with in Chapter 8. Here it is enough to say that Cotswold cottages and small houses are of strict design, with great variation of detail within the overall simplicity. Lines are clear, angles sharp; roofs gable-ended, never markedly hipped. A main feature is the gable, whether big or small. In large houses the gable may be repeated along the front, and returned at the side. A porch, or section of barn, may be enlarged and gabled without the whole roof structure having to be built out to cover it.

Roofs are steep, and tiled with stone roofing slates dug from particular quarries (see Chapter 8). They are hung in graded courses, biggest at the eave and smallest at the ridge. Each size has its own name—Short Wivutts, Long Wivutts, Middle Becks, Short Bachelors. A slate rule showed twenty-six sizes. Inch measurements are more used now than the old names. The stone slates are perfect protection against wind, snow and rain, and heat in summer. Artificial tiles are mostly used in modern building. The plainest house will have a tall chimney, usually with crisply cut capping. Often the older houses have drip stone mouldings over windows, and stone mullions instead of timber or iron. Little porches are very popular in a winter climate of wind and snow.

Good modern building keeps the main principles of the traditional style, using natural stone where possible, or reconstructed stone (see Chapter 4). Planning consent is not usually given for brick facing in the Cotswolds. Occasionally still, stone roofing tiles are used in a choice piece of work, though more often bought from a demolished barn than new. Conservation areas are being established, for the safeguarding of precious areas of towns and villages. The Bledisloe Cup competition for the best kept large or small village in Gloucestershire is organised every year, with plenty of response. Amenity societies are on the increase, and take a part in looking after their own place and working with the Planning Department of the County Council to recognise and encourage Cotswold characteristics in building and landscape.

Modern Social Conditions

Today, Cotswold villages are comfortable and busy. Heights of 800–1,000ft are no hindrance to electricity installations, main services, roads, buses, mobile library vans, ambulances, schools hot-meals service vans, brewers' lorries, television and broadcasting. The danger of being overwhelmed by the modern world, with the M5 on the west and the M4 across the south, is more probable in Cotswold villages than the danger of isolation. Or, if not overwhelmed, being starved by it. Village life is more threatened by modern incomers regarding the village as a place to have a property in rather than the place they live in, and failing to use the buses, support the shops, join village clubs and work in village activities.

As regards development, and the social services which it inevitably requires, a principle of selection is applied at present by the County Council. Not every tiny place has, or can have, a school, village hall, new council housing, and so on. A decision has to be taken, at county level, on which places in each district shall be primary centres, having all main facilities, eg, primary and secondary schools, allocation of council housing and private housing and increased services to cope, roads up to a certain standard, public hall, library, post office, shops, health service and so on; which shall be secondary centres, with, for example, only primary or junior school but transport arranged to a secondary school, smaller allocation of housing and services; and which shall be tertiary, and depend for most facilities except a pillar-box or a pub on the secondary or primary centres. In this third grouping few council houses will be built, and a general village life is not to be looked for. On the other hand, distances in the Cotswolds being nowhere very great, all necessary facilities are well within car range. For medical care, doctors are sufficiently widespread for all villages to be within reach of a surgery, an ambulance, and a doctor's car. Big hospitals at Swindon, Gloucester, Cheltenham, Oxford and even Birmingham ensure that there are plenty of doctors in the Cotswold area. Child welfare centres are maintained by the County Council, district nurses by nursing associations. All these statements relate to the present system of local government, which will undergo big changes in 1974.

North Cotswolds

Let us look more closely at the regions, taking the northern area first. The main block of it is the present North Cotswold Rural district, an area of roughly 130 square miles, with thirty-seven parishes of which only five have much more than 1,000 inhabitants—Chipping Campden, Stow-on-the-Wold, Blockley, Moreton-in-Marsh and Bourton-on-the-Water. Winchcombe, outside the Rural District, is also a primary centre.

Driving down from Birmingham or across the Evesham vale by the A46, you see the jut of Meon Hill blocking the sky at the northern end of the Cotswolds. This end is narrow, 4 miles across, so that Mickleton looks west over the vale of Evesham, and its neighbour Ilmington, clinging to the eastern flank, looks over the valley of the Oxfordshire Stour. Aston Subedge and Weston Subedge are just off the top and over the western edge, sheltering from the winter north and east winds but catching the familiar south-westers. Close to Weston is Saintbury, of particularly pure Cotswold beauty.

All these are tiny places, which in modern times exist for their priceless character and beauty. The primary centre of the area is Chipping Campden, which, besides being the junction of many local roads, has always been a market town. In Anglo-Saxon times it was the centre of local government. During the Middle Ages and sixteenth century the wool trade made the townspeople very prosperous, and the leading merchants expressed their wealth and good life in lavish building. Stone of the finest building quality was quarried locally, for big or small houses for the citizens, trade and guild halls, the pillared Market Hall, inns, mills and shops for business; a grammar school for the young; almshouses for the old and poor; the church for worship. Many of them remain today. The long central street of Chipping Campden, all its varied buildings harmonious in warm grey-gold stone that changes with every changing light of sun and moon, has well been called the most beautiful street in Britain.

In the social reaction against the evils of the late nineteenth-century condition, William Morris and his group of reformers discovered Cotswold villages, and saw, in spite of the agricultural and social decline, a way of life which held better promise than the then unreformed cities. One of these men, C. R. Ashbee, moved a guild of craftsmen down from London to Chipping Campden, and set up fifty working craftsmen in the Silk Mill in Sheep Street, and settled their wives and children nearby (see Chapter 8). The influx of skills made Chipping Campden a centre for art, craft and fine work, with the trade that a fast-growing market for these sustained. Reputation brought the visitors, and today, with improved roads and hotels, the place has a new prosperity as a tourist centre. Campden holds again its Old English and medieval position as the centre of the North Cotswold area.

Its population is coming up to 2,000, though it is still managed by a hard-working Parish Council. It has all the services of a little town. The Grammar School, rebuilt as a co-educational comprehensive school, serves a big area of villages whose children are fetched and returned by bus. Bus services run to Moreton-in-Marsh, Evesham, Stratford-upon-Avon and Cheltenham. The railway station is closed, though the London–Worcester line is open. Oxford, Stratford and Cheltenham provide hospital facilities.

There is local industry as well as craftwork, a Fruit and Vegetable Preservation Research Station, design workshops for industry, and building. Modern housing estates have been built, including a prizewinner for design. Campden keeps up its old festivities. The Campden Morris men dance. In Whit week Scuttlebrook Wake holds sway, and includes the Dover Games on Dover's Hill, 800ft high outside the own. At the Wake the May Queen is crowned, a main event of the local year, as no doubt it was 1,000 years ago.

South of Chipping Campden lies the plateau of the North Cotswolds —medium quality arable land, high, open, shallow soil and little water. Broadway, down off the wolds, is in Worcestershire with richer soil. It is another tourist attraction, of famous and protected beauty. The broad High Street is lined by golden stone houses. Here are the Gordon Russell furniture workshops, well known to modern designers. South, on the escarpment, are Buckland, Stanton and Stanway, all small villages, even hamlets. Here the escarpment is wooded and great beeches and elms frame the golden stone walls and dark olive roofs. Two of the West Country's great houses and a fourteenth-century tithe barn make Stanton and Stanway memorable. They also have modern building and restoration which a modern eye must study to perceive how good modern work can be. Stanton, like Chipping Campden, is more than the sum of its units in its harmony and beauty. Higher up on these austere and noble wolds is Snowshill, very lonesome, with a National Trust house of unusual primitive interior construction.

East across the top of the wolds, past stiff fields of brussels sprouts, is Blockley, little known and of great interest (see Chapter 6). It was once a silk mill village, with eight mills on the stream sunk in the narrow cleft below the houses. It is almost all basically seventeenth- and eighteenth-century building, with an early industrial character rare in the agricultural Cotswolds. It is now a primary centre for its area with plenty of modern housing. A mile and a half south is Bourton-on-the-Hill, 500ft above the road to Moreton-in-Marsh, an enchanting seventeenth- and eighteenth-century place.

Moreton-in-Marsh is a busy town and primary rural centre for this eastern slope of the Cotswolds. The Roman Foss Way is the basis of its central street. Moreton is known for many good hotels and shops, which make it a point for motorists. The Home Office Fire Service Training College is here, and light industry. The Stratford & Moreton Tramroad, opened in 1826, can be traced by enthusiasts. The railway station has survived and is well used for the run to Birmingham.

South again, on the western escarpment, Winchcombe looks west over pastoral country, scoured by south-west gales which fling themselves on the great outliers of the edge towards Tewkesbury and Cheltenham before roaring over the escarpment itself. An old region this, rich in Romano-British villa farms, Winchcombe itself unmistakably a town and no village. It was the eighth-century seat of the kings of Mercia, the middle kingdom of England. Sudeley Castle, a royal Tudor castle, less than a mile down and up the shady lanes from Winchcombe, added to the notableness of the town in former days, as it does now. Modern Winchcombe is a busy fast-growing town, well equipped from its past with many hotels and inns. It has a modern secondary school, hospital, shopping centre, branch library, and active local life. A section of Dowty's engineering works, and of Smith's Electric works, as well as light industry give employment, and Cheltenham is only 7 or 8 miles away.

East from Winchcombe, the most uninhabited area of all the wolds stretches across to Stow-on-the-Wold. At 800 or 900ft, with few roads, the farmland rolls on for miles, silent but for the lapwings and larks, or a distant tractor following the huge smooth curves marked by lines of beech and hawthorn clumps. Cloud shadows move over farms and tiny settlements which hardly break the solitude. Cutsdean, steep grey roofs between open wold and sky, marks the rise of the River Windrush at nearly 700ft. Guiting Power, stepping down between wold and stream, is a secondary rural centre, serving such lonely spots as Temple Guiting, Kineton, Ford, Hawling. Temple Guiting has pleasant modern rural building, a village hall, bus shelter, sports ground and pavilion, all speaking of an active village life. Farming up here is in big units, very up to date (see Chapter 4).

The Windrush leads on through woods to Naunton, murmuring along an almost level fold in the land at 600ft, flowers and birds all the way. Naunton is a place of quarries, where stone roof slates were dug. A former coaching inn, now bypassed, still looks strange in the little place. Going east towards Stow-on-the-Wold, Upper and Lower Slaughter on an arm of the little River Dikler, and Upper and Lower Swell on the Dikler itself are outstanding for their beauty. Close to, or threaded by, the streams, folded in by wooded hills, they are still near enough to the main Foss Way and to Stow to be in the modern world. Indeed, only rigorous control has saved their identity. Lower Slaughter won a Festival of Britain award in 1951 for modern Cotswold village cottages.

All Cotswold roads lead to Stow, they say, and the map shows it. Standing high, 800ft above the valleys of Dikler and Evenlode, it makes a natural eastern entry point for all its district. It is a market town, with fine church and graceful square, almshouses and old narrow alleys, and roads with bus services for Cheltenham, Cirencester, Oxford, Stratford. Two horse fairs are still held here each year, and horses, ponies and riding are very much part of Stow life and the neighbourhood. This is a holiday centre, for motoring and also for walking. Good footpath country slopes away all round it, and there is a youth hostel in the square.

A series of small villages lie off the main roads near Stow on this eastern slope towards Chipping Norton and Oxfordshire. Longborough, Donnington, Broadwell, Evenlode, Adlestrop and Oddington are the main names in a treasury of small gems. Chastleton House marks the great pile of Chastleton Hill and its ancient camp. This is part of the old forest of Wychwood, ancient centre of fairy and folk tales. A feather touch of this character can still be felt in the countryside. Everywhere is very quiet and rural, looking to Stow for modern facilities, each place with a long history, old stones, church, farms, good houses, and huge clumps of dense old trees. Donnington gives its name to a millpond and mill converted to a modern brewery of unique charm and excellent beer.

Bourton-on-the-Water, a primary centre, a mile or so from Lower Slaughter, has made itself a country tourist centre, lively and full of visitors and country business all the summer. The River Windrush flows gently under four stone footbridges with wide grass verges through the middle of Bourton. The Holiday Fellowship has a centre here.

East of Bourton the three Rissingtons—Wick, Little and Great—crouch on the windy wolds at 600 or 700ft. Little Rissington claims the Royal Air Force Central Flying School airfield, high above the A424 from Stow to Burford. West of Bourton you cross the top of the wolds above Cheltenham, marked by tiny world-forgetting settlements of clear identity and being—Aston Blank, Notgrove (church and manor complex here above all ordinary standards), Hazleton, Salperton (nowhere more lonely), Sevenhampton, Brockhampton (just under the 1,000ft line), to complete the northern area.

Central Cotswolds

The central Cotswold area lies on the wolds above Cheltenham, across to Burford on the eastern slope, and down south to Rodmarton, South Cerney and Down Ampney. This is the most traversed and best known part of the Cotswolds, some of it high and bare, the haunt of seagulls and lapwings, some steep and wooded, some river-meadowed and pastoral, and the rough escarpment rearing up at Leckhampton and Birdlip over the vale of Gloucester.

It is marked by four rivers, or streams—Windrush, Coln, Leach and Churn, and the headwaters of the Thames itself, along which the extraction of huge deposits of gravel is turning farm villages into lakeside villages in the Cotswold Water Park. Two small tributary streams—the Sherborne brook and the Duntisbourne—claim their own groups of villages.

Forty-two small places with one country town in this area take up on the one-inch OS map roughly 8in × 13in. All forty-two are stoutly individual—products of long-rooted history over 1,200 years and pre-history far beyond that. The Sherborne brook comes off the Northleach downs at 600ft through Farmington and Sherborne villages to its junction with the gentle Windrush. Sherborne is a tertiary centre, with primary school only and the tertiary rate of development. The Sherborne dances, a very elaborate and developed form of Morris dancing, have been collected and published.

The Windrush here is lazy, wandering, divided, 400ft up. Its name village is a Cotswold beauty, its cottages spreading along the easy hill-side above the river in extraordinary harmony. Nearby are Great and Little Barrington, marked by magnificent stone-tiled farm roofs and huge splendid trees. Taynton, just over the Oxfordshire border, has working stone quarries and houses of cream-coloured newly quarried stone. This is all stone country, masons' country of masons' families and histories (see Chapter 8).

Then comes Burford, like Chipping Campden a glory and a marvellous survival. A medieval wool town at the junction of many roads and on a crossing of the Windrush, in the forest of Wychwood, Burford in the Middle Ages knew great prosperity and built it into houses, halls, church, inns, almshouses, school, using its own countryside stone and timber in a warm harmony that has remained to our time. It was always a road town, and the railway age passed it completely by. In 1876 William Morris came through it. As at Chipping Campden, he saw at once what a treasure England had here in Burford. He and his friends brought about a new public opinion with their teaching, and just in time saved the old town and much of our medieval inheritance in the Cotswolds.

With the return of road travel Burford has boomed. The little town is close packed with old streets and corners. The beautiful High Street slopes down to the road cross. Small, up to date modern-interior shops, mer-chants' houses, good hotels and pubs, quiet squares and narrow corners extend right up to the Windrush bank and the stone bridge. And there it stops. No building straggles on the other bank. Cows graze, and reeds and grass and willows are fresh within a few yards of the town streets.

Burford is prosperous again. The grammar school of 1571, almshouse of 1471, remain, and the church with its Bellfounders' Aisle. There is plenty of modern business, and a brewery still operating locally, though part of a bigger firm. Modern building is concentrated at the upper entrance to Burford on the A40. Here is the big new school and new housing, much of it in natural, not reconstructed, stone. Only 20 miles from Oxford and Swindon, Burford is well placed for contacts and facilities, and is a primary centre for its area.

Ten miles south of the Windrush valley and Burford, the Rivers Leach and Coln run into the Thames, one each side of Lechlade. These are both great trout-fishing streams, and both have well known villages along their lines. The Leach rises near Northleach, which is just off a cross of the Foss Way and the A40 10 miles north of Cirencester. This is the centre of a very unpopulous area, mostly far-scattered farms. The farmer's wife, while she hangs out her washing, sees the track of the wind ruffling through pale barley fields, sheep climbing thin grass slopes divided by grey stone walls, and guesses the weather from the clouds and hazy sky. Northleach is one of the thirteen or so small towns of the Cotswolds, hardly a town but a quiet stone-built place with a few medieval cottages and many old buildings, and a pretty central square. The church is one of the famous Cotswold wool churches, with some very fine modern work in it. Northleach is a primary centre, having a secondary school, a hospital and mobile library service. Business is the ordinary run of country trades, and building.

From here the Leach runs south-east past Aldsworth, through lonely country where the remains of a disused Roman road, Akeman Street, can be traced, down into a steep dip where two hamlets with two churches face each other across the stream—Eastleach Martin and Eastleach Turville. The wide, clear, shallow stream, a clapper bridge, shining carpets of daffodils along the stream banks, skimming swallows, huge dark elms, and the pair of little old churches, make this hidden dip completely picturesque. There is a post office here, and an inn, but no school or other facilities. So too at Southrop, a mile south. These tiny places look to Fairford or Lechlade.

Lechlade is a good-looking little town, flat, circled by its own river, the Leach, and by the Coln, and half a mile away by the Thames itself, so that the oarsman circles half a day through the green fields round the slender spire of the church. It is on a cross of the A361 and A417, 10 miles from the outskirts of Swindon. Four counties meet here— Oxfordshire, Berkshire, Gloucestershire, and Wiltshire. It has about 1,200 inhabitants, and is a local shopping place with spacious market square, a fortnightly cattle market, well modernised old inns, and fifteenth-century church. It is a secondary rural centre, with most facilities, modernised primary school, and a small library. It is a main country pleasure spot for expeditions, picnics on the flat green river banks and

GLOUCESTERSHIRE COLLEGE
OF EDUCATION
LIBRARY

for all river joys. You can hire boats here and there are moorings and slipways. Four miles down the Thames is Kelmscot, William Morris' home and now museum. Road and bus routes link the town with Cirencester, Swindon and Oxford.

The Leach is joined at Lechlade by the River Coln, which has come across the central wolds from its source near Andoversford above Cheltenham. This is a varied river, sometimes quiet and slow through parkland and shallow upland valleys, sometimes spreading out into oozy pastures, sometimes dashing down narrow wooded channels. It is famous for its trout-fishing and for its beautiful villages.

Fairford is the Coln's main town, population around 2,000. It is a primary rural centre, with primary school and comprehensive secondary in new buildings. There is a hall, many inns, some claiming 500 years of business, and restaurants, supported by being within easy road distance of Oxford and by many years of the United States Air Force base at the airfield here. This base has now been withdrawn, and Fairford is a base for the supersonic aircraft Concorde.

Fishing is the great occupation. Among many private owners, the town has its own stretch of water and visitors can hire tickets to fish for a day or longer. Cricket, football, tennis, bowls, hunting and golf fill the country calendar with traditional sport, while close to the town spread the new lakes in old gravel diggings known as the Cotswold Water Park. All kinds of water recreation are growing up, and modern housing is increasing round the water area. Fairford is famous for the windows in its church (Chapter 8), a series of twenty-eight in painted glass, early sixteenth century, depicting the Bible story from Adam and Eve to the Day of Judgment.

You can follow the Coln up from Fairford for 9 or 10 miles to Fossebridge, where the Foss Way crosses it, through the nine beautiful Coln valley villages: Quenington, Hatherop, Coln St Aldwyn, Bibury, Ablington, Winson, Coln Rogers, Coln St Dennis and Fossebridge. These are highly prized places to live in, with cherished standards of appearance in house and street and river access, rough corners planted and waste patches thick with daffodils. All the way the country rises and the wolds become more impressive in village after village; the beechwoods and elms gather round the farms and grey stone houses which lead down tc an old arched stone bridge, a Saxon-Norman village church, a stone-built mill and a 200 to 400 year old manor or priory building from the days of the great sheep runs and wool-shearing on these wolds. Bibury has the National Trust property of Arlington Row cottages (see Chapters 3 and 6).

Page 215 *Restored landscape before and after:* (above) *old Daglingworth camp after World War II;* (below) *the camp removed and the landscape restored*

Page 216 *Present day activities: (above) Cotswolds Warden Service; the chief warden briefs three volunteer wardens before a patrol; (below) power-boat racing on former gravel pits at Fairford, part of the Cotswold Water Park*

No main road runs through this line of villages, which is one reason why they have never been adulterated. But of course they are not to everyone's taste. They are hidden in folds of land and trees, accustomed to snow, fog and wind, and 'there is nothing to do in the evenings'. Only Quenington is a secondary rural centre and has some light industry. Northleach, Fairford and Cirencester serve their needs in education and health; parsons and nurses double up, and the mobile library will clank through the winter roads with chains on for the welcome fortnightly visit. But the villages are thrivingly popular and there is some new building of good quality.

On the other side of the Foss Way the country becomes suddenly wilder and steeper, densely wooded through Chedworth and Withington, rising to 600 and 700ft near Compton Abdale and Shipton Solers and Shipton Oliffe. The Coln is narrowed by the steep land and rushes foam-flecked and dark under huge old trees and through young plantations. The track of the former Midland South Western Junction railway threads these villages. They are all very small, even hamlets, mostly on precipitous hill roads, and mostly the objects of much devotion and care. Chedworth, the secondary rural centre, spreads down a big hillside, thickly wooded to the north where a road leads to the Roman villa which is National Trust property and open to the public. Beyond the tiny Shiptons is Andoversford, on the wide crest overlooking Cheltenham, and here the Coln rises. Andoversford is a very different place, a busy main-road village where the A40 crosses the A436. It is another secondary rural centre.

The other main river of these central wolds is the Churn, longest and most inland tributary of the Thames. It rises at Seven Springs, 5 miles from Andoversford. First it cuts a narrow bed down through Coberley and Cowley, where the Manor house is a conference centre run by the county council, and then goes under the A435 Cirencester-Cheltenham road and comes out into a broad valley of great charm, along which the road also runs, with villages strung along it.

The Churn valley villages are all influenced by Cirencester or Chelten-ham. They have good communications and plenty of facilities and modern housing. However, care and planning control have been exer-cised and they have not lost their character, though they do not com-pare with the Coln villages. Colesbourne and Rendcomb stand in thick stretches of woodland which go over the crest and join up with Withing-ton and Chedworth woods. Rendcomb has a big house which is now a boys' public school. It stands on the hillside above the Churn, looking over the pastures and the cattle and the looping stream, the little weirs

N

and plank footbridges and the anglers motionless as the alders, to the valley road. Rendcomb village, across a two-arched stone bridge, climbs round the shoulder of the wold towards Calmsden.

Next on the way to Cirencester comes North Cerney, with an antique church outstanding even among Cotswold churches, and some good modern housing, though it is only a tertiary centre. This parish is unusual in that it straggles, and is cut in two by the main road. West of the road is Woodmancote among trees, and east is Calmsden, a small exposed cluster like a bird's nest on open turf. Next comes Bagendon, of pre-Roman antiquity, now only a few cottages and farms, one or two houses of great character; and then Baunton, picturesquely placed outside Cirencester off the road on a low wold level below the sky line. Cirencester golf course lies across the road from Baunton. Through Cirencester the Churn runs on into South Cerney and Cerney Wick, joining the Thames outside Cricklade.

Cirencester is one of the best examples of an English country town in its regional style. It stands on the foundations of Corinium, the second largest centre in the Roman province of Britain, at the junction of the Roman Foss Way and Ermin Street. Some medieval buildings and lay-out of little streets remain, and the main central part of the town is a graceful blend of the last three centuries and the present day, using in many cases the basic stonework of earlier times. All is built in the buff-cream limestone of the district, and the town houses show the wealth and taste of the wool merchants and businessmen of the time, and the solid standing of their weavers and workmen (see Chapter 6). Modern work has used reconstituted stone, keeping a harmonious colour. The superb church in the big Market Place is the focal centre of all.

With a population at present of 13,000, Cirencester is a primary centre, and provides all modern business and social facilities. Indeed, it is a very busy place, with much new housing, fast-growing business, and an industrial estate conveniently placed on one edge of the town (see p 135). The fifteenth-century grammar school has been enlarged into a comprehensive secondary school, which serves all the villages round. There is also a range of other schools, and more planned. Cirencester has its own hospital, a branch library, the office of the local newspaper and its printing works, a community centre, cinema, swimming pool, and two big public halls which cater not only for youth and social activites but also for Cirencester's very popular furniture auctions. The large range of local sport includes polo in the Park, golf, a spring race meeting, and hunting with the Vale of White Horse hounds.

Road communications are of course excellent, and bus services through to Gloucester (17 miles), Cheltenham (16 miles) and Swindon (16 miles), though being steadily cut, remain reasonably good in the main part of the day. Hotels and inns are plentiful and varied in standard, and the numbers of restaurants is increasing. There are some guest houses, but not a great deal of cheap accommodation for walkers or cyclists.

The Market Place and old streets round it form a very busy shopping area in charming surroundings. The Abbey grounds behind the church, with a stream of the Churn running through them, are now town property and a big amenity closely accessible. The wide serene rise of Cecily Hill and its fine houses leads to the stately entrance of Lord Bathurst's park and woodlands. These were laid out in the eighteenth century, and extend 5 or more miles across country to join the woods at Sapperton. They form a big timber industry (see p 121). The public are allowed in on foot and horse, with limited access by car. Up here is the polo ground, and the location of many horse- and pony-riding competitions and events, the cricket ground, and the opportunity of good walks in winter or summer.

South of the Market Place the Forum of Corinium has been cleared and rebuilt as an open space, a big car park and roads giving access to the main shopping streets. Here the ancient Mop Fair is held in October. The cattle fair in the spring and the sheep fair in September remain big country events.

Archaeology is naturally a study in this Roman-based town, and digs are conducted in the summer, open to the public. Discovery of big sections of Corinium is going on steadily. The Corinium Museum in Park Street is being greatly enlarged and redesigned as part of a new museum for all ages of the town's history. Situated in the area of the Three Choirs Festival, musical life in Cirencester and its countryside is keen and varied. A civic society looks after the visual standards and amenities. Just outside Cirencester is the Royal Agricultural College, where students can learn farming, forestry and estate management (see p 122). Cirencester caters for a wide country area, whose people crowd the shopping streets on Friday market day. It is distinctly a quality town, different for shopping from Swindon, Gloucester or Cheltenham, and appears to be holding its own among these far bigger rivals.

From Cirencester the great Roman Ermin Street strikes north-west straight over the high wolds regardless of contours to mighty Birdlip Hill at the 975ft top of the escarpment above Gloucester. Three miles out, the little Duntisbourne brook creeps along a fold in the wold to join the Churn. Up its hidden valley are five small hill villages comparable in beauty to the Coln villages—Daglingworth, Duntisbourne Rouse, Middle Duntisbourne, Duntisbourne Leer, and Duntisbourne Abbots. A score of tiny arched bridges cross the brook in field and lane and garden. The churches are hamlet-size, part Saxon, completely endearing. The stream flows down the road in one village, and cars drive in it. Otherwise there is the footpath. Every cottage, every eighth of a hillside acre, counts in the Duntisbournes. This is good farming country.

Further along Ermin Street, on the east, is the turning to Elkstone, with a widely known Norman church and medieval priest-house, a lonely spot on the 850ft contour. Syde and Brimpsfield are off the west of Ermin Street, tiny places with long histories and many antiquities. All these little places share Cirencester's facilities.

On the eastern side of Cirencester, on the slope of the wolds to the Coln valley, are Barnsley, three Ampneys and Poulton. Barnsley Park is one of the great houses on the Cotswolds (see p 243), and also has Roman diggings of interest in the Park. Barnsley, though tiny, has other notable houses and an old church. The Welsh Way, a drovers' road, as in Vaughan Williams' Cotswold opera *Hugh the Drover*, comes down into the village street line.

There are three Ampneys on the A417 outside Cirencester. These have been small farm clusters, named from the Ampney brook. Ampney Crucis is the nucleus village, and has the sixteenth-century house, Ampney Park, an old church and cross, a mill, two pubs, and new housing. Ampney St Peter and Ampney St Mary are close by, all stone cottages beautifully sited off the road on lane and slope. The road zigzags through Poulton, which also keeps much of its beauty hidden on approach lanes. This is a familiar characteristic of central Cotswold villages. The Ampney brook also gives its name to Down Ampney, birthplace of Vaughan Williams, 4 miles south across pastoral country dipping off the Cotswolds into the Thames valley.

The Cotswold Water Park spreads south-west from Fairford, 8 miles or so away, to make South Cerney, Ashton Keynes, Somerford Keynes and Poole Keynes new waterside villages. For centuries, since Domesday Book recorded their pastures and their mills, these have been grass and hay growing, cattle raising, milk and cheese producing, lark- and lapwing-frequented villages. In 50 years the pastures have vanished with the gravel below them, into water (see Chapter 10), and seagulls, swans, and waterfowl have replaced the lapwings (see Chapter 2). Change and consciousness of growth keeps these villages lively. They are all 4–6 miles south of Cirencester and share its services. Gravel extraction and the various industries which stem from it, such as concrete-block making and reconstituting stone, provide employment and keep the young people in the villages. Much new building, under planning control, goes on, mostly in reconstituted stone with artificial but colour-blending tiles. Ashton Keynes is happy in having the young Thames flowing clear under old stone bridges beside its main street. A number of its houses have the flat stone fences made of thin slabs of stone about 2ft × 3ft 6in, or bigger, which were quarried in the Cerney–Ashton Keynes district.

The original centre of these villages is very old, particularly in Somerford Keynes (see Chapters 3 and 8), where record exists of a grant of land in AD 685. At the other end of the historical range, South Cerney, population nearly 2,000, has an army camp, locks of the derelict Thames & Severn Canal, track of the extinct Midland & South Western Junction Railway, early Victorian Gothic clergy almshouses called Edwards' College, a new Junior and Infants' School, a vigorous gravel industry and other light industry. It is a secondary centre, with village hall and many facilities, and sports clubs, three pubs, good bus services, and a busy local life. It has its own mumming play, and an interesting church with an important relic which was found walled up in the tower wall (see Chapter 8). The village has an old stone-built centre of small streets round the road crossing of the Churn, and other old farm and cottage areas. With its hamlet Cerney Wick, it is the last village on the Churn. The three mills are mentioned in Domesday Book.

West of Cirencester for about 12 miles the Cotswolds climb up to about 800ft along the escarpment—wild, rough country with views across the vale of Severn, the Forest of Dean and mid-Wales. A triangle with apex at Cirencester and three sides the A419 to Stroud, the A417 to Gloucester, and the escarpment, contains high wooded wolds cut by deep narrow stream channels, twisting lanes and countless little springs—wonderfully self-contained country different from any of the rolling open sheep land of the Chipping Campden or Stow-on-the-Wold country. It is much less easy and accessible in itself and in transport. One B road and many old lanes thread the grand wooded heights of the main area.

The high ground looks over the Severn, old frontier against the Celts, and every viewpoint is an ancient camp or signal or burial point. These difficult heights were safe for settlements, and small quarries with nearby clusters of stone cottages break the rough ground on seemingly inaccessible ledges and hillsides. Beechwoods sweep from Cranham down the escarpment and east across to the woods of Miserden, Edgeworth and Sapperton, which link up with Cirencester Park. Much of this is National Trust property.

This strange country forms part of the big southern bluff of the Cotswold escarpment. The bluff is split east-west for 7 miles or so, and at the bottom of the rift flows the little River Frome. The upper part of its course is called the Golden Valley for its woods and landscape beauty. When the Cotswold woollen and cloth industry moved into this south-western area in search of waterpower, the mills were built on the streams in the valleys and the hand-working processes spread into the cottages up the slopes. The cobwebs of little lanes speak of the horse and pack taking yarn and fetching cloth from hundreds of homes. The main places now are Painswick and Bisley up on the wolds, and Stroud, Brimscombe and Chalford down in the Frome valley. There are some seventeen smaller villages and farm groups scattered on hilltops under wide skies, or in shades of deep old woods, some on steep ledges, some sunk in silence by a millpond at the bottom of a twisting valley. According to their situation they look for services to Stroud or to Cirencester.

Painswick is a stone-built little town of over 3,000 people, on the Stroud–Cheltenham B4070 road. It is built on a low hill and can be seen across valleys for miles. Once a place of mills and clothiers, it is an extraordinary close fistful of beautiful seventeenth- and eighteenth-century streets and lanes, nooks and corners. Handsome houses throng the town, and adorn the steep slopes of the country close round it. Painswick beacon and all Painswick country bears famous stone, which has travelled far beyond these rough hills, as Painswick people will tell you. The colour is bright and warm. Winter gales and fog from the west cannot deaden the crisp vital beauty of the dark roofs and gables, the milky stone of wall and pillared porch, big steps and little finials which draw the eye on down every street. Of course the church is famous, and so are its bells and yew trees of the churchyard, and the carved tombstones.

Painswick is a very busy place. It is a secondary rural centre, with modern housing, primary school, and central buildings for an institute which organises many activities. Every August it puts on the exhibition of work of the Guild of Gloucestershire Craftsmen, which draws together the best craftwork in the county and is an immense attraction. In music, art and fine craftwork Painswick has something of the vital fructiferous character of Chipping Campden. There are many hotels and guest houses. Its modern building is also of interest.

Painswick valley runs north-south down to Stroud. It is set with stately mills which set forth their belief and pride in their purpose and their work. The next village is Pitchcombe, on a U-turn round a fold in the hills, and then Whiteshill and Randwick on the approach to Stroud. Close to Painswick, on the dizzy edge over the vale of Severn, is Cranham, famous for its beechwoods, and Birdlip at the head of Birdlip hill, where the Roman road plunges 900ft down to Gloucester.

The next north-south valley is Slad, down which the B4070 from

Cheltenham runs, with the little village of Slad on it and farms within
sight. The name of the Slad inn, *The Woolpack*, shows its history. The
next is Toadsmoor valley, which runs up near to Bisley, once the market
centre of all this country. At the time of the Oxford Movement in the
1860s Thomas Keble was vicar of Bisley and the inspirer of a missionary
drive among the little communities of weavers and farmers in this lonely
wooded district. Under him a group of young priests founded several
churches and congregations within the parish of Bisley, so that you will
come across small nineteenth-century churches of great devotion and
character.

Bisley is a most beautiful, quiet, easy little town. Craftsmanship in
stonework seems to have bloomed here in a deep satisfaction and
excellence in each group of houses, each corner, each street line. There are
several big houses, including Over Court and the nearby Lypiatt Park
(see Chapter 8). Nearer to the busy Stroud valley are Eastcombe and
Bussage, both with nineteenth-century churches of Keble's inspiration.
At the eastern end of the valley are Oakridge Lynch and Sapperton.
Oakridge is a hamlet in precipitous hanging woods. Sapperton has
become a name for craftsmen and architects, since the group comprising
the Barnsley brothers, Gimson, Jewson and Waals, settled there in Daneway House at the beginning of this century (see Chapters 8 and 9). They
carried on a craft business of traditional skills, encouraging traditional
life, in the same line of thought as William Morris' at Chipping Campden.
Near Sapperton the source of the River Thames is marked by a statue
in a field at Thames Head.

The Stroud valley is the only industrial area in the Cotswolds. Chapter
6 tells of its past activity in the important wool and cloth business, and
Chapter 5 deals with its industry today. It is a very busy area. The only
transport originally down this mainrift in the escarpment was the Frome
stream (too small for navigation) and a road beside it. Chapter 5 tells
of the building of the Stroudwater and the Thames & Severn canal
through it and then of the Great Western Railway main line. The railway survives, but modern road traffic has sacrificed the canal to its
demand for space. Much of it is drained, and its space used for road
widening or for factories.

The villages along the valley are a mixture of old and new. Old mills,
now modern works, are on the valley bottom by the stream and canal,
with close crammed houses, yards and narrow paths. A little garden may
even bridge the stream. The road runs beside these, and across it the
main part of the villages climbs up the steep valley sides. On the north
side, facing south, thick old trees and hanging gardens are rich and

intricate. Chalford is built in ledges from bottom to top of the valley wall, old footpaths linking cottages. Much beautiful and interesting eighteenth- and nineteenth-century building remains in mills, works, chapels and houses all along the valley, though there has been a great deal of demolition for modern industry. Brimscombe Port has disappeared, the canal basin filled in and warehouses demolished for factory sites. Brimscombe village climbs up the valley side, and looks across at the heights of Minchinhampton and Rodborough. Thrupp joins on to it and runs into the outskirts of Stroud.

Stroud is much the biggest place in the valley and growing fast. Its streets climb steep and narrow from the little river, and only begin to spread out when they reach over the valley wall. It is the centre for the area north and south of the valley, and provides secondary school and technical college, schools for handicapped and backward children, school of art and evening classes. Like Cirencester, it is a shopping centre, sports centre with plenty of hunting and riding, and runs the local football leagues, darts, skittles, etc, for the villages round. The old inns and many remains of the clothing industry, with its supporting trades, give great character to Stroud.

It is totally different from Cirencester, the other main town of the Cotswolds. Cirencester is flat and the streets follow expected lines. Stroud is steeply hilly and has all the individuality of a hill town. It is busy, crowded, always demolishing and building. As you go up the High Street, you come to Upper Stroud, where handsome streets go off at different levels—Gloucester Street, Church Street, Castle Street, and others. The sixteenth-century Town Hall and the parish church and Church Institute make a distinctive area (see Chapter 8). Another is formed by the Subscription Rooms, a very handsome 1833 building, and the Congregational Church of the same period. Stroud is rich in early nineteenth-century religious buildings. It was clearly a go-ahead place, for in the 1890s they built a School of Science and Art, showing the influence of Ruskin, with busts of Faraday, Huxley, Kelvin, Barry Rossetti, Leighton and Turner—an 'advanced' group of masters for the period in a little country town. This building now houses Stroud museum, which presents an excellent collection of old Stroud industry and history. It is still a go-ahead place, and not only in industry. Its autumn festival of religious drama and poetry is well established.

Cross the Stroud valley and you seem to leave modern development and climb back into timeless hill country, as you scale the big bluff of Rodborough and Minchinhampton. Up here are miles of common with old earthworks of a big defensive camp, probably of the first century

AD, against the advance of the Roman invaders. Now the whole area, bounded on the south by the Nailsworth valley, is one for views and clear air, walking, picnics, golf, riding, in fact for rest and refreshment in summer. Wild autumn gales and hard winter weather are also part of it. Magnificent woods enrich every fold and valley. So completely is this high area representative of the Cotswold character that 580 acres of Minchinhampton Common are National Trust property.

Minchinhampton is the main place up here, and is the secondary rural centre. Like its distant neighbours across the narrow-bottomed but wide-topped valley it is an old wool and cloth town. Evidences remain in street names and inn names, fine houses and cottages and worksheds mixed together. The wide market square contains the seventeenth-century Market House, and fine hotel buildings. Surely a Queen Anne post office is rare! Minchinhampton is all stone-built, and much of it stone-tiled, with plenty of modern building in reconstituted stone.

Round it the country is wild and beautiful, thick with woods and up-and-down tumbled land, tiny villages which have no advantages but priceless peace, solitude and sky. St Chloe, Amberley, Box, Pinfarthing, their names speak for them. Many crafts are carried on in these small places, and for services they look to Minchinhampton.

The land slopes south from here to Avening. This is another stretch of country holding the feeling of an older world, like Wychwood near Stow-on-the-Wold. Bleak acres of unhedged field are marked by barrows and standing stones, but Avening itself, a solid little village-town on a dip in the land, is more human and modern. It is only a tertiary centre, but it has a county educational centre where youngsters can have a week's experience of boarding school and do special studies. Beyond it, on the long southern slope of the spur that divides the Bath Avon valley from the Churn and Thames and the Water Park country, is Tetbury, a town and primary centre like Cirencester, 10 miles from Stroud. This is a most charming all-stone town, once an important market centre for the rich cloth waggons and pack trains from all the sheep-raising areas of the West and Midlands. Like Minchinhampton it has a Market House on pillars, and many hotels and houses of two or three centuries ago. The long, gentle curving town streets of creamy stone, the harmony of centuries in uneven heights and styles, the change of level by steps or grass slopes or bridge, give a charm to Tetbury which is instant to the eye. Minchinhampton has something of this character, too, but it is not so gentle to the senses, it knows height and harsh weather, and perhaps has known more poverty. Tetbury is now a little town of outstanding beauty, and also of vigorous industry on its industrial site. As a primary centre it provides all main services, and its ancient grammar school is now turned comprehensive. Communications have always been good, as the town stands on a cross of five A roads on the frontier of Gloucestershire and Wiltshire.

Tetbury is a centre of music and sport. It is in a horse-raising countryside, in the Beaufort Hunt territory, and has maintained a local race-meeting for 200 years. Close to the town is Westonbirt girls' school, which attracts people of musical ability. At Westonbirt, too, is the Arboretum, one of the great collections of Europe; 116 acres have been developed since 1820, with care for grouping, background, density and space. At every season there is some remarkable feature to be seen. It is open to the public.

Turning back to Minchinhampton, and looking west and south, the end of the Cotswold lies before you. The escarpment throws up its most dramatic form here in the west, sweeping on from Minchinhampton heights to 800ft at the brink at Nympsfield and the huge shoulder of Stinchcombe thrusting west over the vale of Berkeley and south over the Bath Avon valley, split by deep cracks where rushing streams, ferns, wild-flowers and tall trees seek the light.

The Nailsworth valley is the chief cleft up from the Frome near Stroud. It climbs up from Dudbridge, through steep wooded sides to Woodchester first (see Chapter 8). This is famous for a splendid Roman pavement which is opened to the public every few years as part of a huge Roman site over which much of Woodchester is built. There was also a considerable glassmaking industry here. More streams leap out on the way up the valley. Nailsworth stands on a meeting point of three, about 5 miles up the valley. Hills rise all round the little town, to form the plateau of Minchinhampton to the north. A good turnpike road was engineered up the valley to Nailsworth, now the A46, but the open country on top of the valley sides is another world from the tight-packed valleys. Nailsworth has always been industrial and not agricultural, because of its site. Water power gave life to early industry—glass, wool, cloth, ironwork. Fine mills, non-conformist chapels, small works, close-built hilly streets, make it a place of vivid character, and plenty of industry keeps it prosperous. It is a secondary rural centre, serving many small places round. One of its streams comes down from Avening, and the other from Kingscote and Horsley. This one has been made to serve as a fish hatchery, and the different water enclosures climb uphill beside the road.

The last few miles west and south-west from Nailsworth heights, across to the edge and Stinchcombe bastion, appear uninterrupted high land as you approach. But the land is split by narrow deep clefts, invisible until you pass the turning or drop down lanes into them. As in the old tales, the sun must strike straight into them from your angle to throw a shadow which reveals them. Climb out of Nailsworth and come across to Nymps-field where the land ends, and you stand as on a ship's deck with only the sky ahead of you. Nympsfield has a group of buildings round the *Rose and Crown* inn, stables and malthouse, from the seventeenth century, and older still is Street Farm. Older than all is the chambered long barrow, which was excavated in 1937, when, as I was told, to make my flesh creep, thirteen skeletons were found 'all sitting down'. Nympsfield provides the airfield for Bristol Gliding Club.

Two miles down on a lower dip of the escarpment is Uley, a long wandering village on a B road, with many springs and streams. It was a mill village, and has many handsome big houses, cottages and farm-houses and interesting remains of cloth working. Close to it is the most beautiful manor house in the Cotswolds, Owlpen Manor, with a little church and graveyard on a ledge behind it. From Owlpen a series of worsening roads will lead you to the region of the Bottoms, eg Waterley Bottom, Tyley Bottom, Ozleworth Bottom. These are clefts, with sheltered hidden paths beside streams, their valley walls rising from 200 to 800ft, flat meadows by the stream grazed by sheep and cattle, wildflowers everywhere along your path and up the sheltered slopes, no sound but the wind in the trees high above, and birds calling as they flit to and fro across the enclosed secure world. A few cottages or converted farmhouses, a tiny pub, will mark a Bottom.

All this incomparable little area is sheltered by the bulk of Stinch-combe Hill, which ends (or begins) the Cotswold escarpment here. On the northern slope is the busy centre of Dursley. This is a primary rural centre, and has increased greatly in population and in business in recent years. A wide spread of local newspapers has its offices and printing works here. Lister's engineering works are here. The town has much old character also, a Market House with open arcades and stone columns, old church and good eighteenth-century houses. It spreads down the roads off the high ground, and faces up the Vale of Berkeley to the mouth of the Stroud valley and the Awre bend of the Severn. Stinch-combe stands above it looking south. The B4060 runs round its bluff here at 400ft. Stinchcombe's people play golf on their renowned course 300ft higher.

The B4060 will lead you to North Nibley and Wotton-under-Edge. Wotton is the bigger, and has a beautiful site backed by wooded cliffs and facing the lower easy slopes of the Cotswold escarpment. On the

heights behind it you can climb up to more prehistoric levels, Bracken-
bury Ditches, and walk in early spring among unusual wildflowers and
the smell of timber cutting. Wotton has many interests, as it shared the
fortunes of the powerful Berkeley Castle and family 6 miles away across
the vale, and also had a wool and cloth industrial life with the rest of
the Cotswolds (see Chapter 6). Katherine Lady Berkeley founded the
school here in 1384; Isaac Pitman lived here and worked out his short-
hand system in Orchard Street; chapels of many denominations show the
independence of life in the people, starting even in 1701 with the old
Town Meeting House. The church is handsome and interesting, with
work by Gimson's Cotswold group of craftsmen from Sapperton, and a
most splendid organ built by Christopher Schirder in 1726 and played
by Handel.

South Cotswolds

From the slopes of Stinchcombe and Minchinhampton the Cotswolds
slope down gently from 700ft to merge into the vale of Sodbury. This
rich quiet countryside links the Bath hills, the Wiltshire downs and the
approaches to Bristol. Sodbury is a Rural District of about twenty small
places and no big one. This may be changed in 1974. Heavy pressure
from traffic arising from the nearness of Swindon, Chippenham, Bristol
and Bath has been relieved by the junction of the M4 and M5 at
Almondsbury near the Severn, and the villages feel the release.

Excluding the new town of Yate on the western boundary of the
district of Sodbury, the population of the whole area is about 20,000.
If you drive south from Stroud or Cirencester on the A46 or A433, after
Tetbury you see rolling farm country, many hedges, cattle, woodland,
lanes signposted to country names and very solitary villages. Doughton,
Shipton Moyne, Willesey, Leighterton, Luckington, Didmarton lie in the
wide wold country, and the tall monument on the steep rise to the west
is at Hawkesbury Upton, and looks over into neighbouring counties.
Hawkesbury Upton is a secondary centre, and Didmarton a tertiary.

Continuing south you come to Great Badminton, famous for the seat
of the Duke of Beaufort, and for the horse shows and trials and public
events which take place in Badminton Park and grounds. The country
round here is rich, well farmed, with magnificent beech windbreaks
visible along the main road. Acton Turville and Castle Combe lie each
side of the Foss Way. Tormarton, Old Sodbury, Little Sodbury and
Horton (see Chapter 8) lie west across the road to Chipping Sodbury.
Most of these little places have populations of about 300.

The ancient town of Chipping Sodbury, with a population of 4,000, stands on a cross of roads from Gloucester, Stroud, Bristol and Bath, so it is well placed for early development. It was granted a market early in the thirteenth century. Its long trading and travel history has left an old town hall, and many interesting inns and old buildings. The town is the district's primary centre for education and other facilities. Good roads and regular contact with people of business, wealth and education have marked this part of the Cotswolds with fine houses, well built farms, inns and small houses, more richly than in the more inaccessible parts further north.

Across the motorway, where the eye is drawn away to the Severn and the great bridge, Pucklechurch, Dyrham, Marshfield and Cold Ashton end the area recognisably Cotswold. Dyrham, a hamlet of 300 people on the wolds at 670ft, has a fine house and park which is National Trust property. Marshfield, also high up, is bigger, with 1,300 people, and is a secondary centre. It was once a borough, and has picturesque and interesting buildings from the seventeenth and eighteenth centuries. Its mumming play has survived. In the parish stands a Three Shires Stone which marks the joining of Gloucestershire, Wiltshire and Somerset. Though the limestone base continues, the self-contained wold characteristics of the Cotswolds cease round here, and the countryside looks to Bristol and Bath.

Acknowledgements to this chapter are on page 310.

8

Architecture

David Verey

Character of the Stone

FOR ABOUT 50 miles from Dyrham to Dover's Hill the Cotswold escarpment presents a virtually unbroken skyline when seen from the Vale. The new M5 Motorway provides a moving panorama for the eyes of the motorist cruising between Bristol and Cheltenham, as it passes close to the bottom of the escarpment. Splendid buildings shelter at the foot of the cliff, and one notices perhaps for the first time that many of the churches in this situation have spires, like Stinchcombe, Standish and Haresfield. The banks are generally too steep for the plough, and careful planting of deciduous woodlands has added to the charm and grandeur of the scene. The whole of the scarp is indented, most markedly from Stonehouse, around the minor valleys of Painswick, Slad, Miserden, Nailsworth, Uley, North Nibley and Hillsley. Deep indentations run right into the Cotswolds, producing broken and picturesque country, and some of the best architecture. This is the western edge of a limestone plateau, which slopes gently to the east and south-east, and merges finally into the clay plains of Oxford.

The limestone of the Cotswolds is composed of small rounded grains of calcium packed together like the roe of a fish. From this resemblance the stone is called oolite, meaning egg-stone. The Inferior Oolite, so called because it is the lower and older stratum of this limestone, is tilted upwards at its western edge. There it forms the scarp, which includes all the highest points; highest of all, and most damaged by indiscriminate and unplanned building, is Cleeve Hill, 1,083ft. Further east it dips under the Great Oolite, the new rock which extends across into Oxfordshire. Some beds of Great Oolite provide fine-grained freestone, which can be cut or carved very easily when freshly quarried, and hardens on exposure. Others provide thin layers of rock which can be split by being left out in the frost, thus producing stone tiles which have always, till now, been used for roofing, and are sometimes called Stonesfield or Cotswold slates, though they are not slate in the geological sense. The correct term should be 'tilestone', for it is in fact a sandy limestone which splits nicely into thin layers; an alternative name would be fissile limestone, meaning that it foliates like the leaves of a book.

From ancient times builders in the Cotswolds had a splendid stone almost everywhere ready to hand. There is no doubt that much of the beauty of the district lies in its old stone churches, barns—some even bigger than churches—manor houses, farms and cottages. The stone colour can shade from yellow, through cream to deep brown. The variations in colour are due to an iron mineral called Limonite, so that where the rock is more ferruginous the colour is a deeper yellow or brown, as, for example, the stone from Coscombe, near Stanway, usually called Guiting stone. The colour is generally warmer in the north Cotswolds and greyer in the south; but everywhere it seems to have the quality of retaining light, and responding to the moods of the day. It grows lichens, deep orange, a light buff, blue grey and pure silver, a diffusion of yellow, red and violet in the sunlight. Everywhere the stone buildings achieve a visual accord with the landscape. It has indeed been said that the landscape plays second fiddle, and this is not only aesthetically true, but in some respects actually so, because trees, plants and shrubs like rhododendrons which will not tolerate lime cannot grow on the Cotswolds.

For those who are interested in our building heritage the Cotswolds occupy a special place, not only for the local architecture but also because some of our best loved national buildings were partly built in Cotswold stone, such as the interior of St Paul's Cathedral, the City churches of London and the Sheldonian Theatre and Colleges in Oxford. The Strongs and the Kempsters owned quarries at Little Barrington, Taynton and Burford, producing in various qualities of hardness the attractively coloured and easily worked oolitic limestone. They not only quarried but wrought and laid their own stone, and were capable of handling important contracts with little supervision from architects. From 1667 they increased their fortunes rapidly owing to the enormous demand for stone and masons for the rebuilding of the City of London. Wren regarded Thomas Strong as the leading builder of his day, and appointed him principal contractor for St Paul's. He laid the foundation stone, but died in 1681, leaving money 'to make a way between the Barrington bridges in Gloucestershire that two men may go a front to carry a corpse in safety'. It is still known as Strong's Causeway. After his brother's death Edward Strong continued his contracts, and became the premier Master Mason of England, laying the last stone on the lantern of St Paul's in 1708.

Their father Valentine Strong, who died in 1662 while working on a

house at Fairford for Andrew Barker, built other buildings in the Cotswolds, of which the manor at Lower Slaughter, though much altered and
enlarged, is the most complete known survival. His tombstone at Fairford
is inscribed with a punning verse:

> Here's one that was an able workman long
> who devised houses built both Fair and Strong
> tho' strong he was a stronger came than he
> and robbed him of his life and fame, we see
> moving an old house, a new one for to rear
> death met him by the way and laid him here.*

When the Strong sons composed these lines, they would not have
realised how far they were to go themselves. From 1667 to 1681 Thomas
Strong, in rebuilding the City of London and selling stone to other
masons and at the same time quantities for Windsor Castle, is estimated
to have dealt in £1,000 per annum. Including all works, the family as a
whole dealt for a total of £183,000, a vast sum in those days.

The quarries at Barrington, Taynton and Upton which supplied so
much of the stone employed by the Strongs and Kempsters had already
been worked from the fourteenth century. They consisted of oolite beds
of varying hardness, lying under a ridge of hills running west either side
of the Windrush river. The stone was used at New College, Oxford, in
1396. It was also supplied for St George's Chapel, Windsor, in 1474,
and at Christchurch, Oxford, in 1535. The Barrington mine was closed
before the end of the nineteenth century; but the quarries at Taynton
were reopened by Mr Philip Lee in recent years and are in production
now. The easily sawn and worked freestone was either extracted by open-
cast quarrying or by tunnel mining, as, for instance, at Quarry Hill,
Bibury, from which stone was taken for Oriel College Library. Wren
often found the supply of Portland stone inadequate, owing to storms
delaying vessels from Portland; but in summer and winter barges could
easily float down the Windrush and Thames to Paul's Wharf in London.
On the north side of Little Barrington village lies a spot near the Fox
Inn known as the Wharf, where the stone from the quarries close at

* Naïve verses are often found on tombstones, even in the twentieth century.
Here is one at France Lynch commemorating a lady who was also connected with
St Paul's:

> This lowly stone doth mark the spot
> Where Mary Digby's soul is not,
> She passed in 1924
> To Jesus' purgatorial store.
> In London on Cecilia's Day
> If at St. Paul's your eyes should stray
> And on Cecilia's banner fall,
> 'Twas Mary Digby made it all.

hand must have been loaded, and several hundred yards lower down on the Windrush there still exists the remains of a sloping weir of stone where the water level could be raised to enable the stone-laden barges to float over to avoid the mill-race below. Some of the stone was also hauled to Radcot Bridge and loaded on to barges on the Thames itself.

Norman

Local buildings are not so well documented as those the Strong family erected elsewhere. Usually the stone, however, came straight out of the ground near the site of the building. It has been said that there has never been any break in continuity between the masons of Belas Knap and the dry-walling of the sheepwalks. This may be; but it does seem that after the departure of the Romans, architecture was temporarily forgotten. Early Saxon stone buildings are very primitive in construction, and for a long time there can have been few domestic buildings in stone. In AD 685 a grant of land at Somerford Keynes was made to St Aldhelm. The Saxon doorway on the north side of the church, therefore, could be the remains of a church of very early date. Unable to construct an arch, a stone lintel carved into the shape of an arch is supported by megalithic jambs which are through-stones going through the thickness of the wall. The Saxons penetrated up the river valleys from the Upper Thames. At Bibury they built a large minster church. The capital on the north side of the tall narrow chancel arch is carved in Ringerike style and dates from the early eleventh century. Many of the motifs used by the Anglo-Saxons are Scandinavian in derivation, and these may include the popular grotesque beak-heads probably originally carved in wood on the wooden Viking churches which must have still existed in England when the Normans came to alter Bibury church. The Norman conquest does not provide a clear-cut change in style; but the Normans brought with them Benedictine monks, thus opening England up to the influences of French civilisation emanating from Cluny, which reached its peak about 1100. Here, however, a quotation from Dr Zarnecki may be useful :

> It has often been said that lavish church decoration was initiated by the Cluniac monasteries . . . but the use of sculpture appears to have been spontaneous throughout western Europe. In England, although the urge for this rich architectural sculpture may have come from the Continent, the actual work was done by native artists. In contrast to the previous period immediately before and after the Conquest, when Norman masons were often employed, there are no indications that foreign masons were working in England during the reign of Henry I

o

(1100–35). Reading Abbey is an illustration of this point, although built under the supervision of monks sent from Cluny, its sculpture bears not the slightest trace of Burgundian influence.

Anglo-Norman masons produced ribbed vaulting even before it was used in France.

An interesting feature of Anglo-Norman architecture is the sculptured tympanum, of which there are many examples in the Cotswold churches. There seems to have been a local exuberance among sculptors and masons. Enriched orders are piled one on top of the other, round the little doorways leading into the small churches, with the carved tympanum containing a mystical meaning in the centre above the door. At Quenington, before the Knights Hospitaller arrived there the church received two tympana which, according to Keyser in *Memorials of Old Gloucestershire* (Ditchfield, p 150), date from the end of the reign of King Stephen. The north doorway is particularly virile. It has three orders of different kinds of chevrons, and one with limpet shells, and the capitals are carved with jacks-on-the-green, symbols of fertility. The tympanum represents the Harrowing of Hell. Christ is prodding Satan, who lies on the ground, and there are three other figures. The scene is lit by a sun-disk with a face in it, to show that even in Hell Christ was supported by the Father's light. The south doorway is a finer composition, all of one piece. The outer arch shows the guilloche pattern and large ringed pellets; on the inner order are many beak-heads as well as the heads of an ox and a horse. The clasping beak-heads are continued down the jambs in a stylised form just as they are at Siddington; but there the tympanum shows the figures of St Peter and St Paul standing before Christ, who presents the keys to one and the book to the other. The Quenington tympanum, however, has the Coronation of the Virgin, one of the earliest existing representations of this subject; she and Christ are seated side by side as He crowns her. On the right is a little domed temple of several storeys, perhaps indicating the Heavenly Mansions like the aedicule carved in the spandrels of the arches on the font at Southrop.

With its vigorous naïve carving filling the space in a somewhat unrelated manner the tympanum also resembles one at Elkstone, where the subject is Christ in Majesty, seated, with the Evangelists' emblems and the Agnus Dei, and the Hand of God above. The Elkstone stone is really a lintel with a canted top, as at Ampney St Mary. The figure carving is rather unskilful when compared with the conventional ornament surrounding it. This includes a row of beak-heads, two human heads and an inverted figure grasping the snouts of its neighbours, which must be partly humorous; the medieval masons had great fun with their grotesques. In the vaulted sanctuary at Elkstone the Romanesque boss was given the form of a head with four mouths, from which the ribs protrude, and to increase the impression of security a belt is fastened across the boss.

The Southrop front, c 1180, has great decorative merit and icono-graphical sophistication, showing French influence in a more digested form. Armoured women trample on vice. The names of the virtues are incised on the trefoil-headed arches and the vices backwards, eg TEMPERANCIA and AIRUXUL; with acanthus leaf and beaded interlacing on the upper part. The sublimest work of the twelfth century, however, is to be found at South Cerney. Here survive the Head and Foot of a wooden rood, described by Lethaby as a 'work of great intensity . . . the earliest piece of wood carving in the country'. It is of exquisite beauty, much finer in treatment than stonework. Generally speaking, however, Anglo-Norman architecture in Gloucestershire does not possess figure sculpture comparable with Herefordshire, except on the capitals at Leonard Stanley, and this wooden crucifix at South Cerney. The North arcade at Bibury has columns and piers irregularly set, probably due to the existence of Saxon porticuses. The eastern respond has a capital most splendidly carved with foliage, c 1180–90, which must derive from Romanesque sources. It is very near the classical Corinthian capital, the most beautiful architectural motif ever devised. The next capitals have the locally more usual trumpet scallops and enriched waterleaf, the chevrons at right-angles. Bibury belonged to the Abbey of Osney from c 1130 to the Dis-solution; this would account for its long chancel, served by several priests, and its many aumbries indicating considerable treasure.

Medieval

The first Early English (thirteenth-century) windows are called lancets, tall and narrow with pointed heads. The east walls at Cherington and Wyck Rissington are good examples of the beginnings of a traceried window. At Cherington the components consist of a central round-headed light with taller lancets on either side and a quatrefoil light above; placing these items closer together it can be seen that a window with mullions would have been invented. At Wyck Rissington there are two pairs of lancets with shaped diamond lights above and a regular diamond or lozenge higher in the centre. All are held together in composition by a circuitously zigzagging dripmould.

The next stage is called Decorated (fourteenth century). A good example of this kind of window survives in the east end at Meysey Hampton, with three tiers of trefoils. The surround is enriched with ballflower, a peculiarly endearing motif, not common in the Cotswolds; but to be found in the south aisle of Gloucester Cathedral, for monastic churches were more independent of trade cycles. At Minchinhampton there is a lovely rose window in the upper part of the south transept, the interior of which is vaulted in stone but in a manner which could more easily have been carried out in wood with scissor trusses. In this stone country in some cases things were done in stone which elsewhere would have been in wood, like the bell turrets at Shorncote and Preston, similar to ones at other places on the stone belt.

Surviving domestic buildings earlier than the beginning of the four-teenth century are rare indeed. However, some of the great barns appear to be earlier than is usually supposed, such as the great barn by Sidding-ton church. Siddington was always in lay hands; but the church passed to the Knights Hospitaller of Quenington by gift of Jordan de Clinton about 1200. The barn is a stone-walled building designed in five bays, and having four transverse timber frames to carry its much repaired roof. The end frames are posted and aisled, with clasping tie-beams, scissor bracing, collars with side-purlins and a ridge-piece. These frames are assembled with open notched-laps. The central pair of frames are base-crucked. These structural details are all attributable to the first half of the thirteenth century; but the most important fact is the existence of open notched-laps on the actual base-cruck timbers, as these joints were not used later. It would therefore seem the Barn was built soon after the site was acquired by the Hospitallers. (Mr C. A. Hewett found that the notched-laps in the roof over the nave of Wells Cathedral change from 'open' to 'secret' form during a pause in the building of the nave between 1210 and 1220. It is unlikely that a religious order of knights such as the Hospitallers would have been out of date in their building methods.)

Some domestic buildings of the Knights Hospitaller at Quenington have survived, including the gatehouse, barn, mill, and pigeoncote. The manor was given to them by Agnes de Lucy in 1193. The pigeoncote is mentioned in 1338. At that time there was a preceptor, two other knights, a chap-lain, three clerks and several servants.

Arlington Row, at Bibury, would appear to have been a barn before it was changed into cottages, and added to at either end. It has several bays, all with crucks, and may be the remains of a barn of the Abbot of Osney.

At the foot of the Cotswolds the great tithe barn at Frocester employs the use of base-crucks. There is documentary evidence for its erection in the time of an Abbot of Gloucester who ruled from 1284 to 1306, and there is part of a barn of about this date at Calcot, near Newington Bagpath, built for the Abbot of Kingswood. The tithe barn at Stanway, built in the fourteenth century by the Abbot of Tewkesbury, has been repaired and is used as a hall and theatre. Other outstandingly splendid medieval barns are to be found, for instance, at Syde, Postlip, and at Farmcote, probably a grange of Hailes Abbey. So even though the monasteries were destroyed, their barns remained, the first of a long series of barns to be built all over the Cotswold hills, and which still have to be dated accurately.

One of the oldest small manor houses is Daneway House, at Sapperton. The earliest recorded reference is in 1339, when Henry de Clifford obtained a licence to celebrate mass in the newly erected oratory at his manor. The hall-house must have been in existence, as the oratory is clearly an addition. The earliest structure is the long rectangular block made up of a hall with a central hearth and a solar off its east end. The simply chamfered arched stone entrance to the screens passage and the set of buttresses which support the west wall appear to be late thirteenth century. The oratory, built on close to the main entrance on the south side, has an ogee trefoil arched entrance typical of the date 1339.

The remains of a castle survive at Beverston, consisting of a quadrangular building with large drum towers at the angles, c 1225. They were improved in the fourteenth century rather than enlarged, and provided with a new gatehouse to the east. The present house occupies the site of a thirteenth-century hall. Sudeley Castle is not older than the fourteenth century, with royal apartments added by Richard III. Buckland Rectory may be as old; but it is chiefly noted for its fifteenth-century hall.

Perpendicular Style

Till recently the accepted view about the beginning of the Perpendicular style was that formulated by the Jacksonian professor of applied mechanics at Cambridge, Robert Willis, in 1865, to the effect that the style originated in the south transept of Gloucester Cathedral. That Edward II was assassinated in Berkeley Castle and buried in Gloucester Cathedral is indisputable; but that his tomb was visited by pilgrims from all parts of England, bearing offerings so great that the abbey was able to rebuild in a suddenly invented new style, is not now considered credible. The pilgrims have been inferred in order to account for the propagation of the style throughout England. Chaucer tells us that in spring people liked going on pilgrimages; but he does not say they went to Gloucester; on the contrary they all went to Canterbury. The fact is that by 1327 the great court masons had a pronounced style of their own. What we see in the Gloucester transept and choir is the style of St Stephen's Chapel, Westminster, which arrived there with the body of the murdered king. Edward III built his father's tomb at Gloucester, introducing enough money at the same time for the Choir to be rebuilt. In view of these circumstances it is fairly obvious that the work was carried out by one of the royal masons, in design at least, and Gloucester becomes first in the field with a development of the latest London ideas. At Gloucester there is an increase in scale with a considerable reduplication of verticals and horizontals. After such a triumph it is not surprising to find that by 1359 Thomas of Gloucester was the King's chief mason at court.

The Perpendicular style found in Gloucester Cathedral as early as 1331–7 went on with little change for 200 years. On the Cotswolds the yields of the wool entirely remodelled great churches like Cirencester, Northleach, Chipping Campden, Fairford, Winchcombe, Lechlade and Chedworth, and large numbers were given Perpendicular windows and towers. The buttresses of the towers are set diagonally at the angles, and the string courses are usually carried boldly across the buttresses instead of dying out behind them. In the later examples there is an exuberance of surface ornament expressed in almost excessive panelling. Coates has an early tower, built before 1361. Other notable examples are at Coberley, Compton Abdale, Kempsford, and Wotton-under-Edge. Wool prices reached their highest level in 1480, so that by the time the Tudors came to the throne great private fortunes had been amassed. Rich wool merchants endowed chantry chapels, many soon to be abolished but not destroyed by the Reformation.* The money was the people's and so it was the naves and chapels which were rebuilt, older work surviving in the chancels. The reconstruction of the nave at Cirencester was carried out at the beginning of the sixteenth century by the merchants of the town whose arms and trademarks can be seen carried by carved angels

* Will of Johan, widow of Thomas Bushe, wool merchant of the Staple of Calais, whose brass is in the nave. Will proved in 1527. She willed to be buried by her husband before the altar of St Anthony. Among her bequests are 'to the Mother Church of S Mary of Worcester a kowe or else 20/-: to the High Altar of my Parish Ch in Northleach 40/-. To the gilding of the Rood loft in my parish ch ten pound. To an honest priest to sing for me 5 years after my decease yearly £6. To my ghostly father the Vicar 2 paire of sheets and 2 towels. To Arthur the Grey Frere yearly during his life 2/- and 2pr sheets & a towel. I will that my chalice and vestments, with all manner of apparel belonging to the same remain in the ch of Northleach & that my priest do sing in them during his time'.

above the great piers of the arcades. The economy of Cirencester was based entirely upon wool from 1300 to 1500. The same can be said of the other towns which have 'wool' churches. The merchants were fortunate in having superb stone to hand and master masons to work it. Some unknown genius must have been at work at Northleach and Chipping Campden, a man who made the Perpendicular style into something individual, by his exaggeration of the normal concave or hollow moulding. This is particularly apparent in the piers and capitals of the arcades of both these churches.

Fairford is best known for its stained glass, all made for the church by Barnard Flower, the King's Master Glasspainter, at the time of its rebuilding, c 1500; but the fabric is in the richest late Perpendicular style, and it also contains that rare thing in the Cotswolds, notable woodwork. On the exterior of the tower are grotesque sculptures and emblems of local occupation, such as the shell of the salt-trader, a hunter's horn and baldric, and of course sheep shears. Many grateful masons carved sheep's heads as corbels in the Cotswold churches.

After the Reformation, from Elizabeth to Anne, very little was done in the way of church building, but what there was is generally in a style of so-called debased Gothic. Several Cotswold towers had to be completely rebuilt in the eighteenth century and with one exception, that of Bourton-on-the-Water which is in classical style by William Marshall, they are all examples of Gothic survival (not revival). Bishop's Cleeve was rebuilt in 1700, Dursley in 1707, Somerford Keynes in 1710, Blockley in 1725.

Domestic

Before the middle of the sixteenth century most of the buildings people lived in were made of timber-framing because, up to that time, even on top of the Cotswolds, there was a good supply of wood. These houses are sometimes found to survive behind a stone casing added in Tudor or later times. Henry VIII's excommunication cut England off from Renaissance art for at least 100 years. Tudor architecture is therefore a kind of domesticated Perpendicular, and nowhere did it reach such perfection in stone as in the Cotswolds. Quite awe-inspiring is the continuity in the technique of domestic stone building. A number of sixteenth-century houses have survived; but their Tudor mannerisms like mullions, finials, four-centred arched doorways, dripmoulds and the like, continued to be used in the seventeenth and eighteenth centuries, making dating sometimes a problem. They also continued in the nineteenth century, though often then there was a kind of meanness of proportion which is detectable. This is not to infer that the Cotswolds were so out-of-touch that the Renaissance was ignored altogether. Far from it; many a Jacobean manor house has its charming, maybe naïve, Renaissance motif. Everywhere there are examples, and often mixed with Gothic survivals. Every town and most villages have their classical houses as well.

The first little building of the new era in Gloucestershire may well be the Ambulatory at Horton Court, situated in the foothills towards Bristol. This was built by one William Knight after he had been sent to Rome in 1527 to promote King Henry's divorce. It looks like an Italian loggia, though the arcade still has flat four-centred Gothic arches. Newark Park at Ozleworth is said to have been built with the stones from Kingswood Abbey. It has a Renaissance doorway with fluted columns and pediment by Smythson, now restored for the National Trust by the American architect Mr Robert Parsons. There must be at least 100 quite sizeable manor-type houses surviving in the Cotswolds which date from between 1550 and 1650, where differences in style are slight or non-existent. Many of them have a little Renaissance detail, either round the door or on a chimneypiece. Whittington Court was probably begun before 1556. The mullioned windows have Renaissance pediments. Chavenage is dated 1576 but is probably older; the main staircase is still the stone-newel type usually found in fifteenth-century houses. The hall chimneypiece, 1608, is Renaissance in character. Stowell Park was rebuilt c 1600, and has a panelled drawing room with an arcaded dado and tiers of Doric and Ionic pilasters. The old town hall in Stroud, late sixteenth century, has a mixture of Gothic and Renaissance motifs. The porch at Ablington Manor, 1590, is gabled and pinnacled in true Gothic style; but it has a classical frieze with portrait heads between the triglyphs. Cold Ashton Manor, 1629, is decorated with strapwork and Corinthian capitals in the hall.

The gabled Cotswold manor house with its yew trees is a romantic dream which for some lucky people has come true. Owlpen in its remote and beautiful valley near the Severn estuary is the epitome of romance. So is Pinbury, described in 1900 as situated in a 'mystery land of difficult hills and deeply wooded valleys dividing the Vale of the White Horse from the Severn and the Welsh borderland'. So is Prinknash: 'It stands on a glorious but impracticable hill, in the midst of a little forest of beech, and commanding Elyseum', wrote Horace Walpole.

After the troubles of the Civil War there was a great boom in building. There was a revival of the wool trade, and the cloth was expanding. Painswick has many houses of this period. It was evidently a fairly important local centre in the Middle Ages, when it had a market and fair, and there was an attempt to create a borough. The later prosperity of the town and its extensive parish, which included the villages of Edge, Sheepscombe and Slad (now made famous by Laurie Lee's *Cider with Rosie*), was based on the cloth industry. The stone used was quarried locally and was also used for buildings in Oxford and London, as well as providing the material for Painswick's unrivalled collection of churchyard tombs—table-tombs of all shapes, even resembling enormous silver tea-caddies, many belonging to the families of the masons themselves—and others in churchyards further afield. The splendid collection at Elmore was made of Painswick stone by Painswick masons.

The well known local family of masons and carvers called Bryan were active throughout the eighteenth century, and must be responsible for many of them. Joseph Bryan lived from 1682 to 1730. He had two sons, John (1716–87), described as 'carver' on his pyramidal tomb, and Joseph (1718–80). In 1748 John designed and built the pair of stone gatepiers with vermiculated panels and ball-finials at the entrance to the churchyard. On the other side stand the Court House, built c 1604 for a clothier, a traditional gabled Cotswold building, but with the added interest of a Court Room built for Chancellor Seaman, who died in 1623. It has a lively Renaissance chimneypiece and a complete set of small-scale panels stencilled with arabesques. To the south is another large house, Castle Hale, gabled, c 1629 and 1653, with an additional classical late Georgian front by Charles Baker, a native and accomplished architect-builder.

The third large house in this area is called Gwynfa, meaning Paradise, and so named by a vicar of Welsh extraction, considerable taste and fortune. It has a nice late eighteenth-century front possessing a central bay with pediment and œil-de-bœuf light, a Venetian window, and a Roman Doric doorcase raised upon a perron. The most extraordinary thing about this house, however, is the fashionable addition of 1909 in 'Cotswold style', but with an Italian loggia and Italian garden complete with ramps to acommodate Edwardian bicycles. It is in fact Castle Hale in reverse, showing how fashion had come a complete circle and returned to the vernacular. When I first went to live in this house in 1917, every room had a William Morris wallpaper, and below the chair rails the dados were covered with a fine kind of straw matting, the gas lighting had incandescent mantles, the water closets were flushed by pressing a brass pedal, there were carved angels from Oberammergau in the chapel, there was a billiard room, and a soundproof telephone room containing one weird instrument; and up two flights of stairs—one could still get out into the garden, so steep was the hill on which the house was built—there were parish rooms for boys' clubs and meetings.

Painswick is full of delights and surprises, not least of which are the mill houses in the valley below, or the splendid rococo plaster work in the Palladian house called The Beacon. In 1820 there were twenty-five mills working in the parish, but it escaped subsequent nineteenth-century development, owing to the competition of Stroud and the failure of a scheme to bring the railway (see also Chapter 6).

Painswick House, set in a hilly wooded park is slightly apart from the town on the slopes of the Beacon. It was originally known as Buenos Ayres, and consisted of a squarish classical house of the 1730s. Its provenance has not been finally decided, except that Bristol is obviously the direction in which to look. The romantic setting was fully utilised in the layout of a perambulation through now enormous beech trees across a ravine, from Gothick folly to Gothick arch, past a Gothick seat or an urn carved with putti, or a statue of Pan. In the 1830s Basevi added flanking wings on to the house, repeating the boldly rusticated and pedimented windows of the central block. Inside, the rooms are on a very grand scale for a house of this size, and Basevi's dining room is severe and magnificent, with a Corinthian order and coffered ceiling.

Basevi is said also to have designed the Stroud Subscription Room in 1833, but it was built by the Painswick architect Charles Baker—a dignified five-bay facade, articulated by nicely varied quoins, and with a pedimented centrepiece with three tall round-arched windows to the ballroom on the *piano nobile*. Stroud was originally included in the manor and ecclesiastical parish of Bisley, which was anciently of some importance. Among the outlying farmsteads of the parish are an unusual number of houses which are still basically medieval buildings, such as Througham Slad; while the south of the parish provides a classic example of squatter development in the eight small villages which sprang up on the fringes of two large commons. Most of the inhabitants of these villages were cottage weavers, working for the cloth mills in the Chalford valley below, and in the early nineteenth century many were reduced to extreme poverty, a situation which was partly relieved by emigration to New South Wales. For instance, some of the relations of the architect Benjamin Bucknall emigrated. John Keble's brother Tom, who was vicar of Bisley from 1827, gathered round him the group of Tractarian clergy who became known as the 'Bisley School', and during his incumbency provided daughter churches for the villages in the south of the parish such as Bussage, which was paid for by a group of High Church undergraduates, and France Lynch, designed by Bodley.

The most remarkable house in the Bisley area is Nether Lypiatt Manor, 1702–5. It was built for a judge named Coxe and is the perfect 'grand' house in miniature, apparently influenced by Coleshill, which the judge may have passed on his way to London. The house is only 46ft square, but comprises a full cellar-storey, a basement above ground, a principal floor or modest English version of the *piano nobile*, a bedroom floor and an attic with dormers in the hipped roof. The big central chimneystack is intended to take the place of the belvedere in large houses like Coleshill. Sacheverell Sitwell's comment cannot be omitted : 'No house would compose so beautifully for a glass transparency, with wrought iron gates in front flanked by a pair of little formal pavilions', and he added, for he new it well, 'with an interior where music will for ever linger as it was the home of Violet Gordon Woodhouse', who in her day was a well known player of the clavichord.

Eighteenth-century mansions on the Cotswolds are few and far between, and have nothing to do with local tradition except in their skilful handling of stone. The most interesting early Georgian houses are those which reflect the Baroque tendencies of Vanbrugh before Lord Burlington put a stop to them. Barnsley Park is perhaps the most splendid example, 1720–31. Built in stone from the huge underground mine at Quarry Hill between Barnsley and Bibury, the mouldings and carvings are as fresh today as when they were cut. We know that the house was built for Henry Perrot, who married a niece of the first Duke of Chandos ('Princely Chandos, that great patron of the liberal arts'); but we do not know who was his architect. As the family was closely knit, and as the Duke was building his palace at Canons at the same time, employing all the great architects of the day, it is hardly credible that one of these was not employed at Barnsley, probably John James. There are similarities with his other works, such as Appeldurcombe in the Isle of Wight, now a ruin, and perhaps even more relevant to Barnsley's entrance front, Kingston Maurwood in Dorset, 1717. It has nine bays, the central three projecting forward, with four giant Corinthian pilasters supporting a bold cornice. The ground floor has arched openings with powerful keystones, and the attic storey, again divided by pilasters, has a heavy projecting pediment. Either side the first floor windows are crowned with pediments. The south front has projecting bays on either side, and is therefore quite a contrast, although there are similar giant Corinthian pilasters at the corners and between each of the windows. The E front has a bowed centre. The hall fills the centre of the entrance front and is sumptuously decorated with modelled stucco by the Italians Artari and Bagutti, similar to their work at Clandon.

There are three mansions at the Bristol end of the Cotswolds which are equal in magnificence to any in England, in spite of the absence of great Whig families. Badminton dates from the Restoration and was in progress of building when the third Marquis of Worcester was created first Duke of Beaufort in 1682. The final touches were added by Kent in the 1740s, and he designed the superb Worcester Lodge. Most of the park buildings, including a house built of tree trunks and the huge castellated barns, were designed by Thomas Wright after Kent's death. This was high fashion and Dyrham is earlier than this, and Dodington later. Much has been written about both and they are open to the public. At the other extreme end of the northernmost part of the county there are three private mansions : Barrington, with its park buildings probably by Kent; Daylesford, built for Warren Hastings; and Northwick, altered by Lord Burlington. There is also the well known Mogul-inspired house Sezincote, built of an almost orange-coloured ashlar.

The Industrial Revolution did not bring wealth to the Cotswolds, in fact, if anything, its effect was impoverishing. The architecture of the small towns, therefore, has survived the Victorian age with little change. Places like Cirencester and Tetbury went through a period of semi-stagnation.

Churches and country houses, however, were built; but the most interesting Victorian house was never finished. This is Woodchester Park. Its architect Benjamin Bucknall who was born at Rodborough in 1833 is the only English architect who could be described as a disciple of Viollet-le-Duc. Bucknall thought 'Pugin was a true artist and distinguished architect, the first to make people see their barbarism and to indicate the true principles so well known in the past but till now forgotten. Unfortunately his death has largely stopped this progressive trend and the only true way now is through Viollet-le-Duc's books'. Bucknall accepted Pugin's doctrine that construction should not be hidden, but he also benefited from Viollet-le-Duc's much deeper knowledge and analysis of Gothic as a rational system of building in stone.

At Woodchester he set out to achieve what Pugin had never attempted, a country house built of stone throughout, walled with stone, roofed with stone and vaulted with stone, with stone staircases, stone gutters, stone downpipes, and even a stone bath. Woodchester also is one of the first Victorian buildings in which the architect showed an interest in local traditions. The detail of the chapel is based on a study of the early fourteenth-century transept at nearby Minchinhampton church. The main outline of the house, with its generous gables, square-headed windows and roofs covered in local stone tiles, is unmistakably Cotswold. The stone is superb oolitic limestone, probably quarried at Minchinhampton. In spite of the big square-headed windows and lierne vaults, there are touches of early French Gothic here and there; the gargoyles—genuine water-spouting gargoyles—were inspired by the ones Viollet-le-Duc put on Notre Dame at Paris. The south front is a real Gothic wall of glass supported on a stone framework; on the ground floor the glazing is continuous from end to end, except where it is divided by buttresses; these buttresses are put there to hold the building up, in contrast to the decorative buttresses which too many Victorian architects were fond of attaching to their buildings. 'To Bucknall', writes Dr Mark Girouard, 'the point of Gothic was that it was a system of construction; to revive the detail without the construction was to play at fancy-dress architecture.' His masterpiece, however uneconomic and uninhabitable, was virtually indestructible. Unloved, unlived in and unmaintained, it has lasted for over 100 years and is still almost in mint condition.

Bucknall also must have designed Tocknells House near Painswick; it is so similar to Woodchester but on a much smaller scale. There still may be other houses by him to be discovered, though this is not necessarily so, because he spent the last 20 years of his life in Algiers. Bucknall's client, Mr Leigh, bought the Woodchester estate from Lord Ducie, who built an enormous house at Tortworth, 1849–52, employing Teulon as his architect. The old square Georgian house at Woodchester was pulled down.

The reputation of such houses was at rock bottom in mid-Victorian years. The dominant philosophy was Pugin's—that elevation should be subservient to plan, and that the different elements of a house should be expressed externally as 'distinct and beautiful features'. But how many elements of a house needed a distinct expression; the opportunities for exaggeration were endless. At the same time the picturesque tradition was far from dead. As Dr Girouard has pointed out, 'the most interesting high-Victorian houses are those which experiment with new ways of visual organisation, but keep a sensible dialogue going between practical and visual standards'. Tortworth (1849–52) is a good example of a house which combines strong Puginesque influence with picturesque showmanship. The different parts of the house are given separate expression with frantic enthusiasm, but are combined together in a picturesque composition building up to the huge pyramidal tower, which contains a sensational wooden Gothic staircase winding round all four walls. The entrance front is approached through an archway which once had carved on it the word WELCOME, removed when the house became a prison, but perhaps quite important as a morale-booster to Lord Ducie's guests if they had an inkling of the aesthetic austerity of some of the bedrooms.

Victorian architects were increasingly conscious of skyline. The potentialities of the diagonal line (as in a gable) naturally led to the exploitation of roofs. Quar Wood, built near Stow-on-the-Wold in 1857 by Pearson, had a combination of roofs or different shapes—gable, hipped gable, pyramid, spirelet and wedge—a dramatic essay in rising and falling skyline. The house was illustrated in Eastlake's book soon after it was built; but its qualities were later forgotten and then became so unrecognised that nobody raised the smallest protest when in 1953 it was emasculated into neo-Cotswold of the most banal variety.

Cotswold Style

What is the Cotswold style? The picturesque element is certainly of prime importance, with its emphasis on diagonals. In Georgian times, when classical architecture was the fashion, the roof line was hidden behind a parapet. Then came the *cottage-orné*, which was a conscious return to the picturesque based on vernacular cottage architecture. Vernacular building was basically functional. In the Cotswolds it was a continuation of the Gothic way of building, simplified for domestic requirements, and perfected in Elizabethan and Jacobean times. In spite of the Renaissance, in spite of Georgian fashion and Victorian revivals, the Gothic way survived. There are many examples of Gothic survival, as opposed to revival. Eclecticism was rife in the nineteenth century, and towards the end of the period the Cotswold style itself was consciously revived. Batsford Park by Sir Ernest George and Peto (1888–93) is a clever 'working up' of the Tudor-Gothic style into a country house in the grand scale, which at first sight might be genuine sixteenth-century work. The house was designed to 'avoid prettiness and fanciful features', unlike George and Peto's earlier stables close by. Here Guy Dawber was employed as clerk-of-works and here he learnt all about Cotswold building in stone. About the turn of the century he was building several houses of his own design in either Cotswold style, like the Old Stone House at Oddington and Hill Place at Lower Swell, or in Queen Anne, like Eyford Park, and Burdocks at Fairford. The style 'Queen Anne' for domestic buildings had a considerable vogue, but the term was used to include a style of building which was really a revival of something earlier and akin to Gothic—it was anyway more like the English or Dutch seventeenth-century style than Georgian.

Chipping Campden in 1902 became the centre of the Guild of Handi-crafts, founded by C. R. Ashbee, who had become involved in the philo-sophy of craftsmanship and honest work. In all 150 men, women and children came from London, among them about fifty working guildsmen. The influence of Ashbee, and later of Frederick Landseer Griggs, has left a lasting impression on Campden; in fact it is not easy to determine what is old and what is new.

William Morris's social-aesthetic principles are familiar: 'Art must be for the people, not for the connoisseur; it must be by the people not by unassisted individual genius. This is how the conditions of art were in the middle ages, and unless such conditions could be restored in the nineteenth century, there was no hope of a decent art or a decent life.' Morris thought architecture 'the master-art and one of the most important things a man could turn his hand to'. His hand, we note, not his mind. It may be an accidental turn of phrase, but it is very telling all the same. The crafts which make up architecture were closer to Morris's heart than the intellectual power of designing. So the aspect of architecture which interested him most is that every work of architecture is a work of cooperation. This was the outcome of his veneration for the Middle Ages. 'The ancient buildings of the middle ages were the work of associated labour and thought of the people.' In Morris's day the great architect was carefully guarded from the common troubles of common men. How true this is of an age in which an architect of repute designed churches, public buildings, country houses and villas, but scarcely ever houses for the common man. Yet this is not really what Morris was pleading for. He was a born craftsman, and he turned his plea in the direction of craft. 'Architecture must be cherished by all the crafts whereby men make things which they intend shall be beautiful, and shall last some-what beyond the passing day.'

This no doubt was the kind of lecture Morris delivered to the Secularist Society in Leicester one Sunday in 1884, when among his audience was an architectural student called Ernest Gimson, aged nineteen. Morris afterwards advised him to go into the London office of J. D. Sedding, which was next door to the headquarters of William Morris & Co. From this time onwards Morris was the profound influence on Gimson's life. In Sedding's office Gimson met Ernest Barnsley, whose brother Sidney was articled to the famous architect Norman Shaw. Gimson was put on the committee of the Society for the Preservation of Ancient Buildings, founded by Morris originally to prevent architects scraping medieval plaster off the interior walls of old churches. Here Gimson met all the clever young men of this persuasion—Philip Webb, Lethaby, and Detmar

Blow who had travelled with Ruskin, and afterwards also came to live and build in the Cotswolds.

Not only was Gimson an architect but he also designed furniture. In the London Exhibition of the Arts and Crafts Society in 1890 he exhibited some excellent pieces, and the short-lived firm called Kenton & Co was formed by him and his friends, including Sidney Barnsley. Ernest Barnsley set up as an architect in Birmingham. To design furniture was one thing; but to get it made to the required standard in material and workmanship was quite another. For this reason the firm of Kenton came to an end, but experience had been gained and it was not a financial loss. To Gimson and Sidney Barnsley architecture and the crafts were so interdependent that they could not settle down to an ordinary architectural practice in London. In the unspoilt country where tradition in building and the surviving crafts, such as wheelwrights' work and blacksmithing, still held good, which was the case at Sapperton, they felt they could find the right setting for a real revival of building and the handicrafts, free from the taint of commercialism or the deadly monotony of machine production. So they came to Gloucestershire, all three of them, for Ernest Barnsley having had little success in Birmingham, joined them at Pinbury Park near Sapperton.

It proved the ideal place for their purpose. For the next 25 years they lived and worked at Sapperton. Gimson absorbed everything in nature around him. Socially he was all the time 'drawing together and invigorating whatever threads of true village life were still discernible'. His time was largely taken up with designing for his cabinetmakers, such as Peter Waals, the Dutch foreman, whose standard of workmanship was so high that everything had to be as near perfect as possible, and for his blacksmith Alfred Bucknell. Gimson's gospel was that of Morris, a healthy enjoyment for all in making useful and beautiful things; but he could never follow Morris into the ways of mass-production, and so his furniture was expensive and ony within the reach of the well-to-do. He and the Barnsleys all built houses for themselves on Lord Bathurst's estate at Sapperton. The addition which they built on to Pinbury contains the drawing room with its beautiful carved stone chimneypiece, modelled plaster frieze, and ceiling, with motifs all taken straight from nature and which Gimson worked himself, and the splendidly proportioned bay-window looking out towards the great yews of the Nun's Walk. He died aged fifty-four in 1919, just in time not to see the shattering of his Utopia.

The Barnsleys and Norman Jewson carried on with their architectural practice. Ernest Barnsley built the great house at Rodmarton for the

Hon Claud Biddulph, begun in 1909—a splendid country house which has grown out of the craft movement with magnificent use of stone and timber. After the Barnsleys' deaths Jewson continued to build many very good houses, and these houses are among the best in what is now recognised as the Cotswold style.

Notes to this chapter are on page 310.

P

9

The Visitor's Cotswolds

John D. F. Green

THE VISITOR to the Cotswolds, whether by motor car, bicycle or afoot, should first study their topography. He must appreciate that they climb to the west to a sudden escarpment that overlooks the Severn valley and on into Wales; that there are few natural passes through them, except at Stroud and Cheltenham and into the Evesham Vale at Winchcombe. Most of the western edge is a rough fall of some 1,000ft, not always easy to ascend, but offering in places a wonderful reward in the distant prospect. In the east the Cotswolds slope imperceptibly into the basin of the Thames, glowing in the warm architectural charm of relatively lowland places like Burford and Fairford. From the western escarpment all springs with the exception of those in the Stroud valleys flow east to swell the Thames. For this reason the Cotswolds hold many putative sources of that river.

This then is the simplified clue : know the Cotswolds by its rivers and you will know all. Of these, the Churn, the Coln and the Windrush are the most important, but they have many tributaries within their own private valleys which often have to be forded in villages of infinite charm like the Duntisbournes, the Swells and the Leaches. The principal river that flows west is the Frome, long industrialised by the Stroud cloth trade.

Churn Valley

The Churn is one of the reputed sources of the Thames, and the point where it rises at Seven Springs is, in fact, the most distant source from London. It is only 4 miles here from Cheltenham, which lies under the Cotswolds in the Severn vale.

The great houses of the Churn valley were Cowley Manor and Colesbourne and Rendcomb Parks. Cowley Manor is now a Gloucestershire County Council conference centre. The mansion is Italianate in style; with terraced gardens where waterplants are cultivated. Colesbourne, the next estate, was owned at one time by the botanist H. J. Elwes, who, with Professor Henry, wrote the classic *Trees of Great Britain and Ireland*. This interest at Colesbourne has recently been revived by a reclassification of the present trees, which has revealed specimens culled from Elwes' lifetime of travel, some of which are unique in Britain.

From Colesbourne one may leave the valley and visit the bleak upland village of Elkstone. This is near Ermin Street, and so, expectedly, a site of Roman occupation. However, it is the church which merits the visit, being one of the best examples of Norman parish architecture to be found in Gloucestershire. Looking through the rounded arches of its aisleless nave one grasps that sense of civilised assurance that made the Norman occupation of rural England so dramatic. The combination of Gothic faith and Frankish certainty was a predestination from which there was to be no return. Elkstone church has this special message, particularly as one leaves it by the south doorway.

To return to the Churn; next to Colesbourne stands anther Italianate mansion, on a high wold overlooking the road. This is Rendcombe Park, now a successful public school which was developed in the 1920s. Rendcomb village climbs over the wold beside it, towards the old salt road called the White Way. After Rendcomb the Churn winds its way through the village of North Cerney, whose church is another essential visit. It can be seen standing back behind its lych-gate, some 200yd from the road. Its restoration represents the lifework of Will Croome, who for many years in the middle of this century was chairman of the Cathedral Advisory Committee for England, and a Trustee of the Historical Churches Preservation Trust. Beyond the church is the Queen Anne rectory, bearing the arms of the patron of the living, University College, Oxford. It is sad that the modern main road ever separated this lovely group from the River Churn, the Manor Farm and the Bathurst Arms.

At North Cerney one is free to follow the main road into Cirencester or to turn west at Perrott's Brook into the Cirencester woods, which run from Daglingworth virtually to the summit of the Stroud valley. Cirencester is the main town of the Cotswolds, and the chief place on the Churn. It is a graceful limestone town, and keeps an easy character in spite of good shops, crowded streets on market day, and constantly improving business. It stands squarely on the site of Roman Corinium, and the foundations of Roman shops, houses or street lines are readily exposed in any site-clearance. Interest in its Roman remains has drawn visitors for many centuries, but today more than ever. Archeological digs take place every summer, and the museum is lively and beautifully arranged. Cirencester's timeless attraction has been its splendid church in the Market Place at the heart of the town, the finest wool church of them all. Many old streets of seventeenth- and eighteenth-century houses, large and small, lead out from the centre. Here you can buy lardy-cakes, a Gloucestershire speciality, and find one of the best saddlers in England. The grounds of the medieval abbey immediately behind the church have become the property of the town since 1945, and form a green stretch with fine timber through which the Churn runs.

Cirencester Park itself has been a main adornment of the town since it was laid out in the early eighteenth century by Lord Bathurst, with the advice of Alexander Pope who, like Shenstone and other eighteenth-century poets, specialised in landscapes. Lord Bathurst's mansion stands close to the town, and the Park opens behind it, leading along woodland rides that continue 5 or more miles across country to link up with the beechwoods at Sapperton. The public are allowed access on foot and hore, with some access for cars. The handling of the beechwoods is of particular interest to foresters and naturalists who wish to study the natural regeneration of species on the limestone. In Cirencester Park (or Oakley Park as it was formerly known) one can find Pope's seat (one of several charming stone pavilions), a former toll house on the old line of the Bath Road, and on the farther side Pinbury Park, the house of Gloucestershire's first historian, Sir Robert Atkyns, who is buried in nearby Sapperton. Pinbury was for some years the home of the Poet Laureate John Masefield.

The Cirencester Park Polo Club has its grounds in the Park. This broad expanse of open turf surrounded by clumps of noble trees is surely the most beautiful sports ground in England. It is off the Tetbury road, and the public can come in to what is always a popular summer attraction. The town's cricket ground is also in the Park. Recently, equestrian events have been staged in the Park and promise to become more important. The far-stretching woods serve a serious purpose for timber, but in May 1972 Lord Bathurst, recognising the new demands upon the Cotswolds occasioned by the tourist development, opened a Leisure Park to demonstrate the work of the countryside to visitors. All round the year Cirencester Park means for Cirencester and its visitors bluebells and summer green, picnics and birdsong, autumn rambles after nuts and blackberries, fiery beech avenues streaming on October gales, or winter meets of hounds in bitter damp fog, with a faint sun struggling through glittering cobwebs in every bracken spray. The unexpected is ever present, be it the crash and startle of horse or deer in the mist.

Coln Valley

Two days spent in the Coln valley would perhaps give the visitor his best reward in terms of Cotswold atmosphere. This small stream that flows off the high slopes to the east of Cleeve Hill and into the village of Withington is called the Clevely brook. Thereafter it is correct to know it as the Coln. The church end of Withington village has considerable character. One must exercise imagination to appreciate its isolated and sequestered charm at the time when William Cobbett lost his heart to it in his *Rural Rides*. There was no direct road to Cheltenham then, and the Bishop of Worcester owned the Manor, which was not separated from the Church.

The great house in the parish of Withington was always Compton Casey, which for 200 years was the home of the Howe family, bearers of the now extinct peerage of Chedworth. Well maintained, the surviving third of the former mansion is a farmhouse which can be walked round within its wonderfully lost valley. On the northern slopes the clumps of beeches in the deer park are still visible, as is the old park wall itself, which leads over the hill to Compton Abdale fringed with ancient limes. Around the house is a moat formed by the river, and some rough orchards which were formerly landscaped gardens. The clipped yews that once surrounded the bowling green are now ungainly trees alive at sundown with wood-pigeons. To enjoy and understand Compton Casey one should have in hand the plan of the house and gardens of 1712 which is reproduced from Atkyns' *History of Gloucestershire*. Why Compton Casey was allowed to decline may seem a mystery to our generation but we forget that until the Romantic Movement hills and views were thought more appropriate to shepherds than to gentlemen, or, we should say, to educated people.

A mile further up the river is Stowell Park, the home of Lord Vestey. The present mansion was built in the 1860s, and incorporated an old house with Jacobean features and a fine staircase. The church is diminutive and very old, and its dimness glimmers with wall-paintings. Stowell and its neighbour Yanworth are two hamlets that, except for some larger farm buildings, seem never to have changed.

On the southern slopes of the Chedworth woods, scarcely 2 miles from the Foss Way itself, some Roman established what is perhaps the best preserved and largest domestic villa site in Britain (see Chapter 3). Why so much remains is due to the accident of fate which sometime or other allowed a slide of Fuller's earth to smother it. It was discovered in 1864 when a gamekeeper was looking for his lost ferret. The stump of a tree still bestrides one of the walls in the dressing room or *apodyterium*, showing exactly how the ground plan was revealed. Since 1924 the villa has belonged to the National Trust and is one of its most visited possessions. It is unique in being of very late occupation, continuing well into the fourth century and so posing all the questions of the missing link between the decline of world order in distant Rome and the dawn of our own more parochial history.

Chedworth village lies, not in the main valley of the Coln but in a small one that is adjacent. It will be found spread along its own hillsides, not closely clustered in Cotswold form but more like parts of the Stroud valley in character. If time permits the visitor to make the steep descent, the group setting of the Manor, the church and Church Row is a fine example of English village settlement. It is approached by an ancient medieval street known as Queen Street, because here Elizabeth of York came on her way to see the Perpendicular additions to the church which were completed in 1485, the year of her husband's, Henry VII's, accession. Chedworth today, wrapped in geographical isolation, is a village with an intensely self-sufficient life which includes every kind of parochial organisation from its ancient Silver Band to its indefatigable bell-ringers, who fill the distant wolds with basic music.

At Fossebridge, still in the parish of Chedworth, the break is made between the upper Coln, or the Coln of the ancient woodland, and the river that gives its name to villages which are internationally famed. The ring of their names—Coln St Dennis, Coln Rogers, Ablington, Bibury, Coln St Aldwyn and Quenington—conjures a warmth of feeling at once uniquely domestic and civilised lying amidst the contrast of gaunt and exposed wolds.

The first of the Colns downstream is Coln St Dennis. The church with heavily buttressed tower is of Norman origin and stands in front of a small village green. The road to Coln Rogers leads over the river, which has now become a presentable trout stream. The Coln, typical of limestone streams, is much fished, but unlike the sunnier chalk streams of Hampshire lacks the richer plant life, and is for the most part a mayfly stream of limited season. Crayfish used to abound in it as in all Cotswold streams, and were much favoured in hostelries like the Fossebridge Hotel and the *Swan* at Bibury up to the time of World War I.

A short way along the road to Bibury the hamlet of Calcot lies across the river, all stone, tightly clustered and treeless with a fine barn at its centre. Next comes Coln Rogers against a north background of wooded slopes, with a church that contains Saxon work, and beside it an

Elizabethan vicarage. At Winson nearby lived for many years Robert Henriques, one of whose novels, *Through the Valley*, suggests in particular this part of the Cotswolds, usually known as 'the Valley' by its inhabitants.

Of more direct literary fame, however, is the next hamlet of Ablington, for this is the Cotswold Village itself. Here is the scene of *A Cotswold Village*, written by its squire Arthur Gibbs in 1898. Gibbs died suddenly at the age of thirty-one. He was a young man of wealth, equally at home with horse or rod or gun, but of high intelligence and considerable poetic feeling. He accepted with compassion and insight the social position that for so short a span of life he was privileged to enjoy. He tells of the country customs of his youth, the mummers' plays, village cricket matches, the Chedworth band and local politics, all of which he saw with the same enlivened sympathy as Richard Jefferies, if from a different social angle. His old manor house is a gem of Elizabethan architecture, infinitely modest and richly ochred. The entrance porch contains the five heads of the Tudor monarchy, with Elizabeth herself in the centre.

If *A Cotswold Village* charmed our grandparents, it certainly created for succeeding generations the consciousness of a Cotswold style. This in turn has been reflected in the architecture of restoration, with its gables, pitched roofs, drip-courses and dovecotes. Nowhere is this more apparent to the visitor than at Bibury, although it is perhaps better not to visit it in August. The National Trust owns Arlington Row, the scene of Lesley's picture in the Royal Academy in 1898, the same year that *A Cotswold Village* was published. Facing west out of the shadows, its lichen-coated stone only momentarily catches the sunlight and is nearly indiscernible from the background from which it is hewn. Arlington Row is the quintessence of English cottage architecture (see Chapter 8). Across the meadow at night and morning, drenched in clinging mist, the illusion of disappearance is almost rivalled by that of Bibury Court itself, the fine Elizabethan house which is now a hotel. Arlington Mill has been saved, restored and made into a folk museum, containing mill machinery, farm implements and other tools, examples of wallpaper and domestic items. One room has examples of Ernest Gimson's work at Daneway, of which we shall learn more. Bibury Church lies close to the Court in a fold of the river. Among some corbels that have been removed in past restorations, and which are usually custered around the font, is one of a ram's head. This may well be the best evidence we have of the appearance of the breed whose fleeces made the Cotswolds famous.

After Bibury one reaches the large estates at Williamstrip and Hatherop. Here is an atmosphere of firm proprietorship and restrained grandeur, with deer and high elms and iron railings. The two mansions, of

Earl St Aldwyn at Williamstrip and of Sir Thomas Bazley at Hatherop
Castle, stand almost opposite in Hatherop village, with their land spreading away in opposite directions. The river here flows in a deep defile round
the high ground on which the church and manor at Coln St Aldwyn
stand, and then curves majestically into the village of Quenington through
falling banks of beech trees. Quenington has become considerably residential of recent years and typical of the new style of Cotswold village
development. Still dominating it, however, is the fourteenth century
Preceptory site of the order of the Knights of St John, where the gatehouse still stands. The Hospitallers spread their influence wide over the
Cotswolds in the Middle Ages. They were often associated with clumps
of ash on high ground, and beds of wild colchicum or autumn crocus,
which was used as a drug. One of their distant and exposed chantry
chapels was on the beacon at Chedworth, where it was then visible along
the lower Coln, and a local variant of the proverb about 'fog on the hill'
was 'when St John puts on his hat Bibury boys beware of that'.

All roads have now become relatively flat because the Thames valley
has been reached. Here lies Fairford, in spirit a Cotswold town although
it lies on the edge of the river gravels and faces towards Swindon, which
is now having an unknown social influence upon all this neighbourhood.
Fairford's market square and commercial frontages bear the mark of
Georgian rural England, with its demure civility. The tradition otherwise
is of the wool men and the fifteenth century, and despite its being the
present home of Concorde and supersonic aircraft, its fame resides in
twenty-eight church windows.

The glass in Fairford church is unique both in its quality and extent.
The glazing is attributed to the munificence of John Tame, a wool
stapler who was rebuilding the church towards the end of the fifteenth
century as the Wars of the Roses were drawing to their close. The windows
are certainly Flemish in so far as glass firing was an advanced Flemish
art, but this was the period of King's College, Cambridge, and the
Henry VII chapel at Westminster, when many famous English artists
were also working in glass. All the internal evidence suggests that the
windows were designed for Fairford, and may have been associated
with the King himself. Henry VII had acquired in 1487 from the
Countess of Warwick, daughter of the Kingmaker (Neville, Earl of
Warwick, 1428–71), 114 manors sequestrated after the battle of Barnet,
and Fairford was one of fourteen in the county of Gloucester. It may be
of significance that Henry VII's image appears at this exact period on
corbels in both the contemporary churches of Northleach and Chedworth.

John Tame intended his windows to read as a picture story from the

Bible, and they certainly represent a rich man's contribution to the new enlightenment. The glazier's art was so new and effective that, like television in our day, it bid fair to rival the appeal of prose to our reason by adding the seduction of visual sense. Notwithstanding, and even divested of all religious intent, the Fairford windows would remain art of a universal order, completely resolved, exquisite in textural quality and arresting in design. In such a case there is no need to question the origins or motives of their authors; it is sufficient that they should exist.

Leach Valley

Associated with the Coln and characteristic of the smaller Cotswold rivers is the Leach. Drayton wrote :

> Clear Coln and lively Leach so down from Cotswold's plain
> At Lechdale linking hands come likewise to support
> The mother of great Thames.

The Leach rises near Northleach in a beautiful small hamlet called Hampnett.

Northleach was another of England's noted wool towns. Its church is closely related to that of its sister staple town at Chipping Campden. Each has the same slender octagonal columns to support a wide span of roof. Northleach certainly bears comparison with the greatest of the wool churches of eastern England and its south porch is one of the best examples of fifteenth-century architecture to be found in all England. It is ascetic despite its elegance, and breathes an intellectual Gothic confidence, as if to dispute the need for any Renaissance. Above it is a priest's, or sacristan's cell, which is approached from the south aisle by a newel stairway. The room has a large fireplace with an ingeniously disguised chimney.

The most important feature of Northleach church is the monumental brasses of the wool men. These recall vividly the social background of these men of the late Middle Ages, their wealth and piety coupled with intense personal pride amidst a tragic awareness of human transience. The woolpacks on which they stand, the stapler's marks, the arms of the City of Calais (which was still English), the mixed Latin and English inscriptions and Roman and Arabic numerals, the puns, and the etchings of the sheep themselves, can be absorbed for hours until a whole moment of historical transition comes alive with startling immediacy. It seems impossible to believe that this was a period of supreme unrest, when bitter internecine wars were drawing to their close.

Though little more than a village in size, Northleach has an ancient municipal structure, with elected officers bearing medieval titles, and a Court Leet as well as its modern parish council. On the Foss Way stands a big building which was built in the late eighteenth century by that wealthy clothier, dilettante and reformer, Sir Onesiphorous Paul, whose strange Christian name is commemorated on his memorial in Gloucester Cathedral. Northleach despite its size has a grammar school, a hospital, and a bench of magistrates.

The Leach flows on past many well known farms of high reputation, like Aldsworth, where the last pure-bred flock of Cotswold sheep were to be found until recently. The twin villages of Eastleach Martin and East-leach Turville cluster on its banks. The stepping bridge is often illustrated in the guidebooks. These, and nearby Southrop, bring to mind the name of John Keble and the Oxford Movement. He was vicar of Eastleach and Burthorpe and later of Southrop. He knew the country from child-hood, having been born at Fairford and brought up in the vicarage at Coln St Aldwyn. If there was something peculiarly English in what Keble brought to the revived Anglican faith, with its distinctive Pre-Raphaelite environment, this was echoed by his neighbour William Morris at Kelm-scot, which lies nearby, close to the point where the Leach finally reaches the Thames.

North Cotswolds

The Cotswolds in the north differ from the southern Cotswolds in a quite decisive manner. It is not because of geology, nor of climate, nor of the style of the architecture, though stucco and pebbledash are used more freely in the damper south. The differences are cultural. The north Cotswolds belong to the West Midlands and are part of the old kingdom of Mercia. Today their tourist patronage is still Midland-based, as the Birmingham and Warwickshire numberplates on the cars at weekends indicate. The southern Cotswolds belong in spirit to King Alfred's Wessex and the softer world of Wiltshire limestone still typified at Castle Combe.

The Cotswold town which should have no doubt where it stands in this dilemma is Winchcombe on the western escarpment and north of Cheltenham. Winchcombe once shared with Coventry and Lichfield the honour of being a royal capital of Mercia. The legends of the Mercian kings have persisted there through the centuries. The Tudor royal castle of Sudeley close by will not disappoint the visitor despite the fact that much of it is ruin. Like Kenilworth it is deeply impressive in its scale and setting, and one walks easily back into the Tudor past. Nearby, too, are the remains of the Abbey of Hailes, one of the great Cistercian monasteries like Tintern, Rievaulx and Fountains. Its possession of a relic of the Holy Blood had made it famous throughout medieval England as a centre for pilgrimage. The *George* hotel at Winchcombe, with its gallery round the courtyard, was said to have been a pilgrims' inn.

From Hailes one follows the foothills past Stanway and Stanton to Broadway. Stanway, with the oriel window of its hall and its gatehouse said to be designed by Inigo Jones, is probably the best early Jacobean house in Gloucestershire. The nearby tithe barn, built in the late fourteenth century for the Abbey of Tewkesbury, is also a structural triumph of span. Its massive stone roof is still supported on the original oak principals. Stanton is another of the limestone villages which approaches architectural perfection. It owed much to its rebuilding by an architect-squire, Sir Phillip Stott. The work was carried out in the 1920s, which was a good period for restoration, since many skilled craftsmen were unemployed.

Today the undisputed capital of the north Cotswolds is Chipping Campden. The wealth of Campden in the golden days of wool would have been prodigious. The leading wool merchants or factors each had their headquarters in London and their warehouses in Calais. Of these, William Grevel is proclaimed on his monument in the church to be the 'flower of the wool merchants of all England' and 'former citizen of London'. Another magnificent tomb commemorates the woolman Sir Baptist Hicks, also of London, and his 'dear consort' Elizabeth Viscountess Campden. In the town the Market Hall and the almshouses, the old Grammar School and Grevel's house are among an amazing number of examples of late medieval architecture. Because of this endowment Campden was much under the influence of the rediscovery of the Cotswold idiom in architecture by Dawber and others at the turn of the century. It was blessed at this time by the presence of C. R. Ashbee and his Guild of Handicrafts, who worked in the Silk Mill. Here was another echo of the agony of William Morris groaning above the rattle of the shuttles and the roar of the blast furnaces that formed the unresolved harmony of nineteenth-century England. Much skilled work was done in Campden as a result, and is still carried on. Mr Hart's metalwork has become internationally known, and Sir Gordon Russell's influence on design has been widely felt. Sir Gordon was born at Snowshill and lives in Campden. There is no doubt that the feel of places like Campden and Bibury has done much to inspire our own times to preserve the Cotswolds by declaring them an Area of Outstanding Natural Beauty, although the beauty lies as much in artefact as in nature and is quite inseparable from it.

Outside Campden is Dover's Hill. In the seventeenth century Robert Dover, an energetic Captain in the Army, and anti-Puritan, organised a sports meeting up on this commanding table which continued for 200 years as a big local event called the Dover or the Cotswold Games. They are mentioned in Drayton's *Polyalbion* and in many local writings. They were always linked with Campden's Whitsuntide merrymaking known as Scuttlebrook Wake. Their fame spread throughout the Midlands, until gradually ruffians from the Back Country used the occasion annually to demoralise and play havoc with the neighbourhood. By the end of the 1830s as many as 30,000 people are said to have arrived and camped. The Games were officially closed in 1841, but have been revived today in their original form as a sports meeting only, and they still take place at Whitsuntide.

After Broadway, which lies in the county of Worcester, the road leads through Willersey and on to the two Subedges, Weston and Aston, and Mickleton. While these villages, and little Saintbury, a perfect Cotswold hamlet, still owe everything to the idiom of the limestone, they stand upon the ridged and furrowed clays of the Midland shires. The oak trees become shapely with their feet in the deeper clay, and the elms exceed their height on the brashy wolds. Beyond Mickleton is Meon Hill, an ancient camp and last outpost of the Cotswolds, being only a few miles from Stratford-on-Avon.

The Rev Richard Graves of Mickleton planted, among other pleasures that his friend the poet Shenstone inspired, the avenue that leads to Kiftsgate on the hillside overhanging Mickleton. Beyond Kiftsgate, itself a most famous garden, at Hidcote Bartrim are the Hidcote gardens, now the property of the National Trust, and the result of the lifetime's work of the horticulturalist Laurence Johnstone. Hidcote, in its use of hedges and its range of alkaline-tolerant plants, has over the last half century had a profound influence on Cotswold gardening in particular and on English gardening in general. Both it and Kiftsgate should be seen.

In the church at Mickleton is the quaint memorial of that early blue-stocking, Utrecia Smith. She was the daughter of the curate who had taught Richard Graves his Latin, and inspired Shenstone's *Ode to Ophelia*.

The final circuit round the Warwickshire border at Ilmington and back to the Foss Way could include a visit to Ebrington, whose ancient manor house is still the home of Earl Fortescue. In Ebrington church is the tomb of his ancestor John Fortescue, Chancellor of England in the fifteenth century and author of the first English law book. A Lancastrian in sentiment, he had submitted to Edward IV after the battle of Tewkesbury, and was allowed to live out his retirement at Ebrington, where he died an old man in 1471. Ebrington, like Chudleigh in Devon, is a village about which funny stories are told. It's in Ebrington that folk must have manured the church tower to make it grow, and where they grow the hedges tall to keep the cuckoo in.

Windrush Valley

In the high country above the Stanway Woods there lies an expanse of woldland that is among the most typical of the Cotswold scene. It is here that the Windrush rises. The fields are large and in places featureless, and used to be well stocked with hares and partridges, with the result that shooting and coursing provided the winter's diversion. Large corn farms like Trafalgar, reminiscently named, have come back into their own since World War II, but with them methods that the partridge no longer enjoys. Continued prosperity has also brought maturity in the form of shelter planting to many upland sites. However, a village like Cutsdean remains one of those exposed fortresses of stone that darken into invisibility when drenched with rain, and mark the site of ancient habitations in the open sheepwalk of other days. The whole scene breathes the spirit of the wolds. Through it passes that most rewarding of all drives, from Cirencester along the White Way and on to Snowshill and the Tower at Broadway. This is a journey of such wild seclusion and disregarded time that it has few equals in southern England. It is the kind of scenic route along the high escarpment that would be spoiled forever by overtrimming the verges or improving the track. It is not so long ago that this road was gated for most of its length. It certainly offers the visitor from the wide lands of the New World a glimpse of England's own outback as it was before the motor car cut it back to present size.

The first sizeable Windrush village to be reached, and perhaps the most unspoilt, is Temple Guiting. As its name suggests, it was an outpost of the crusading Order of the Knights Templar, which once operated from the Temple in London. When the Templars were disbanded all over Europe, their lands were sequestrated and often granted to the Knights Hospitaller, a more restrained Order which was to be richly represented along the courses of the Cotswold rivers. Temple Guiting was granted to the Knights of St John at Quenington. Its church was practically rebuilt in the eighteenth century in a Renaissance style, unusual in the Cotswolds, but it suits its parklike setting, and while we cannot be certain of what we have lost, it appears that at the time no one had any regret.

Lower Guiting, or Guiting Power as it is often called, is a sister village of different character. It is typical of the larger agricultural villages of the Cotswolds. The cottages have a distinctive simplicity which is enhanced by their grouping, set back upon an expanse of manorial waste that serves them for a village green. Some 50 years ago Guiting was forgotten and distressed, as was frequently the case during the years of agricultural depression, when the Cotswolds were among the most marginal of all English farmlands. Of recent years a degree of wealth has returned to all such villages, and the two Guitings, so different in their way, have also regained a state of well-being without self-consciousness. Close to the Guitings come the ancient Guiting woods, now worked by the Forestry Commission, and round them are many satellite hamlets like low-lying Kineton and upland Farmcot. On the hill at Bemborough is the Cotswold Farm Park, a new venture established to preserve local breeds of farm animals threatened with extinction—such as the Old Gloucester cattle (whose milk made the Double Gloucester cheese); Longhorn cattle, the ancient Midland breed; Spotted Jacob's sheep; certain breeds of poultry, and farmhorses.

The Windrush flows on through Naunton and by way of Harford Bridge to Bourton-on-the-Water. Bourton, by virtue of its good hotels and shops, is something more than a village. It has never been an administrative centre like Northleach or Stow-on-the-Wold, but it is very much a place for visitors. The river here widens into a formal canal which runs through the middle of the town. It is the eighteenth-century flavour of its stone bridges that gives to Bourton its affinity with Burford and Fairford, all limestone towns in their private valleys, where the plain seems imminent and yet the winds seem still. It is unfortunate that Bourton's church suffered rebuilding in poor neo-Gothic taste in the second half of the nineteenth century, and it has also lost its association with a manorial precinct, which deprives any village of its token of continuity and sense of place.

Nowadays Bourton is a town with problems. It has become a 'honeypot', like Bibury, in the words of the Department of the Environment, and siphons off the coachloads of tourists, for whom it caters so well that other villages for miles round are undoubtedly relieved of pressure upon their own amenities. Tourist attractions abound. One of these is Birdland, which is no vulgar gimmick but a local man's sensitive and scrupulous contribution to the growing interest in wild life. The model village is another attraction. The working of gravel pits has made life hideous for Bourton residents, but when extraction ceases, the pits will shelter wild life and provide recreation.

The so-called Bourton Vale, which is the only broad stretch of vale to be found on the high Cotswolds, is part conditioned by the dual river system formed by the Windrush's little tributaries Dikler and Eye. These streams are true village-makers, inducing settlement along their sequestered banks and offering shelter of the most exclusive kind by the disciplined use of stone. The Dikler rises north-west of Stow in the lakes at Donnington and flows south. On its banks are Upper and Lower Swell. The Eye in turn flows east and waters the Slaughters. These are four villages of the highest architectural quality, which is much enhanced in places by the water frontages. All are thronged with tourists in summer, but at other times of year may be enjoyed at will. High above them to the east is the bleak and ancient town of Stow-on-the-Wold.

Stow, on the Foss Way, is a very ancient settlement. It was an eighteenth-century joke that Stow lacked earth, fire and water, but had plenty of air, but the Roman legions had earlier known that this was scarcely kind, as relics of their occupation show. Stow church is certainly the most commanding landmark in the Cotswolds. The spacious marketplace seems to have given Stow a new retailing life in the age of out-of-town shopping, and the motorcar has certainly redressed the balance of its lost railway station. Before both cars and trains Stow's fame rested upon its horse fairs held in May and October–November. Their charter goes back to the days of King Edward III (1327–77), and they continue on a lesser scale today.

East of Bourton are the Rissingtons, three charming villages grappling the undercliff of the Wolds. Little Rissington has the Royal Air Force Central Flying School on the flat tableland above. The lights of Rissington at night can be seen from high ground in most parts of the northern Cotswolds. On Bourton's southern flank, which separates the Windrush from the Sherborne valley, is the hill hamlet of Clapton, distinguished over many years for growing strawberries, and strawberries certainly thrive on the alkaline limestone soil. Linking Clapton to Great Rissington is forgotten New Bridge lane spanning the meandering Windrush in a valley infinitely lost.

Again to the east at Windrush village the river meets the Sherborne brook. Here the visitor might complete the journey to Burford by first leaving the river and following the Foss Way back to Farmington to enter another charmingly private valley which is still a part of the Windrush system. Here one can see the Cotswolds farmed as they used to be, extensively and with style. From Farmington to Haycroft Bottom the road leads to Sherborne. Sherborne Park was the seat of the Dutton family for many centuries but has now become an institution. The Duttons promoted the famous Bibury Club, a race-meeting as old as Newmarket itself and patronised by King Charles II. In 1681 when Parliament met at Oxford the Newmarket Spring Meeting was transferred to Bibury racecourse. The romantic allure of Bibury races inspired several well known Victorian prints such as 'The Ruling Passion' and 'The Day of Reckoning' by Edmund Waller, a talented Victorian artist whose family were squires of Farmington. Waller was an artist ahead of his time as a realistic painter of animals. He used to study his horses in the riding school in Cheltenham, and paint the Cotswold hounds in their old kennels at Whaddon Lane, in between, we are told, bouts of revelry at local inns. Cheltenham in those days had its sporting *demi-monde*, while the fame of Fred Archer lingered in Prestbury and before Adam Lindsay Gordon had gone to Australia.

Before Burford is reached the road leads past the Barringtons, two most attractive villages lying on the hillside. The house set in the park at Great Barrington is architecturally and in its situation one of the most pleasing in a county generally not rich in the grand Georgian style. It was built by George II's Lord Chancellor, Earl Talbot, who is buried in the church. There is a charming tablet to Earl Talbot's daughter in the chancel, which contains a fine medallion by Nollekens.

Just across the Gloucestershire boundary one comes upon Taynton, the Oxfordshire village hewn out of the stone of which it is formed, and sympathetically modelled by the mason's tools. There seems to be more than mere skill in the evolution of such a place that fulfils so perfectly the simple domestic needs of its time. Its famous quarry, from whose stone Blenheim was built, lies outside the village, and a fine ridge of building stone runs all the way from Farmington along the north bank of the Sherborne brook. This has left its mark in the social as well as the structural idiom of the villages. In such a world the mason was master, and the poor farmworker little regarded. The apprenticed craftsman was always known as 'Mr' So-and-So and never 'Smith' or 'Brown', and no one ever forgot it. The subsoil made the man.

It is this which makes Burford the fitting end of the Windrush pilgrimage. In Burford's single broad street one studies the unfolding history of Cotswold life over a period of 500 years. Details may change with time; styles of mullion, gable, dormer and porch evolve, but the material that came up from the ground below in blocks of limestone or frost-rent slats forms the whole exterior from foundation to the eaves. Burford has also its old Grammar School buildings, its almshouses given by the King-maker and its Priory where Speaker Lenthall (1591–1662) lived (he was held in the curule chair of the House of Commons during the Long Parliament and has caused every Speaker to be 'reluctant' since). However, most famous of all the names in English history to be associated with Burford is surely that of Lucius Carey Viscount Falkland 'the incomparable young man' of Clarendon's eulogy. Brought up at the Priory, young Falkland was the reputed author of the remark that seems to sum up all that this part of the Cotswolds suggests: 'When it is not necessary to change it i necessary not to change'.

Burford has survived to carry out the truth of this old wisdom, and is now a most prized centre of the Cotswolds for beauty, architecture and crafts (see Chapter 7).

Frome or Stroud Valley

The main Cotswold river which does not flow into the Thames is the Frome, and it was the little Frome that created Stroud as an international centre of the cloth trade. Its source lies far from Stroud in a spring near the high escarpment at the Cranham woods near Birdlip. It flows back into a mysterious country nearly as far as Cirencester before it decides to turn west again towards Chalford. The head of the Frome is surrounded by the high wooded landscape of Miserden, with its ancient mansion itself set in tidy farmland. Although new houses have been added, Miserden is still one of those villages that have kept themselves correct architecturally, and has been able to resist those package-deal components that threaten Cotswold architecture at the present time. Nearby Cranham has two big events, a deer-roast and feast, and a cheese-rolling when the stout of leg and wind race each other down the steep hill after the revolving cheeses.

The river on its way to Stroud flows round an incredibly isolated plateau of which Bisley is the centre. The whole area is full of good houses and old yeoman farms lying at the head of deep re-entrants like the Slad valley. Near Miserden itself are good houses like Sudgrove and Wishanger. At Bisley there is Jayne's Court, and Lypiatt Park, where the Gunpowder Plot is said to have been concocted. Generally the architecture is of a higher order here than in the eastern Cotswolds, largely no doubt because it came under the middle-class influence of the cloth trade, and also because its well sheltered combes were more fertile in the eighteenth century than the open sheepwalks of the wolds. Certainly the opposite is true today, when large flat fields give mechanised argiculture the advantage. This is also a precipitous John Peel kind of country with steeply wooded ledges which, although it lies in Cotswold Hunt territory, is better traversed on foot or on a stout pony than negotiated by a fast horse. A quaint feature here for many years was the Tolstoyan settlement of Whiteway colony, which refused to use or accept

Q

money or government or public services and relied instead upon its own self-help. Its story has been told by one of the founders, Nellie Shaw, in her book *Whiteway*, which also tells how a vicar of Miserden came forward to help the colonists, then extremely unpopular, by providing such basic human needs as burial.

From Miserden the little Frome descends in a series of falling pools through Edgeworth to Daneway, into one of those utterly lost valleys of the Cotswolds that lies across the road to nowhere. Before World War II, when all Cotswold roads were of crushed limestone which washed away on the hills with every storm of rain, the tourist never ventured into such a fastness. In a bad winter the inhabitant just waited for the thaw. Today it is possible to enter it by narrow but reasonable roads. Nevertheless there is still a gingerbread forest snugness here, an element of mystery as smoke rises from habitations sunk deep in the folds of beechwoods.

In the heart of such a world is Daneway House, aspiring to be the most romantic house in all the Cotswold country with its two rivals Owlpen Manor and Compton Casey. For many years Daneway was a craft centre of national renown. It was here, some time before the 1914 war, that Ernest Gimson and the Barnsley brothers enjoyed their fruitful association. Disciples of William Morris, whom Gimson had just known, they were young architects who eschewed the mass-produced at the time when it was beginning to dominate our national economy. At the Arts and Crafts Exhibition in 1890 Ernest Gimson had exhibited his first notable pieces of furniture (see Chapter 8). It was his philosophy to unite architecture with the furnishings it would house and to achieve the highest standard of workmanship in the use of unalloyed materials. When the three friends first came to the Cotswolds they found the atmosphere which they sought, a tradition of craftsmanship and natural materials like oak and stone waiting to be married. After some years at Pinbury Park, which was leased to them by Lord Bathurst, Gimson moved to the old saw-mills at Daneway, where he established his workshops, using the house as a showroom and sharing it with the gamekeeper. Sidney Barnsley worked on his own, making furniture of exquisite finish. Ernest Barnsley returned to architecture, doing some local work, but notably at Rodmarton Manor, which was one of the few big houses to be newly built in the period before the 1914 war. All three men lived at Sapperton in cottages improved to their own design, and each today lies buried in its churchyard. They exerted a strong influence on local craft in the Cotswolds and upon the conscience of the contract builder. As a result there are left behind many native families who are still doing fine architectural craftwork. The now very popular exhibition of the work of the Guild of Gloucestershire Craftsmen that is held each August in Painswick was stimulated by the Gimson tradition. Today students and young artists make their pilgrimage to Sapperton, but they find nothing but the tombstones and Rodmarton Manor, the last place where much of the Daneway group's work is kept together.

Between the heights of Oakridge in the north and Frampton Mansel on the south bank the Frome links with the Thames & Severn Canal and the Great Western Railway to enter a valley rich in industrial archaeology. Some of the canal locks are themselves fascinating, pitted with alkali and hirsute with algae, but still revealing the clean-cut anatomy of the millwright's craft. Many of the mills are as good architecturally as their owners' houses, and as lofty and clean in design. Beechwoods all along the north bank fall to the deep valley level, giving it the name of the Golden Valley from the glory of the beech leaves in autumn. Early industrial tradition is noticeable, too, in the parallel Nailsworth valley, where the Frome's sister stream, the little Avon, flows down from Cherington lakes through the attractive defile of Avening. Here Longford's mill recalls the former close association between the industrial proprietor and his business that retained for industry the personal touch of village life. The Playnes of Longford were part of the Stroud millocracy of families, of whom the Pauls and the Shepherds before and the Marleys and Winterbothams later were among those whose capital sustained the neighbourhood. Theirs was the golden age of West of England cloth, when the fine uniforms of Europe's aristocratic armies came from the Stroud valleys, and it was said that a review by the Czar on a wet day might so stain the white jackets of the Imperial Guard that the news would bring drunkenness to Stroud at the prospect of weeks of renewed work and wages. This, too, it must be remembered, was the age of hunting pink and the billiard table, the cloth of both being products of Stroud's skill. Today it is Australian wool that fills the warehouses, but makes cloths so fine that much becomes dresses for women and the lightest evening wear at that (see Chapter 6).

Rising up south from the Stroud valley are Minchinhampton and Rodborough Commons, an elevated plateau of close-grazed turf where one gains the impression of communion with sky rather than earth. From them one looks across a void to the prominences of Selsley Hill in the south and Haresfield Beacon in the west, both having grand views of the Severn glinting as it winds its serpentine course along Gloucester Vale. On this plateau is Minchinhampton, now a very residential district, but formerly another wool town with a fine Market Hall like those at Tetbury, Dursley, and Chipping Campden. Gatcombe Park, which overhangs the Nailsworth valley, was once the home of David Ricardo, the economist, a disciple of Adam Smith and the father of modern banking. Amberley, another village on the ridge, is the Enderby of *John Halifax, Gentleman*.

North of the Stroud valley the two re-entrants to the Cotswolds are the Slad and Painswick valleys. Slad valley cuts deeply back towards Bisley and is famous now as the setting of Laurie Lee's *Cider with Rosie*. Painswick is another small Cotswold town of outstanding interest and beauty. Its churchyard is famed for its yews, reputedly ninety-nine but hard to count. They were there in the eighteenth century, and Samuel Rudder recalls how elegant ladies sat beside them in the sun. Painswick has fine houses both in the town and in the valleys round, all closely linked with the cloth trade. The Court House behind the church is where King Charles I slept on his march to Gloucester in 1643. When Essex relieved the county town and Severn bastion, it was to Painswick that the King returned, in dejected spirits, a month later.

Stroud today may have the dismembered charm of a Lowry painting. It is certainly a victim of the age of *laissez-faire* and was choked from want of planning when the high-pitched red brick houses were built into its steep hillsides. Cinder paths, deserted mills and rushy ponds mark the old origins. The people, however, are brisk and forthright, and less devious than typical Cotswold folk. Much of this stems from the private world of wool, and its associations with the Yorkshire and Wiltshire towns in the past. Politics in Stroud were formerly mannerless and violent. A notable Conservative champion was once the late Sir Stafford Cripps's father, who later became Lord Parmoor, and his opponent in those days was Charles Peter Allen, Asquith's President of the Board of Trade, who lived at Whiteshill. Stroud today is politically more docile, but its industry is vigorous and expanding, and very diversified. Employment is among the highest in the country, and the town boasts the only general cultural festival in Gloucestershire, of poetry and drama, which takes place in the late autumn.

South Cotswolds

South of Stroud the long river valleys have ended and the flat brashy tableland comprises what colloquially is called 'Beaufortshire'. This is because it lies in the land of the Beaufort Hunt and has long come under the influence of Badminton, the seat of the Dukes of Beaufort. Badminton has for centuries been a centre for lovers of field sports and equestrian skills. There is a well known sporting print of the chimney sweep at

Chipping Sodbury saying, 'Sorry, gentlemen, I can't vote for you 'cause I 'unts with the Duke'. Today Badminton is particularly well known for the three-day equestrian event that, with royal participation, has stimulated the interest which has brought Britain many new Olympic honours.

The vale that lies beneath the high escarpment of the southern Cotswolds is the Vale of Berkeley, and in the distance is Berkeley Castle, flanked by two more modern kinds of power stations, of the atomic variety along the Severn estuary. The promontories of the hills above the Vale are sharp and isolated, offering magnificent views of the great river with the Black Mountains of Wales in the distance. Such scenic points are Hawkesbury, Nibley, Stinchcombe, and, further along the ridge, Selsley Common. At Hawkesbury is the Somerset monument; the Post Office tower at Ozleworth is a new pinnacle in the landscape; the Tyndale monument at Nibley commemorates the local man who first translated the Bible into our natural tongue; and the golf course at Stinchcombe (a spur extending out into the Vale above Dursley) provides perhaps the finest panoramic view in the whole of southern England.

A feature of this escarpment is the towns which lie just beneath it on the lias beds where the springs break out, places like Wotton-under-Edge, Dursley, Uley and Woodchester. Each carries sharply the authentic style of the limestone architecture, although the sharp hauls from them seem to emphasise their snug aversion to the windswept world above. All again had connections in the past with weaving and spinning. Tall cottages built in the banks often had a floor added to make room for the more modest hand looms. This may be seen in particular at Wotton--under-Edge, a market town which received its charter as long ago as 1252. Wotton, with many good buildings and narrow streets, shops and public houses, stands in need of modern planning, especially now that the M5 along the Berkeley Vale has made it more accessible than at any time in its self-sufficient past.

On the ledge above Wotton is the hill village of Alderley, which contains one or two distinguished houses, particularly the Grange where Matthew Hale was born (1609–76). Hale was Lord Chief Justice of England and one of the most important figures in the establishment of English law in the period of Civil War and Restoration. His *History of the Common Law* was published after he had died and been buried in Alderley churchyard. His descendants still own land in Alderley, although their big estate has been broken up and the present head of the family is a New Zealander.

Possibly no part of England is more wild and unimpaired than this underledge of the southern Cotswolds. Ozleworth valley cannot be crossed and scarcely penetrated, but the hexagonal Norman tower of its small church standing within the stable enclosure of the big house is unique. Boxwell on the other bank must also be one of the few places in which virtually nothing has changed since Prince Rupert was a frequent visitor and Charles II spent his night there after the battle of Worcester. It is still owned by the same family. Newark Park belongs to the National Trust.

On the far side of Stinchcombe Hill lie two more cloth towns, Dursley and Uley. Dursley has grown greatly because Lister's engineering works, once a humble foundry, are placed there (see p 132). Uley's clothing days are over and most of its inhabitants now work at Lister's, but some of its fame rests upon the presence of Owlpen Manor. This is a modest but perfectly gabled sixteenth-century manor house. It is hard to say what makes it so romantic, but such it is, and even Rudder wrote in the eighteenth century : 'It is a kind of gloomy retreat, the church and the house lie dispersedly at the top of a deep narrow coombe almost environed by steep hills, covered with hanging beechwoods and forming a kind of amphitheatre'. A wonderful view of this amphitheatre is obtained from the main road out of Dursley as one climbs the flank of Stinchcombe Hill.

Beyond Uley lie Nympsfield and Woodchester, and down the defile of Woodchester Park one is back again in the clothing valley of Nailsworth. Woodchester is known for its huge Roman settlement, of which one magnificent mosaic pavement is opened for public view once in several years. Then as the crow flies one is soon back to Horsley, and up on the wolds again, as one passes the ancient manorial farmhouse of Chavenage. One has no doubt that here again are the limestone hills which bred the sheep that made the cloth mills possible.

As the Cotswolds level out in their course towards the Foss Way again and towards the Wiltshire border, the land improves in quality and the influence of grass begins to assert itself. Such free galloping terrain has always favoured horse-raising and the hunting of the fox. Here the houses, too, become much more than the modest manors in the farmland. There is Westonbirt, Lewis Vulliamy's masterpiece, built between 1840 and 1870 for a member of the ancient and wealthy family of Holford. Westonbirt was architecturally matched with R. S. Holford's London residence—Dorchester House in Park Lane, now the Dorchester Hotel and possibly the finest of all London's vanished private houses. Westonbirt remains a fashionable girls' school. But more famous is its Arboretum, which is always open to the public. This is a unique national possession, now cared for by the Forestry Commission.

R. S. Holford's passion for architecture was responsible for many less lavish country house conversions in this part of the world, including the *White Hart* at Tetbury. In all of them Lewis Vulliamy had a hand. Because of the better land on the Wiltshire side of the Cotswolds, the initial endowment of each farmhouse was greater than in the poorer parts of the oolitic plateau. Doughton on the Tetbury road is probably a fair example of one that escaped alteration because a second house was built opposite to it on the other side of the road.

Notes to this chapter are on page 310.

10

The Planner's View: the Foreseeable Future

Norman Collins

As LONG AGO as 1945 the late John Dower in his famous report to the then Minister of Town and Country Planning referred to the Cotswolds as an area of high amenity value which, in his estimation, 'was deserving and requiring the special concern of local and central planning authorities in order to safeguard its landscape beauty, farm use and wild life and to increase appropriately facilities for open air recreation'. The Dower Report was concerned with problems relating to the establishment of National Parks in England and Wales, but the author drew attention to other areas where the scenery was not so wild which he thought required special protection. When Sir Arthur Hobhouse's Committee made recommendations to the Minister on the Dower Report in 1947, it described these tracts of outstanding landscape beauty as Conservation Areas. Selecting the Cotswolds as one such area, the Committee particularly remarked that it fell short of the National Park standard because it lacked wildness.

Most of the recommendations of the Hobhouse Committee were made statutory by the National Parks and Access to the Countryside Act in 1949, but there were inevitable changes in emphasis and definition, particularly with regard to the Conservation Areas. The Report had referred to these as areas 'whose contribution to the wider enjoyment of the countryside is so important that special measures should be taken to preserve their natural beauty'. Perhaps this reference inspired the name 'Areas of Outstanding Natural Beauty' which was substituted for Conservation Areas in the Act.

In 1966 the designation of the Cotswolds as the largest Area of Outstanding Natural Beauty gave statutory effect to a situation which had in fact been recognised for a very long time. The county councils concerned, always conscious of the beauty of the Cotswolds, had taken every available opportunity to safeguard the remarkable character and beauty of the area. In 1947 the Town and Country Planning Act made it possible to include Areas of Great Landscape Value in development plans and large parts of the Cotswolds were defined in this way. Showing the Cotswolds as an Area of Great Landscape Value presumed a particularly strict control on development to protect the scenic amenities—for example, the siting, design and materials of buildings had to be carefully considered, but this did not intend that initiative in good architectural design should be stifled. It should be understood that farm buildings are for the most part exempt from planning control, and I will have a little more to say about this later. Advertisements, mineral workings, camping sites and other types of development, such as overhead power lines, which might have a considerable impact on the scenery, were most carefully controlled to ensure the least possible damage to the local amenities.

The conservation of woodlands in the Cotswolds has been one of the county council's particular concerns, and trees have been preserved by order where there appeared to be threat of felling. In other places landowners have been encouraged to enter into dedication agreements with the Forestry Commission to ensure the long-term maintenance of the landscape.

In 1968 the Countryside Act consolidated the earlier legislation and set up the Countryside Commission with powers to encourage the provision and improvement of facilities for recreation in the countryside. The county councils have been encouraged in their endeavours by the support of their district councils, and the local amenity societies. Broadly the effect of the AONB designation strengthens the local authorities in resisting pressure for unsuitable development. The Countryside Commission expects planning powers to be used with particular regard for the preservation and enhancement of scenic beauty. There are no special administrative arrangements following upon designation but planning authorities may, if they wish, set up a special committee to deal with the area and may delegate such powers to that committee as they think fit. As the Cotswold AONB extends into a number of counties, a Joint Advisory Committee was appointed to include members who were not county councillors.

In an Area of Outstanding Natural Beauty the powers and duties of local planning authorities are the same as those in any other area but they may exercise powers available to them under the Countryside and other Acts in so far as they relate to the preservation and enhancement of natural beauty. It would be possible, for example, for any county council concerned to make orders restricting traffic in the interests of amenity, and when one considers the expected increase in the number of motor cars in association with the certainty of greater public leisure, this would seem likely to become very important at some time in the future.

Grants are also available to local authorities for planting trees, the treatment of derelict land, for access orders or agreements and the acquisition of land for access.

It must, however, be appreciated that all these measures are not intended to bring about any change in the general character of the Cotswolds. They certainly result in intensifying the consciousness of the beauties which already exist, but farming and the other uses of land go on. New forms of land use and development continue to be the subject of control by the local planning authorities but always with specific reference to the objectives which I have explained.

Characteristics of Landscape and Villages

Enhancement of the appearance of the Cotswolds is therefore an important planning objective. The improvement in the appearance of derelict land and the clearance of eyesores has the curious result that unless people have known the area before the clearance there is virtually no way for them to assess the change. Memories of an ugliness of the past, like those of a horrible event, tend to lapse into oblivion. I wonder how many people remember the squalid acres of semi-derelict wartime buildings which used to defile the Daglingworth countryside along Ermin Street until the mid-1960s (p 215) or, for that matter, the insistent line of great black poles which carried a telephone cable along the same road from Birdlip to Cirencester. These horrors have disappeared, but sometimes the removal of eyesores can be a very tedious and time-consuming business. More often than not there are legal difficulties relating to compensation claims and hardship. Nevertheless, gradually and determinedly the planning authorities make effective changes for the better. Even improvements to the roads across the Cotswolds produce, in their wake, other compensations which the general public takes for granted. Mile upon mile of new Cotswold dry-stone walling measure the improved highway's progress across the uplands at a cost of about £10 per yd run : a high price indeed, and like all other craftwork getting costlier year by year. But surely the restoration of part of the traditional scenery of the Cotswolds, in locations where it has the greatest possible effect on passers-by, must be worth it.

So the designation of the Cotswolds AONB engrossed in the approved development plans of the counties concerned ensures the future conservation of this unique agricultural upland. But there are towns, communities and smaller settlements in the Cotswolds which, with the country-side around, form a complex social organism extremely sensitive to economic pressures. In fact a study of this situation reveals in micro-cosm the fundamental change that has occurred all over the western world in comparatively recent times. Town and country are no longer separate. We have, in fact, a symbiotic situation where town and country are tending to complement each other and establish a new balance to replace the old hierarchical system of settlements. The rebalancing pro-cess is still far from complete and the need for it is certainly less great in some areas than in others. In general those areas which suffered very badly in the Industrial Revolution are suffering the greatest upheaval now.

The Industrial Revolution hardly affected the appearance of Cots-wold landscape and villages. The dry-stone walls, the weft and warp of the Cotswold landscape fabric, did not arise until the Agrarian Revolu-tion of the eighteenth century and the enclosures which followed it. Tradition has it that the height of walls was determined by the height a sheep could jump, although the period was essentially one where arable fields began to replace pasture, barley being the crop which flourished best on the thin brashy soils.

The sporting tradition of the Cotswold 'squirearchy', leading to the planting of coverts and shelter belts for the breeding and rearing of game birds, has also had a considerable influence on the landscape as we know it today. The great fox-hunting tradition also has had its subtle effects on the scenery.

In fact, with obvious qualifications, the countryside and the settlements in the Cotswolds are much the same today as they were some hundreds of years ago. The Cotswolds' fortunate survival after the Industrial Revolution may be contrasted with the urban devastation of the West Riding, where vast quantities of coal happened to be near to the sheep runs on the moorlands. So the Cotswolds survived the Industrial Revolu-tion. The big question is will they survive the Technological Revolution?

New Pressures

Before describing some of the features which could affect the future of the Cotswolds, let me briefly distinguish between the two manufacturing revolutions. In the first Industrial Revolution the towns and cities grew rapidly, with vast increase of population and quantities of cheap labour drawn from the agricultural countryside. Communications were still difficult. Although the railways and canals passed through the countryside, there were still vast areas of remote land, of difficult terrain by-passed by the civil engineers looking for easy gradients. One such area was the Cotswolds, and this, no doubt, helped it to maintain a regional identity and individual character which other areas, criss-crossed by the new railways, failed to do.

In the nineteenth century the cities were already committed to an industrial future but the countryside, especially areas like the Cotswolds, which were comparatively remote, still belonged to the past. The transition in the twentieth century of these areas and their symbiosis with the urban economies has in consequence been less violent, allowing them gradually to assimilate the new situation and to adjust their way of life in an industrially orientated economy.

Farming today is an essential part of the industrial economy dependent upon urban manufacturing. In addition all country dwellers are now being influenced by exactly the same mass media as townspeople. The ability to move about is just as totally integrated thanks to the motor car, which is no longer a luxury but an absolute necessity for a large majority of the population. Indeed the new mobility has done more than anything else to integrate town and country. The process of integration has gone on sufficiently long and with such compound intensity that it is now possible to identify a very significant change in the town/country relationship which will have great importance in determining what could happen in the future. No longer are the towns concentrations of settlements in the countryside of an agricultural society. Now the countryside has become the hinterland of an urban-based society. This society is very heavily concentrated in the urban areas, but modern systems of highly mechanised scientific agriculture have multiplied the output of crops and stock. Quite contrary to what some alarmists predict, the agricultural experts maintain that even higher productivity will be possible from marginally reduced areas of farmland as a consequence of urban encroachments. The increasing urban population is also looking forward to greater personal affluence coupled with a great deal more leisure time. Not only has modern technology enabled greater productivity on the farm, it has also released the workers from countless hard and muscle-operated jobs in the factory and the field and emancipated the housewife from the backbreaking chores of running the home. It really all adds up to more and more leisure time for everyone, with considerable extra purchasing power becoming available as well. It was the economist Keynes who said, 'to those who sweat for their daily bread leisure is a longed-for sweet—until they get it!' This sums up the situation and establishes the *dramatis personae* for my scenario about the future of the Cotswolds.

However, before we can make any forecast, it is important to state the assumptions quite clearly. First we will assume that the status of the Cotswolds as an agricultural area of outstanding natural beauty will continue. Some may say that this is obviously going to be the case. But when one remembers that recently there has been serious concern about the future status of our National Parks, particularly with regard to the winning of valuable minerals, one can appreciate more vividly that a *status quo* for the Cotswolds is not such an inevitable situation after all. Our second assumption will be that the national economy will continue to prosper, ie, with a sound balance of payments and satisfactory gross national productivity. The third assumption is that, by the most up-to-date estimate, the population of Great Britain will increase by about one-fifth by the end of the century to a total of about 64 millions.

If these assumptions prove to be right, the following things could happen. By the year 2000 the West Midlands conurbation centred on Birmingham could grow from 5 to 6 millions; greater London from 11 to 13 millions and its spread reach one-third of the way across the country; and the population of the Severn vale from Tewkesbury to Bristol, including the projected Severnside, could reach nearly 2 millions. By that time the number of cars on the roads will have nearly trebled, the working week will have fallen to about 36 hours, and the completed motorway system will allow people to travel fast to anywhere they wish. Millions of people will be within easy reach of any beauty region. Add to this the world's tourists every summer. No area will be inaccessible or even remote. Any places or regions which manage to survive with a distinctive character will be sought out and invaded by everyone.

New Types of Resident

This is already happening, and particularly in regions like the Cotswolds where the beauty lies in buildings rather than the landscape. Our landscape here is attractive but not really remarkable. However, the buildings, walls, cottages, manor houses, barns and churches made of the local stone have produced an organic regional scenery of outstanding and unique quality. Buildings can be bought and sold, whereas landscape cannot. Already the significant indicators of the region's special attraction are becoming evident. Cotswold stone houses and cottages command higher and higher prices in the real estate market. There seems to be no limit to the price people will pay to possess a place with a character of its own in the Cotswolds. If there is one thing about the future which may be forecast with certainty, it is that the limestone buildings, turning gold in any Cotswold sunset are, in fact, gilt-edged for all time. It could be said that each attractive Cotswold stone village is, in fact, a complex and precious antique in multiple ownership.

This demand for a little place in the Cotswolds has a number of facets which may be distinguished. There is the retirement home; the semi-retirement or second home; and the home of the longer-distance commuter. Whoever may be the occupant of that home, the situation is usually the same. There is a very high investment upon acquisition and further high investment in restoration and renovation. Because character residences in the Cotswolds are at a premium and command very high prices, the newer occupants tend to be in the higher socio-economic groups, and the houses are well restored in good taste. The pseudo-antique coach lamps occasionally sprout from either side of the stone doorways—perhaps too frequently for the ardent conservationist—but much more important fundamental reconstruction, such as the insertion of damp-proof courses, roofing insulation and underfelt beneath stone slats, and the installation of central heating, completely outweighs such occasional transgressions into prettification. The Cotswold villages, in fact, have never been in such good condition or so well cared for in centuries. The demand for a scarce commodity engenders conservation as well as inflation!

The new affluent Cotswold residents have virtually replaced the farm labourers, the original inhabitants of the old stone villages. They have gone to the towns or live in the reconstructed stone council houses well round the corner from genuine Cotswold stone village streets. For better or for worse the newcomers are part of the present and the future scene. They are certainly becoming integrated in the life of the small towns and villages, but in a way they represent a new way of life superimposed on the farming economy of the area, which is continuing prosperously and efficiently, thanks to a well capitalised and technically well equipped agricultural industry. What will happen to this agricultural economy in the next 20 or 30 years? The land will certainly go on being worked, but there will be changes, many of them so drastic that they could shatter the dreams of those sentimentalists who cherish an illusion of the perpetuation of the Cotswolds as we know them today. Some say that the farmers are destroying the countryside. It depends upon one's viewpoint. Certainly there will be changes. Like industry, farming in the future will be fundamentally different from farming as we know it today. After all, agriculture is just another industry, even though it is dealing with cyclical processes based upon a basic land resource and the vagaries of climate. Large-scale mechanised farming requires fields of up to 50 acres in extent to be efficient. Hedgerows, trees and, particularly in the Cotswolds, stone walls would have to be cleared away to achieve these dimensions. Picturesque old barns and cowsheds could be replaced by huge and often high factory type structures. Wildlife eco-systems could be destroyed by various methods of crop control. People will continue to complain bitterly about Cotswold farmers wanting to erect enormous grain silos and other large buildings to produce cattle by factory farming methods at competitive prices, and at the same time, when they buy home-killed meat at the butchers, complain that even now it is far too expensive. Perhaps the same people will agitate about the industrialists on Severnside producing fertilisers to maintain the farmland scenery which they enjoy, because it is claimed that the chemical works will pollute the clean Cotswold air.

The farmers for their part will protest about trespass and encroachment on their land by thoughtless irresponsible townsfolk having a day out in the Cotswolds. The planners will certainly be blamed by everyone for failing to resolve all these conflicts. Conflicts are usually simple to identify but to reconcile divergent opinions and to resolve conflicts is always much more difficult. In future, as pressures build up, it will nearly always become a matter of finding acceptable compromises between conflicting demands. The integration of the car-borne masses determined to enjoy themselves in a countryside where farmers continue at work all the time will be a difficult but essential exercise.

New Demands by Visiting Population

Virtually everyone will come to the Cotswolds in cars or motor-coaches. Why will they come? How long will they come for? When will they come? Surveys and analyses carried out in the Planning Departments covering the Cotswolds have already revealed some interesting facts. People are very gregarious by nature. They want to see the picturesque villages, historical places, and the stately homes and gardens. They want nice places to picnic—as near to their cars as possible. Picnic places offering a prospect of a sheet of water or river close by are always in demand. Similarly a place to stop showing a spectacular viewpoint across the countryside or an unusual activity, such as gliding, is very popular.

In my Study *Outdoor Recreation and the Gloucestershire Countryside* three types of recreational demands were identified. Firstly, for local people, say to take an evening drive through the Cotswolds or to play a game of golf on Cleeve Common; secondly, regional demands by people prepared to travel some distance to seek recreation, and already using the motorways; finally, national demands by people on longer holidays. At present, the Cotswolds tend to have a transit characteristic, as many people car-camping or in caravans choose to visit them on their way to other places. However, it is expected that the Cotswolds will become much more of a holiday place in their own right, where people will want to stay for longer holiday periods. In the Study a number of ideas were put forward suggesting ways of resolving some of the anticipated conflicts between residents and visitors. Many of the ideas were confirmed by the 1968 Countryside Act. I have already mentioned that this Act established a Countryside Commission to survey and enhance the natural beauty of the countryside and to encourage the provision and improvement of facilities for everyone's enjoyment. There are also powers in the Act for local authorities and private owners to provide and maintain Country Parks and picnic areas. Country Parks are areas of suitable territory, at least 25 acres in extent, not too far away from large urban concentrations and capable of accommodating large numbers of car-borne visitors out in the country for recreation. Even before the Government's white paper *Leisure in the Countryside* gave a clear indication of the likely content of the Act, Gloucestershire and its neighbouring authorities had determined objectives and priorities for the conservation of the Cotswolds and the development of its recreational resources.

These resources lie in the fine landscape, the attractive villages, the nature reserves, commons and historic sites and remains of all kinds. Many ancient routes, such as the Cotswold Ridgeway and Salt Way, cross the area and link the sites of camps, burial mounds and defensive positions of prehistoric, Roman and more recent times.

Scenic routes for the cyclist, motorist, horseman and rambler are needed to take advantage of the resources whilst avoiding the normal traffic routes in the area. Car parks are needed on the edges of the more popular villages as well as others carefully sited and screened in the countryside itself. As little traffic as possible should travel through the villages. Along the escarpment existing viewpoints, where there is access, could be combined with picnic sites and served by scenic routes, parking facilities and information centres.

Such development needs great care in siting and design. The vulnerable sky line of the escarpment seen from the vale demands that car parks and development be located below or behind it or associated with mature tree groups, with provision for further planting. In the Cotswolds themselves the long expansive views demand keeping any development off sky lines and uplands, unless screened by trees, and this policy has been pursued by the local planning authorities.

Although they are excluded from the Area of Outstanding Natural Beauty, the Stroud valleys are physically a part of the Cotswolds. The escarpment has been cut into by the River Frome and its tributaries, producing a number of deep valleys in which the settlements of Stroud, Thrupp, Chalford and Nailsworth have developed. Between the two main valleys—Golden Valley and Nailsworth Valley—rise the extensive commons of Minchinhampton, Selsley and Rodborough, most of which are in National Trust ownership. The commons, used for grazing, are very popular for recreation. They attract great numbers of motorists, horse riders, golfers and picnickers, particularly at weekends, and a problem of conflict between the various activities arises.

In the valleys themselves there is scope for creating a linear linked park system based on the disused Stroudwater canal and River Frome. Footpath links between such a system and the commons on the hilltops could be improved to provide pleasant walks out from the settlements into the surrounding countryside.

Industrial Archaeology and Local History

In 1964 a conference held by the Council for British Archaeology considered the problem of many early industrial buildings which, now obsolete, were rapidly being destroyed by redevelopment or neglect. The Conference agreed that these sites, representative as they were of the origins of the Industrial Revolution, had national significance, and serious effort should be made to preserve them. Later that year the Gloucestershire County Council gave support to this view when it aided a survey of industrial archaeology in the Stroud valleys by the newly formed Gloucestershire Society for Industrial Archaeology. The principal aim of the local planning authority was to initiate the restoration of important industrial buildings and secure an improvement in the overall physical amenity of the valleys. It was considered that the appearance of the old mills and their settings could be improved without resorting to expensive structural alterations or extensive landscaping. In many cases improvements could be achieved by the removal of derelict outbuildings, the clearance of accumulated debris, the removal of advertisements and the renewal of fences and walls. At a meeting late in 1964 members and officials of the district councils supported the Stroud Valleys Facelift project and explored means of achieving the desired aims. Subsequently an exhibition was held under the auspices of the Council for the Preservation of Rural England (Protection was later substituted for Preservation), the County Planning Authority and the Gloucestershire

R

Society for Industrial Archaeology, which illustrated many examples of dereliction along the valleys. In addition it was demonstrated how minor improvements around the mills could act as focal points for extending improvements elsewhere.

Since that time many industrialists and other property owners have co-operated in implementing these ideas. Sites have been cleared of rubbish, advertisements removed, trees planted and a host of other improvements carried out. Substantial lengths of the Thames & Severn Canal have been cleared out by volunteer labour, aided by the County Highways Department, and points of interest such as the Round House, Chalford, have been landscaped. However, much remains still to be done and it is the intention of the county council, in association with other interested parties and volunteers, to continue this work of improvement. Newcomers to the Stroud valley will be unaware of some of the improvements carried out. A closer inspection, however, will reveal the existence of young trees, the newness of rebuilt walls and attractive stretches of new water.

In view of its many interests the Chalford valley with its River Frome has received most attention so far in Operation Facelift. From the steep-sided and well wooded valley the river flows swiftly westwards to the vale of Berkeley and the River Severn. In spite of considerable pasture-land and woodland this is not a rural valley in the strictest sense, since from the early eighteenth century the Cotswold wool and cloth trade moved from the upland wolds in search of water power for mills, and mill after mill was built on the Frome and its neighbouring streams. For years this 'Stroud valley' contained the largest woollen and cloth industry in England, which led the world in such manufactures and trade. Upstream from the urban areas of Stroud, the sunny south-facing slopes are scattered with houses of many styles, sizes and ages—millowners', mill operatives', cottage spinners' and weavers'. Small twisting lanes, which speak of cottage industries, drop into the valley and connect with the main Cirencester road. The Thames & Severn Canal was cut through the narrow valley in 1789, and the Great Western Railway main line from London to Gloucester opened through here in 1845. So every yard of the 'Stroud valley' is precious for some aspect of English local life and history.

Gloucestershire County Council has published a leaflet about a Guided Walk along the Chalford valley, which is the upper part of the Stroud valley. This describes all the places of interest by means of a number of 'way marks' along the route keyed to easily identifiable points on a sketch map. This is but one example of a number of similar exercises which have been completed by the planners, very often in collaboration with local experts in voluntary organisations. These studies have the principal objective of making the Cotswolds more interesting and enjoyable for everyone, seekers as well as holidaymakers.

There is another interesting guide to the Cooper's Hill Nature Reserve, which is owned by the Gloucestershire County Council and set on a Cotswold promontory overlooking the Severn vale. The Nature Conservancy and the Gloucestershire Trust for Nature Conservation set up a Nature Trail in the Reserve, which is described in the guide. Cooper's Hill is, of course, famous for the Whitsuntide cheese-rolling contest. The origins of the game are lost in history, but it attracts very large numbers of people to see athletic young daredevils of both sexes chase and tumble after the hard cheese rolling down the hill from near the maypole on the summit. Usually ceremonies or festivals occur on only one day of the year. The Cranham Feast and Dover's Games at Chipping Campden, for example, attract very large numbers of people in their cars and there is inevitably a certain amount of traffic congestion on the day of the event. The major problem is always dealing with motor-car congestion and car parking. For special events space can usually be found by opening up a few fields nearby. This sort of temporary car parking facility usually suffices, but if the British Tourist Authority sets out to promote such essentially English ceremonies the resultant interest could give cause for reviving more old ones or inventing new ones. This has certainly happened in other countries, which have recognised that indigenous folklore has a particular tourist appeal. Cheeses could be rolled down Cooper's Hill on a number of occasions in the summer for the tourist's pleasure if some local profits were guaranteed and it were demonstrably in the interests of national tourism. The Cooper's Hill maypole could be plaited by local folk dancers as well. If this were to occur, then there would certainly be serious car parking and other public assembly problems for the planners to solve in a more permanent way.

Commons

On the Cotswold commons the motor car is notoriously well represented in the lists of leisure conflicts. Public rights over common land are well known to be complex. The general public's rights of access over commons are, contrary to popular belief, very often narrowly proscribed by statute, and rights can be confined to local inhabitants. Because local-use rights and public-leisure claims on commons can produce serious conflicts, Gloucestershire planners have commenced a series of studies of the more important Cotswold commons used by the public for a wide variety of recreational pursuits.

Cleeve Common is by far the largest on the Cotswolds. It is, in fact, 1,332 acres in extent, which is well over twice the size of Minchinhampton Common, the next largest. So first of all we studied Cleeve Common and a consultative report with recommendations about its use and recreation potential was published in 1971. The report distinguished priority work to be done, and not surprisingly a new car park with lavatories came high on the list. The Common, it was thought, would benefit enormously from effective wardening. This could probably best be done on horseback, bearing in mind the vast extent and loneliness of some parts of the area. Effective informatory signposting would also help, again because of the very great expanse of the Common.

The Area of Outstanding Natural Beauty has a full-time warden who is in charge of the Cotswold Voluntary Warden Service. This service was set up in 1968, and there are now about 200 keen and helpful volunteers concerned to ensure that the Cotswolds are properly looked after. On Cleeve Common legal difficulties, identified in the Study, will have to be overcome before the Warden Service can carry out patrols. When this is possible, there will have to be a new set of bye-laws drawn up with the cooperation of the Cleeve Common Conservators. The contents of these bye-laws will have to be the subject of detailed consideration, but it would appear *inter alia* that they should prohibit the driving of motor vehicles over the common, and the riding of horses over certain parts, especially over the golf course and where walkers have right of way. There will, of course, be special bridle-ways for riding, and clearly the informatory signs to distinguish who may do what and where will be a very important supplement to the bye-laws.

The Cotswold wardens are now helping the planners with survey work preliminary to their preparing similar reports on other commons. During the summer of 1971 some of the wardens helped to carry out 'on-the-spot' enquiries to find out why people were visiting Painswick Common, where they came from, and other information—another example of how planners are glad to collaborate with other people in their interesting work.

Cotswold Water Park

Most of the big commons on the Cotswolds are along its high western edge. There is another important and very special recreational resource on the eastern side of the dip-slope near the head waters of the Thames.

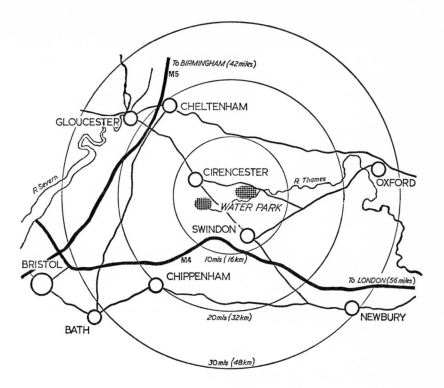

Fig 28. The Cotswold Water Park.

In the Upper Thames valley gravel has been worked extensively since the 1920s in areas where the water table is very close to the surface. After the gravel has been dug, extensive lakes are formed, and these form two principal concentrations centred around South Cerney and between Fairford and Lechlade. Already there are nearly 1,000 acres of water in the two zones, which together cover 24 square miles, and by the late 1980s there could be nearly 4,000 acres of lakes with very great potential for inland water recreation.

The decision that the area in the Upper Thames valley between Cirencester and Swindon should become a water park (Fig 28) was made in 1967 at the first meeting of the Cotswold Water Park Joint Committee. This Committee consists of representatives of Gloucestershire and Wiltshire County Councils, Cirencester Rural District Council and Cricklade and Wotton Bassett Rural District Council.

The area is regionally well placed. At present about 2 million people live within one hour's travelling time of the Park, and with completion of M4 and M5 motorways, the South Midland and West London areas are now only about 1½ hours' journey away.

The Cotswold Water Park Master Plan, approved in 1970, sets out more fully than would be appropriate here the background problems and proposals. In brief, the aims are that the area should become a water park serving the interests of aquatic sportsmen, naturalists and others who wish to enjoy a stretch of inland water. To achieve this, it is necessary for the authorities concerned to ensure proper resolution of the conflicting demands of all the users, and generally to make every endeavour to achieve realisation of the plan.

In addition to the various active water sports, for which planning will be flexible, so that varying demands in the future may be met, it is envisaged that the following will be catered for in the Park: angling, wildlife study, walking, riding, spectators, casual visitors and picnickers. Strategically sited holiday caravan and camping sites, and a marina on the River Thames where it becomes navigable at Lechlade, are likely developments. One lake is already being used by the Education Committee of Gloucestershire County Council, as a recreational water-sports training area for school and youth organisations; and the area generally is highly regarded by the Nature Conservancy for its potential for research and education.

Two areas within the Water Park have been designated as County Parks under the Countryside Act 1968. One of these, Keynes Park, has now been acquired by Gloucestershire and developed for sailing and other quiet pursuits.

By far the larger part of the area, however, will have to be developed by private enterprise. The recreational after-use of lakes on a commercial scale requires a separate planning permission; any applications will be considered within the context of the Plan, and permissions will be subject to conditions appropriate to its realisation.

The gravel beds, which overlie the Oxford Clay, are associated with the Cotswold rivers Churn, Coln and Leach, where these streams level out into the Upper Thames basin. Light and fertile soils, with damp alluvial pastures, form an essentially flat landscape, with only one or two low hills for relief. Fields tend to be small, with tall hedgerows and associated hedgerow trees, and small woodlands here and there.

The villages are in the main attractive, with considerable historic and architectural interest. The fifteenth-century stained glass in Fairford Church, for instance, is a regular visitors' attraction.

The gravel traffic in and out of the Water Park has caused considerable disturbance in the villages, and wear and tear on minor roads. The aim of improvements to the road network, such as the new Spine Road in the South Cerney area, is not only to improve access to the Park for recreational uses, but also to exclude gravel and recreation traffic from the villages. The Fairford and Lechlade bypasses are also important, bearing in mind that there could be 15,000 vehicles in the Water Park on a peak recreation day.

Hydrology

Hydrological problems associated with the movement of underground and surface water are important influences on the size and extent of individual gravel workings and the lakes resulting from them.

The gravel beds in the Water Park area are saturated with underground water and the surface or water table is often within 2 feet or so of ground level (Fig 29). This water table has a surface approximately

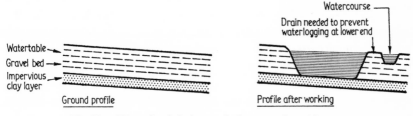

Fig 29.   Water levels before and after gravel working.

parallel to the ground. When the ground is excavated, exposing a free water surface, this surface for all practical purposes may be taken as level. The 'rest' level of water in an excavation will be such as to achieve equilibrium between :

(a) the increased inflow through the gravels induced by lower water levels at the upper end of the pit, and

(b) the increased outflow at the lower end of the pit.

Under certain circumstances, particularly in short lakes in flat areas, this balance can be achieved within existing ground levels, without affecting surface water flows in the area. Where extraction has resulted in a long lake with a significant difference in ground level between the upper and lower ends, water will flow over the downstream perimeter of the lake, causing waterlogging on the adjacent ground. The water level can be lowered and waterlogging avoided by providing a drain from the lake to a nearby watercourse.

The plotting of a series of levels and longitudinal sections, which has been done, will enable careful control to be exercised over the size of further pits and the extent to which existing ones can be linked.

The land drainage system in the area is complex. It is necessary at times to leave main drainage channels undisturbed, and a 30ft reservation may be left either side where otherwise it would have been profitable to link workings to create a larger pit. Working pits should only be connected to watercourses by properly designed systems, to avoid sediment being carried into the watercourse and thereby upsetting the hydraulic gradient.

Close liaison is maintained with the Thames Conservancy, and official consultations are held with them when planning applications are considered for gravel workings in this area.

Landscaping after Gravel Work

As I have said, gravel has been worked in the area since the 1920s. Up to the 1950s it was usually excavated by mechanical shovels, which left shallows and small islands in the water, and gently shelving sides. Some of these early pits were restored to agricultural use; others have become partly or completely grown over with willow scrub. By 1960 most excavation was being done by crane-grabs, which leave the pits with vertical sides and deep water right to the edge. Some of the older shallow pits have been reworked by this method. Both types of pit have proved of interest to the naturalist, different plant species tending to colonise, and different birds being attracted to, each type (see Chapter 2).

The objective of development control has (for some years) been to enhance the after-use of the pits for recreation. Conditions have been imposed, with planning permissions requiring the grading of the shore line to more gradual slopes; the retention of trees where possible; and the carrying out of landscaping schemes. Due to the time-scale of working, however, these landscape recovery schemes are only now beginning to become effective.

In 1971 Amey's, a large gravel operator in the Park, made a gift of a worked-out pit near Lechlade to the Gloucestershire Trust for Nature Conservation in memory of a deceased member of the firm. This pit had previously been used as an unofficial nature reserve, by agreement between the Trust and the firm.

For a number of reasons, it is intended that ecologically appropriate planting should be used throughout the Water Park (see Chapter 2). It is fortunate that the natural colonists of worked-out pits, the willows, are among the fastest growing shrubs and trees, and for cheap and quick effect sets can be used. Another advantage of the willows is their capacity for self-renewal after vandalism. No doubt, management for sailing, nature reserves, even public access, will necessarily include control of the growth in due course.

Ecologically based planting is the most likely to succeed on the rather difficult soils remaining after working. These include undisturbed ground with thin topsoil and gravelly subsoil; graded-out mounds of overburden with or without topsoil; damp and swampy areas; gravelly banks of lakes, subject to fluctuating water levels and erosion to varying extents; and the lake margins, which may be gravelly or silty. All soils are base rich, the drainage water and the gravel itself both deriving from the oolitic limestone of the Cotswolds. Visually, the effect of ecological planting will be preferable to a collection of exotic species, which could produce a tame gardenesque appearance less satisfying to those seeking the refreshment of the countryside. In areas of more concentrated development such as camping and caravan sites, the more ornamental varieties of willow, maple and other local genera may be introduced.

Planning for Recreation

In this flat area the provision of viewpoints is important. Old bridges over a disused railway line have been retained for this purpose, and where material is available artificial hills may be created. These need not be very high to be effective, and could also meet another need— shelter. Wind exposure is one problem resulting from the removal of hedges and trees in gravel working. Planting for shelter will also be needed, with care that it does not interfere with sailing.

Where road widening becomes necessary, hedges and trees will be preserved wherever possible and desirable. On the other hand, in strategic positions, lengths of roadside hedge will be removed to allow views across the lakes.

For picnicking, swimming, paddling and for visual reasons, lakeside banks need grading out to shallow slopes, shelving as gradually as possible under water. For other uses, such as sailing and angling, banks may be steeper. These variable demands with suitable landscaping and structuring will gradually establish individual shoreline characters for the different lakes.

Car parks are an obvious requirement, but they need not be obtrusive, if screened and broken up by planting. In this area, gravel is the most suitable surface, and all that may be needed will be to strip off the top-soil. In some places it is possible that grass may not stand up to car-parking wear. The new plastic net reinforcements in the grass roots could be suitable if they proved economical.

Buildings; Aquatic Zoo

The ultimate objective will be to have new buildings of high architectural quality. Washing plant and aggregate stockpiles often remain beside a pit where extraction has ceased and recreational uses have already become established. This is unfortunate, both visually and aurally, but the situation persists until the cost of hauling exceeds the cost of moving the plant to another site. In the short term, while money is scarce, temporary buildings may have to be tolerated. They need not necessarily be unsightly. Even some of the gravel-washing plant suitably painted and augmented could create exciting structural accents in the large-scale Water Park landscape.

On the outskirts of South Cerney, one of the villages bordering the Water Park, there is a potential for a small lakeside housing development when gravel working ceases. This will be an opportunity for architecture appropriate to the waterside, and for strong careful detailing of the water's edge.

Finally, a brief comment about the interesting and challenging idea for the lakes which will be formed around the River Isis (Thames) south of Somerford Keynes. Within this area it is proposed that an aquatic nature reserve could be established, where a protected habitat could be provided for native wetland birds and mammals in danger of extinction. They could be encouraged to breed and provide new stock for release elsewhere. Other interesting mammals could be introduced, and it would be hoped that the exhibition side could help finance the scientific and educational side of the project.

To aid observation of the creatures in their natural habitat, elevated walkways could be constructed above the water, and it would also be possible to make observation tunnels under the water, where lighting could be installed.

This location would afford a great opportunity to establish an aquatic wildlife centre unique in this country, where conservation and preservation ideas could be practised whilst providing an opportunity for close observation by the general public.

Improvement of the Countryside

When the gravel reserves have been exhausted and the Water Park completed, the result could well be an area vastly more attractive to look

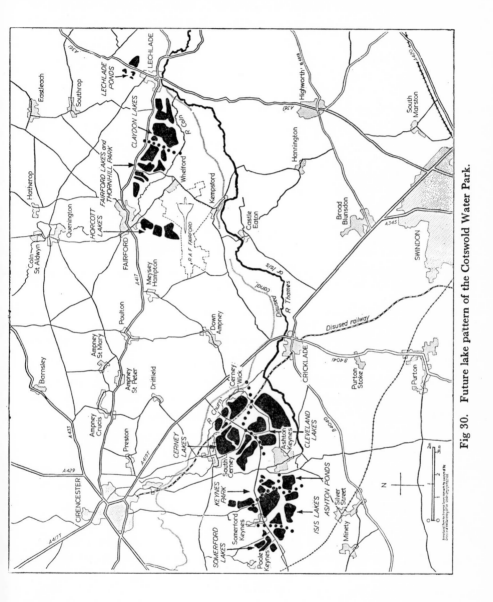

Fig 30. Future lake pattern of the Cotswold Water Park.

at than it was before (Fig 30). As well as providing an enormous variety of water-based facilities for large numbers of people, the Nature Conservancy's Wetland Habitat Team believe that the Water Park will be the finest site in the country of all-round biological interest as well as for research and education. There is no doubt that it will become a very important nature reserve as well as an expansive nesting and over-wintering place for waterfowl.

Eventually the Park may attract other developments, such as hotels, restaurants and the like. This is the stage when it is hoped that some really significant architecture will be built. The project is now developing at an accelerating pace. The development and maintenance of the new recreational resources require skilled management and experienced stewardship. The local authorities with the Countryside Commission's encouragement are developing Country Parks in the lake complex, but the major developers will be the gravel operators. There is a very happy partnership between the gravel firms and the local authorities, who are all excited about the prospects and keen to ensure that the Water Park is a great success in every respect. Of course there are other similar developments going on elsewhere, but not on the scale of the Cotswold Water Park. The experience and know-how which we have acquired is being freely offered to other schemes.

Recreation

In the Gloucestershire Outdoor Recreation Study we identified the leisure activities which usually take place in the countryside, under two distinct headings: (1) essentially fixed location, such as caravanning, camping and gliding, and (2) free-ranging activities, such as walking, riding, cycling and motoring. In the first group the activity was of prime importance but in the second group the countryside itself was the determining element. The various activities in these two groups were studied and exhaustive analysis produced several conclusions, which were as follows:

> The countryside can absorb many fixed location activities, but the siting of some of them will need great care. Conflict between activities should be avoided where possible and disturbance (e.g. by motor cycle scrambling) kept to a minimum. Nearly all the activities depend upon the use of a private car or coach to carry participants and spectators to the location. This causes problems unless the activities have good access from main roads and adequate car parking at the site.

Car parks are a major need at road access points to commons, near sites used for crowd-drawing activities such as gliding, cycling and scrambling, along scenic routes and in walking and water activity areas. The design of such car parks should be in sympathy with their surroundings, with as great a use of natural materials and natural screening as possible.

Other facilities are also needed; picnic areas, camp sites, refreshment facilities, toilets and information services are basic needs if outdoor recreation demands are to bet met in an acceptable way. The provision of such facilities will also be in the interests of the countryside itself, for by encouraging people to places designed or adapted to cater for them, trespass and abuse of the land may be reduced elsewhere.

Routes through the countryside need to be improved to increase their potential for recreation. Pleasure motorists should have a network of clearly defined scenic routes from which they may choose an itinerary. Such routes should be signposted and have along them the kind of facilities mentioned above. Walkers and horse riders should have a choice between long or short distance footpath and bridle-way routes for exploring the countryside. For those walkers who come by car to the countryside, and for the pleasure motorists who may want a short walk, the footpath network should connect with rural car parks. Cyclists could also use these car parks in association with starting and finishing points for races. Separate routes for cyclists in the countryside should be considered, linking similar routes in urban areas and with County Country Parks. To quote the Study :

> It is evident that many facilities are needed in common by several activities. Economy of land could well result. In many cases different activities could happily take place on adjacent land and benefit from the economies of shared car parking and facilities. County Country Parks could fulfil this role, providing land for a wide range of activities within the Park, and as a focal point for scenic routes, long distance footpaths and bridle-paths in the countryside around.

A typical project which it is hoped to carry out is on an escarpment site near the National Trust land at Frocester Hill. This scheme is but one in a series which will be related to a Cotswold scenic route, following roads which run close to the edge of the escarpment, and afford spectacular viewpoints across the Severn vale. The car parks, well tucked away to prevent windscreen reflection from the vale, and picnic areas along the western edge of the Cotswolds, will also be linked to the Cotswold Way. This long-distance walk, comprising existing footpaths and bridle-ways, connected by short lengths of minor roads, runs nearly 100 miles along the escarpment, and is already substantially signed and way-marked, thanks to the work of a large number of volunteers col-

GLOUCESTERSHIRE COLLEGE OF EDUCATION LIBRARY

laborating with county officers. It is confidently expected that the Cotswold Way will be designated by the Countryside Commission as a National Long Distance Footpath.

Camping Sites

During the past decade there has been a rapid growth in the number of people taking holidays away from home. An increasing proportion of these are using a caravan or tent for overnight accommodation, either whilst touring or *en route* for a holiday destination. The Cotswolds because of their renowned beauty, and because they are strategically placed between the Midlands conurbation and the resorts of the South West, are likely to attract an increasing number of campers and caravanners. In meeting their needs there is always a danger that the amenities which they (and others) seek to enjoy may be destroyed in the process.

The need for a plan to resolve this potential conflict was recognised by the Joint Advisory Committee, which resolved 'that the Technical Officers be requested to consider the question of holiday caravan sites within the Area of Outstanding Natural Beauty and submit a report thereon to the Joint Committee'. This report was published in mid-1970 and drew attention to the following important matters :

The demand for new sites to serve caravan and tent campers wanting to explore the Cotswolds is likely to increase considerably over the next decade. Although there is no evidence that the few sites so far established have seriously affected amenities, future pressures could easily adversely alter the position, unless the constituent authorities are prepared to channel them to the right locations. To do this, there must be clear and consistent policies for the control of new caravan and tent camping sites over the whole of the AONB and adjoining areas, supplemented where necessary by positive action to meet the demand in ways which will not detract from the natural beauty of the region.

In formulating policies for the control of new camping sites, the basic purpose behind the designation of the Cotswolds as an Area of Outstanding Natural Beauty—to preserve and enhance that natural beauty —must never be overlooked. Camping sites are unlikely to enhance natural beauty, consequently there must be very few locations within an AONB where the presence of a camping site would not detract from it in some degree. It could therefore be argued, that within the AONB there should be a general presumption against the establishment of new camping sites.

Nevertheless, all kinds of campers will appear increasingly in the Cotswolds, and if not catered for adequately, will become a nuisance to landowners, farmers and local authorities. The constituent authorities have a duty to make provision for new camping sites, as far as that is consistent with preserving and enhancing the Cotswolds' natural beauty. One method would be to encourage, where acceptable, the establishment of suitably located camping sites in areas adjoining the AONB but within easy reach of it and related to the main tourist routes. However, such provision would not cover parts of the Cotswolds, and it may be necessary to establish a few new sites within the AONB itself, of minimal impact on the landscape.

Large permanent camping sites are obviously unacceptable in the Cotswolds, and a proliferation of small sites could be equally disastrous in a more insidious way. Where new sites are proved to be necessary, a balance will have to be struck. These sites will have to be large enough to make the provision of reasonable facilities economic, yet small enough, given the right location and landscaping, to be completely unobtrusive. Their location could be identified by appropriately located international signs.

Need for Planning Control

The Cotswolds have been an area of tourist attraction for a long while, catering for the quiet forms of open-air recreation. Increased population and accessibility are likely to increase the numbers of those coming for a holiday to the Cotswolds, particularly the second holiday, or a few days' break. But there are dangers that the pressures of tourism could lead to development which would destroy the very qualities that attract people to the area. The heritage of the Cotswolds must be preserved at all cost, but the cost will be high in land and buildings maintenance. Maintenance needs money, and that needs economic prosperity. Tourism can add to this, but if allowed to go unreined, at a price. It is for the planners to strike the balance. But there is a further safeguard against spoliation and exploitation—the traditions of Cotswold land stewardship. Local reverence for the past has guarded the inheritance of stone craft and architecture for centuries. There is every sign that this concern will persist, and the Cotswold style will develop a contemporary character as it did in the seventeenth, eighteenth and nineteenth centuries, while remaining recognisably itself.

Cotswold Identity

The architectural vernacular of the Cotswolds is entirely derived from traditional building in the local limestone. The skills of the old stonemasons, like many other country crafts, are gradually disappearing. The quarrying of the natural stone for the roofing slats and the walls of buildings has, with a few notable exceptions, also ceased. Many of the quarries are still operative, but they are being worked for limestone aggregate needed in the manufacture of reconstructed stone.

In 1965 Gloucestershire County Planning Committee appointed a working party to study the various types of reconstructed stone blocks used as substitutes for natural stone and to determine which were satisfactory and therefore acceptable for use in the Cotswolds. At the inaugural meeting of the Cotswold AONB Joint Advisory Committee it was agreed that the Gloucestershire Cotswold Building Materials Report should be the guide for development control policy. The adoption of this policy indicated the fundamental change so far as building in the Cotswolds was concerned. No longer could a planning authority continue to insist upon the use of local limestone to face all new buildings in the Cotswolds. The stone was just not being quarried, nor were there stone-walling masons about. Planning authorities had to come to terms with the realities of the situation, regrettable as that might be to some devout conservationists.

The manufacture of reconstructed stone blocks was revolutionised by the use of plastic moulds with vibrated casting techniques. These are now so advanced that some of the new blocks are almost indistinguishable from natural stone. The blocks do not weather so well as real stone, but bearing in mind that this is not available in sufficient quantity at acceptable prices, the substitute material is reasonably acceptable. The study identified sub-regional colour change in Cotswold stonework. This tends to be a warm honey colour in the north, grading through shades of silver-grey towards the south. It was concluded that reconstructed stone blocks simulating these weathered colours with comparatively low relief were the most acceptable. Having the most suitable reconstructed stone block, however, did not necessarily guarantee a satisfactory finished appearance to a wall. The guide gives some useful advice about laying the blocks and jointing them. As in natural stonework, the best results depend on laying the reconstructed stone blocks in courses with the larger ones at the base of the wall. The jointing plays a very important part in the overall appearance of the wall, and the mortar should be similar in colour or slightly lighter than the surrounding stonework. Although it is difficult to generalise, the most successful joint is a simple flush one either rubbed, bagged or flushed roughly with a piece of stick.

The Building Materials Guide also has useful information about roofing buildings in the Cotswolds. The general conclusion is that the colour is of overriding importance. Plain roofing tiles or simulated concrete slats should match the local weathered Cotswold stone slats of the locality as closely as possible. Colour, it seems, is more important than the shape of the tiles, although the interlocking types of tile are not very suitable for buildings in the region.

In the classic Cotswold villages, where conservation of the architectural vernacular is paramount, the use of reconstructed stone or other substitute materials for the traditional ones may not be suitable. The infilling of odd plots or the replacement of derelict buildings with new ones requires architectural skill and sensitive use of the traditional building materials, and in these cases suitable natural stone will have to be obtained from the quarries for walls and roofing. Sometimes secondhand stone slats from demolished Cotswold buildings can be obtained from local builders, who carefully store these now somewhat scarce roofing materials.

Sometimes an 'invisible mending' technique will be appropriate when building anew. This is very often essential when filling a gap caused by a demolition in a continuous Cotswold frontage. Visitors to Cirencester would be unlikely to notice that Baxter's, the butcher's shop in Castle Street, is a completely new building. In other places a bold contemporary architectural approach can be quite successful. Moreton-in-Marsh and Northleach fire stations are new Cotswold buildings unashamedly expressing their function in complete harmony with the surrounding traditional Cotswold buildings. The Triangle contemporary housing development in Cirencester won a Civic Trust Award.

Some people may think that all new buildings in the Cotswolds should copy existing ones. There is, however, no real justification for barring modern architecture from the Cotswolds. After all, tradition is an evolving thing. The objective must always be to design a building which naturally fits its site and is in complete harmony with the surrounding landscape. Materials which give no sharp contrast in colour always help to create this harmony.

In Gloucestershire, after the Civic Amenities Act became law in 1967, a provisional list describing the proposed conservation areas was published by the Planning Department. Perhaps, not surprisingly, out of 120 places selected no fewer than 75 per cent were in the Cotswolds. The designation of the scheduled places has been progressing ever since, and the help of the amenity societies and the local authorities has been a great encouragement. The broad objectives of the conservation programme are, of course, to preserve and wherever possible enhance the amenities and special architectural character of the designated areas of towns and villages. So often in these places it is the walls, gates, fences,

s

outbuildings, trees and ground textures, grass, cobbles, paving and the like which add so much to the special character of the place. Thoughtless, albeit minor, development by an authority, a statutory undertaker, advertiser or an individual can have a very serious effect upon a delicate architectural and textural balance. Planners hope that by publishing an analysis of the genius loci of the conservation area and by pointing out some of the desiderata likely to affect the local character, it may be possible to enhance the place through future development initiatives. The designation of conservation areas may, in fact, be regarded as the pre-liminary positive action by individuals and authorities to preserve and enhance its character and appearance in every possible way. Some pro-posals for new development likely to affect the character of a conservation area to a significant extent could be of general public concern. Planning authorities will give public notice of such applications, indicating the nature of the development proposed and taking account of any representa-tions they may receive before deciding whether or not to give permission.

Conclusion

Agriculture is likely to continue to be the economic backbone of the area, and a prosperous farming community is most likely to contribute towards the conservation of the physical environment. The prices farms in the Cotswolds fetch is evidence that farming can be made, and is being made, to pay. It has been said : 'The prosperity of the Cotswolds belongs to the past and to the present.' I would add 'and to the future'.

Some change is inevitable—social, economical and physical. More Cotswold cottages will be occupied by retired people, commuters or used as second homes. Agricultural employment may drop even further, but farms can never be run entirely by pressing buttons. There may be some growth in other employment, industrial and service, but large numbers are unlikely to be involved. Some buildings will disappear, some new buildings will arise, but the pace of change will be slower than in other parts, such as the Severn Vale. Basically the Cotswolds will remain as they are today, and the Cotswolds of the early twenty-first century should be easily recognisable from the numerous graphic descriptions of the Cotswolds of the early 1970s.

Notes to this chapter are on page 311.

Notes, References, Sources and Acknowledgements

CHAPTER 1

(Pages 21–47)

Geology and Physical Environment: J. W. Murray and A. B. Hawkins

Ackermann, K. J. and Cave, R. 'Superficial deposits and structures including landslip, in the Stroud District, Gloucestershire', *Proc Geol Ass*, 78 (1968), 567–86

Ager, D. V. 'The genus *Gibbirhynchia* in the British Domerian', *Proc Geol Ass*, 65 (1954), 25–51

Ager, D. V. 'Field meeting in the Central Cotswolds', *Proc Geol Ass*, 66 (1956), 336–65

Arkell, W. J. *The Jurassic System in Great Britain* (Clarendon Press, Oxford, 1933)

Arkell, W. J. and Donovan, D. T. 'The Fuller's Earth of the Cotswolds, and its relation to the Great Oolite', *Q Jl geol Soc Lond*, 107 (1951), 227–53

Buckman, S. S. 'On the Cotswold, Midford and Yeovil Sands, and the division between Lias and Oolite', *Q Jl geol Soc Lond*, 45 (1889), 440–73

Davies, D. K. 'Shelf sedimentation: An example from the Jurassic of Britain', *J Sediment Petrol*, 39 (1969), 1344–70

Dreghorn, W. *Geology explained in the Severn Vale and Cotswolds* (David & Charles, Newton Abbot, 1967)

Green, G. W. and Melville, R. V. 'The stratigraphy of the Stowell Park borehole (1949–51)', *Bull Geol Surv*, UK, 11 (1956), 1–33

Hancock, P. L. 'Jointing in the Jurassic limestones of the Cotswold Hills', *Proc Geol Ass*, 80 (1969), 219–42

Hawkins, A. B. and Kellaway, G. A. 'Field meeting at Bristol and Bath with special reference to new evidence of glaciation', *Proc Geol Ass*, 82 (1971), 267–92

Kellaway, G. A., Horton, A. and Poole, E. G. 'The development of some Pleistocene structures in the Cotswolds and Upper Thames Basin', *Bull Geol Surv*, UK, 37 (1971), 1–28

Kellaway, G. A. and Welch, F. B. A. 'British Regional Geology: Bristol and Gloucester District', *Geol Surv* (1948), 91pp

Kent, P. E. 'A structure contour map of the surface of the buried pre-Permian rocks of England and Wales', *Proc Geol Ass*, 40 (1949), 87–104

McKerrow, W. S., Ager, D. V. and Donovan, D. T. 'Geology of the Cotswold Hills', *Geol Ass Guide*, 36 (1964), 1–26

Martin, A. J. 'Bathonian sedimentation in southern England', *Proc Geol Ass*, 78 (1967), 473–88

Murray, J. W. 'The Inferior Oolite of the Cotswold scarp, Wotton-under-Edge to Leckhampton', *Proc Bristol Nat Soc*, 31 (1969), 535–49

Richardson, L. 'Wells and Springs of Gloucestershire', *Mem Geol Surv*, UK (1930), 292pp

CHAPTER 2

(Pages 48–75)

Wild Life : C. M. Swaine

NOTES ON SCIENTIFIC NAMES OF SPECIES MENTIONED IN THE TEXT

THE English names of animal species belonging to several groups are now more or less standardised. If the corresponding scientific names are required, they may be found in the following reference books :

Mammals : *The Handbook of British Mammals,* ed Southern (Blackwell)
Birds : *A Field Guide to the Birds of Britain and Europe,* Peterson *et al* (Collins)
Amphibia and Reptiles : *The British Amphibians and Reptiles,* Smith (Collins)
Fishes : *The Fishes of the British Isles,* Jenkins (Warne)
Butterflies : *A Field Guide to the Butterflies of Britain and Europe,* Higgins and Riley (Collins)

The English names of flowering plants and ferns are only now acquiring an adequate degree of standardisation for general use. Those used in the present account are taken from the following work, where the corresponding scientific names may be found :

The Pocket Guide to Wild Flowers, McClintock and Fitter (Collins)

SCIENTIFIC NAMES OF OTHER SPECIES MENTIONED IN THE TEXT

Bacon beetle	*Dermestes lardarius*
Black-lined Orthetrum	*Orthetrum cancellatum*
Blood-red Sympetrum	*Sympetrum sanguineum*
Cistus forester	*Procris geryon*
Cockroach	*Blatta orientalis, Periplaneta americana*
Dark bush-cricket	*Pholidoptera griseoaptera*
Death-cap toadstool	*Amanita phalloides*
Emperor dragonfly	*Anax imperator*
Eyed hawkmoth	*Smerinthus ocellata*
Fresh-water crayfish	*Astacus fluviatilis*
Fresh-water shrimp	*Gammarus pulex*

Glow-worm	*Lampyris noctiluca*
Green-drake mayfly	*Ephemera danica*
Humming-bird hawkmoth	*Macroglossa stellatarum*
Leopard moth	*Zeuzera pyrina*
Lime hawkmoth	*Mimas tiliae*
Lobster moth	*Stauropus fagi*
Lunar hornet clearwing	*Sphecia bembeciformis*
Oak bush-cricket	*Meconema thalassina*
Orange-tailed clearwing	*Aegeria andrenaeformis*
Poplar hawkmoth	*Laothoe populi*
Privet hawkmoth	*Sphinx ligustri*
Roman snail	*Helix pomatia*
Rufous grasshopper	*Gomphocerippus rufus*
Silver-Y moth	*Plusia gamma*
Water boatman	*Notonecta* and *Corixa* spp
Water scorpion	*Nepa cinerea*
Water stick-insect	*Ranatra linearis*

BIBLIOGRAPHY

Gibbs, J. A. *A Cotswold Village* (1898)
Mellersh, W. L. *A Treatise on the Birds of Gloucestershire* (1902)
Payne, G. E. *Gloucestershire: A survey* (nd)
Playne, H. C. *Birds of the Stroud District*, Leaflet No 12, Cowle Museum, Stroud (1944)
Riddelsdell, H. J., Hedley, G. W. and Price, W. R. *Flora of Gloucestershire* (1948)
Swaine, C. M. *Birds and Bird Watching in Gloucestershire* (1969)
Witchell, C. A., and Strugnell, W. B. *The Fauna and Flora of Gloucestershire* (1892)
Numerous references to the wild life of the Cotswolds are to be found in the *Proceedings, Journal* and other publications of the Bristol Naturalists' Society, The Cotteswold Naturalists' Field Club and the North Gloucestershire Naturalists' Society, and in the *Gloucestershire Bird Report*, published by the last-named organisation.

ACKNOWLEDGEMENTS

I AM grateful to Mrs S. C. Holland for certain information concerning plants, and to Messrs G. Douglas, M. J. D'Oyly and A. Richardson for assistance in connection with the treatment of fishes, mammals and Lepidoptera respectively.

CHAPTER 3
(Pages 76–109)
From Prehistory to AD *1500* : I. F. Smith, Bruce Eagles, Kathleen Morgan
Prehistory

1 A handaxe from Elkstone (*Archaeological Review*, 4 [1969], 21) does, however, suggest limited penetration of the Cotswolds during the

Pleistocene period; most Palaeolithic finds are from river valleys peripheral to the hills (listed in D. A. Roe, *A Gazetteer of British Lower and Middle Palaeolithic Sites*, CBA Research Report 8 [1968])

2 Guess-dates, based on radiocarbon determinations for Mesolithic sites in neighbouring areas : Thatcham, Berkshire, 8415 BC ± 170 (Q–659) to 6150 BC ± 180 (BM–65) and Cherhill, Wiltshire, 5280 BC ± 140 (BM–447)

3 A synthesis of the finds and distribution in Gloucestershire is given in *Trans BGAS*, LXXXIX (1970), 5–10. Detailed lists will be found in J. J. Wymer (ed) *A Gazetteer of British Mesolithic Sites* (CBA Research Report forthcoming)

4 *Trans BGAS*, LXXXIX (1970), 8–9

5 A. G. Smith *in* D. Walker and R. G. West (eds). *Studies in the Vegetational History of the British Isles: Essays in Honour of Harry Godwin* (Cambridge, 1970), 81–96

6 Radiocarbon assays demonstrate that Neolithic economy had been established in most parts of the British Isles before 3000 BC. This and other dates mentioned in connection with sites and finds prior to the first century AD are expressed in terms of radiocarbon years, now known not to correspond with calendar years. Universally acceptable corrections remain to be worked out, but it may be noted that the true age of a site dated by radiocarbon to 3000 BC is likely to be around 3700 BC

7 J. G. Evans *in* D. D. A. Simpson (ed). *Economy and Settlement in Neolithic and Early Bronze Age Britain and Europe* (Leicester, 1971), 34, 40, 62–4

8 J. Murray. *The First European Agriculture, a Study of the Osteological and Botanical Evidence until 2000* BC (Edinburgh, 1970), Table No 146

9 At Ascott-under-Wychwood (information from Mr Don Benson); Burn Ground, Hampnett (W. F. Grimes. *Excavations on Defence Sites*, I [1960], 41–101); an upper stone in Corinium Museum is said to have come from Jack Barrow, Duntisbourne Abbots

10 J. Murray, op cit, Table No 145

11 Preliminary account in *Current Archaeology*, 24 (1971), 7–10

12 *Trans BGAS*, LXIII (1942), 172–89

13 *Proc CNFC*, V (1870), 285; VI, 218

14 *Trans BGAS*, LXXXIII (1964), 5–33; LXXXV (1966), 209–13

15 A tabulated summary giving numbers and sources of imported stone axes from Gloucestershire will be found in *Proceedings of the Prehistoric Society*, XXXVIII (1972), 247

16 Inventory for Gloucestershire in *Trans BGAS*, LXXIX, Part 1 (1960), 3–149; inventory for the Cotswold-Severn group as a whole in T. G. E. Powell *et al. Megalithic Enquiries in the West of Britain* (Liverpool, 1969), Appendix A. The present map omits twenty-one sites that appear in the above-mentioned inventories for Gloucestershire. These are mostly unexcavated, sometimes destroyed, sites for which the evidence seems especially dubious; a few excavated monuments, apparently related to the chambered tombs but lacking evidence of funerary use, are also omitted

17 J. X. W. P. Corcoran *in* T. G. E. Powell *et al*, op cit, Chapters 2 and 3
18 *Current Archaeology*, 24 (1971), 10
19 The estimate is supported by another radiocarbon date of *c* 2800 BC for Wayland's Smithy, Berkshire, another tomb of the Cotswold-Severn group (*Antiquity*, XXXIX [1965], 126–33)
20 J. X. W. P. Corcoran, op cit, Chapter 3, *seriatim*
21 Indicated by the incorporation of Late Neolithic pottery in the final blocking at Notgrove, Nympsfield and probably some others
22 For evidence of this practice from Cotswold-Severn tombs, see S. Piggott. *The West Kennet Long Barrow, Excavations 1955–56* (HMSO, 1962), 66
23 R. J. C. Atkinson *in* J. M. Coles and D. D. A. Simpson (eds). *Studies in Ancient Europe: Essays presented to Stuart Piggott* (Leicester, 1968), 92
24 P. Dixon. *Crickley Hill: Third Report, 1971* (Committee for Research into the Iron Age in the North-West Cotswolds, Cheltenham, 1971), 7–10; *Antiquity*, XLVI (1972), 50
25 I. F. Smith *in* D. D. A. Simpson (ed). *Economy and Settlement in Neolithic and Early Bronze Age Britain and Europe* (Leicester, 1971), 96–101
26 *Trans BGAS*, LXXVI (1957), 141–6
27 *Archaeological Journal*, CXXVI (1969), 21
28 Excavated by Mrs M. U. Jones; it contained sherds of Grooved Ware, now in the Ashmolean Museum, Oxford
29 *Trans BGAS*, LXXXVII (1968), 14–28
30 *Antiquaries Journal*, XII (1932), 280
31 W. Stukeley. *Abury, a Temple of the British Druids, with some others Described* (London, 1743), Tab III; A. Thom, *Megalithic Sites in Britain* (Oxford, 1967), Fig 6:8
32 *Trans BGAS*, LXXIX, Part 1 (1960), 31
33 Ibid, 30
34 To the lists for Gloucestershire and Oxfordshire published by D. L. Clarke. *Beaker Pottery of Great Britain and Ireland*, Vol 2 (1970), 482, 493–4, may be added three recent finds in Gloucestershire : a large fragment from Crickley Hill (P. Dixon, op cit, 12), a damaged specimen from a secondary interment in the Sale's Lot chambered tomb, Withington (*Trans BGAS*, LXXXV [1966], 24), and a complete specimen found without associations at Hall's Road, Leckhampton (*Trans BGAS*, LXXXV [1966], 216)
35 For distribution of barbed-and-tanged arrowheads in the Swell district, see sources cited in note 14
36 I. F. Smith *in* P. J. Fowler (ed). *Archaeology and the Landscape: Essays for L. V. Grinsell* (1972), 157–67
37 Particulars of excavated round barrows are listed in *Trans BGAS*, LXXIX, Part 1 (1960), 99–139, with the exception of a report in *Trans BGAS*, LXXXVI (1967), 16–41, on a bell barrow subsequently excavated in the parish of Temple Guiting
38 There is no published corpus of bronzes for the area. The well known Monkswood hoard of 'Ornament Horizon' bronzes, datable *c* 1200 BC,

was found in the southern Cotswolds, just inside the Somerset county boundary (*Proc Society of Antiquaries of London*, 2nd series, XV [1895], 357–60; *Proc Prehistoric Society*, XXV [1959], 144–9). A Late Bronze Age hoard of eight socketed axes from Bourton-on-the-Water includes five of 'South Welsh' type (*Antiquaries Journal*, XII [1932], 279–93, Fig 3; XV [1935], 196–7

39   Bristol Museum Information Sheet no A7.70

40   A sixth century BC date seems appropriate for the Early Iron Age pottery from the hill forts on Crickley and Leckhampton Hills (*Proc CNFC*, XXXVI [1970–71], 24). Some of the pottery from Chastleton Camp, thought to derive from a Bronze Age tradition, could be earlier (D. W. Harding, *The Iron Age in the Upper Thames Basin* [Oxford, 1972], 74). A socketed bronze chisel from Meon Hill (*Archaeologia*, V [1779], 118) hints at the possibility of an initial phase in the Late Bronze Age for this hill fort

41   Particulars of Iron Age monuments and finds in the Gloucestershire Cotswolds will be found in the forthcoming publication by the Royal Commission on Historical Monuments (England), *An Inventory of Ancient and Historical Monuments in Gloucestershire. I. Iron Age and Romano-British Monuments in the Cotswold Area* (HMSO). For hill forts in the Oxfordshire Cotswolds, see *Oxoniensia*, XXXI (1966), 28–42. An account of Meon Hill, Warwickshire, appeared in *Trans Birmingham Archaeological Society*, XXXII (1906), 101–15

42   Reappraisal by RCHM (Eng) of Gloucestershire hill forts included on the Ordnance Survey's *Map of Southern Britain in the Iron Age* (1962) has resulted in the elimination of sixteen sites from this category. Two 'new' hill forts have been discovered since publication of the Ordnance Survey's map

43   An interim account of recent work at the hill forts on Crickley and Leckhampton Hills is available in *Proc CNFC*, XXXVI (1970–71), 18–23; further details for Crickley Hill will be found in the sources cited in note 24, and for Leckhampton in *Trans BGAS*, XC (1971), 5–21

44   Preliminary descriptions and plans in *Antiquity*, XLVII (1973), 56–9. A storage pit and small finds which are indicative of settlement are recorded from the hill fort on Shenberrow Hill, but no house-plans were recovered in the small cuttings made. Hearths, stone pavements and the post-holes of unidentified structures were found at Chastleton Camp

45   The evidence consists mainly of finds of pottery; there is also a bone weaving-comb from Copse Hill, Lower or Upper Slaughter (*Trans BGAS*, LXXXIII [1964], 11); wattle-marked daub was noted at King's Beeches, Southam (*Proc CNFC*, XV [1904], 49–67

46   D. W. Harding. *The Iron Age in the Upper Thames Basin* (Oxford, 1972), 24

47   *Oxoniensia*, XI/XII (1946–47), 44–64; D. W. Harding, op cit, 30

48   Antiquity, V (1931), 489–91

49   *Proc Prehistoric Society*, XXXIII (1967), 328

50   Ibid, 330

51 *Trans BGAS*, V (1880–1), 137–41; *Proc CNFC*, VIII (1881–2), 81–2.
    Part of a gold torque may have come from another grave (*Proc Pre-
    historic Society*, XV [1949], 188–90)
52 British Museum, *Guide to Early Iron Age Antiquities* (1925), 146
53 W. M. Wylie. *Fairford Graves* (1852), 15; Pl V : 7
54 *Antiquaries Journal*, XVIII (1938), 75–6
55 In the original account (E. M. Clifford, *Bagendon, a Belgic Oppidum*,
    Cambridge, 1961) it is suggested that the area delimited by the dykes
    was 200 acres. Dykes discovered subsequently and apparently forming
    part of the system may indicate that the area controlled was of the
    order of 500 acres

Romano-British and early Anglo-Saxon Occupation

56 Discussed by C. F. C. Hawkes in E. M. Clifford, op cit, 56–67
57 *Archaeological Journal*, CXV (1960), 49–98, and *Britannia*, I (1970),
    179–97
58 The major series of excavations at Cirencester are described in interim
    reports in *Antiquaries Journal*, XLI (1961)—XLIX (1969), and
    Britannia, I (1970). These accounts give references to earlier excava-
    tions
59 Bibliographies of individual Romano-British sites will be found in the
    forthcoming Inventory by RCHM (Eng), see note 41. For Kingscote,
    see also *Trans BGAS* XCI (1972), 60–91
60 An oblong ditched enclosure of some 10 acres adjacent to the Foss Way.
    Finds of the first century include butt-beakers
61 The evidence comprises a Claudian coin, early first-century pottery and
    a V-shaped ditch. No military equipment is recorded
62 VCH, *Oxfordshire* I (1939), 330; *Archaeological News Letter*, April,
    1948
63 ie, occupied (in the late Empire at least) by the *coloni*, agricultural serfs,
    who were the backbone of the labour force on a villa estate
64 M. J. T. Lewis. *Temples in Roman Britain* (1966)
65 Corinium Museum, unpublished : B958
66 J. M. C. Toynbee in Olive M. Griffiths. *Daglingworth: The Story of a
    Cotswold Village* (1959), 3–7, and J. M. C. Toynbee. *Art in Britain
    under the Romans* (1964), passim
67 Cheltenham Museum, unpublished : sword, 1924 : 46(A); ploughshare,
    1924 : 46(B)
68 D. Atkinson, *Trans BGAS*, LXXVI (1957), 21–34
69 D. J. Smith, in *La Mosaïque Gréco-Romaine* (Centre National de la
    Recherche Scientifique, Paris, 1965), 95–116; and in *The Roman Villa
    in Britain* (ed A. L. F. Rivet, 1969), 97–102, 112–13, 115–16; *Antiquaries
    Journal*, XLIX (1969), 235–43. D. E. Johnston, *Trans BGAS*, LXXXVI
    (1967), 102–6
70 J. P. C. Kent. in R. H. M. Dolley (ed). *Anglo-Saxon Coins*, 2
71 Briefly mentioned in *Britannia*, I (1970), 293; II (1971), 275. Further
    information kindly given by the excavator, Mr D. J. Viner
72 *Medieval Archaeology*, V (1961), 1–70

73   *Trans BGAS*, LXXVIII (1959), 53, 84–5, including environmental details by Canon L. W. Grensted
74   *Trans BGAS*, LXXXII (1963), 163. Dr G. C. Dunning thought the pot might be twelfth century but an earlier date is possible in view of the grass-tempered fabric
75   *Antiquaries Journal*, XII (1932), 284–93
76   *Oxoniensia*, III (1938), 168
77   *Trans BGAS*, LXXI (1952), 13–87
78   A full bibliography is available in A. Meaney. *A Gazetteer of Early Anglo-Saxon Burial Sites* (1964). In addition, a burial with a spearhead was found in Barrington Park in 1942 (Ashmolean Museum records); burials were cut through the Foss Way at Bourton (*Proc CNFC*, XXXIII [1960–1], 166); and an inhumation cemetery has been excavated by Cheltenham Museum at Bishop's Cleeve
79   Many of the grave goods are in the Corinium Museum
80   Recorded in *The Anglo-Saxon Chronicle* under that year (ed D. Whitelock, 1965)
81   H. P. R. Finberg. *Roman and Saxon Withington*, Dept of English Local History Occasional Papers No 8 (University of Leicester, 1955)

ACKNOWLEDGEMENTS TO 'PREHISTORY' AND 'ROMANO-BRITISH ... OCCUPATION'

MATERIAL relating to Iron Age and Romano-British settlement in the Gloucestershire Cotswolds (excluding Cirencester town) is derived from the Inventory shortly to be published by the Royal Commission on Historical Monuments (England); thanks are expressed for permission to make use of the Commission's records. The writers alone are responsible for interpretations put forward here. Thanks are also offered to Mrs H. E. O'Neil, Mr L. V. Grinsell and the Hon Editor of the *Transactions of the Bristol and Gloucestershire Archaeological Society* for permission to adapt barrow distribution maps first published in that journal.

AD 700 to 1500

Darby, H. C. and Terrett, I. B. *Domesday Geography of Midland England* (Cambridge, 1954)
Domesday Book, Vol i (Record Com)
Finberg, H. P. R. *Gloucestershire Studies* (1957)
Gloucestershire Subsidy Roll, 1327 (privately printed, 1856)
Grundy. *Saxon Charters and Field Names* (BGAS, 1935)
Hilton, R. H. *A Medieval Society* (1966)
Rahtz, P. A. 'Upton, Gloucestershire, 1959–1964', *Trans BGAS*, lxxxv
Smith, A. H. (ed). *Place Names of Gloucestershire* (Cambridge, 1964)
Taylor, C. S. *Domesday Survey of Gloucestershire* (1889)
Victoria History of the County of Gloucester, Vol 6, ed C. R. Elrington (1965)

CHAPTER 4

(Pages 110–38)

Farming and Industry—Past and Present : Frank H. Garner and Michael W. Ingram

Farming

Batty, F. W. *Forest of Dean* (1952)
Bristol University Reconstruction Research Group, *Gloucester, Somerset and Wilts Survey*, 2 vols (1949)
Dreghorn, W. *Geology Explained in Severn Vale and the Cotswolds* (1967)
4 June Returns for England and Wales (HMSO published annually)
Gibbs, J. A. *A Cotswold Village* (1898)
Hart, C. *The Industrial History of Dean* (1971)
Henriques, R. *The Cotswolds* (1950)
Kellaway and Welch. *Geology Survey and Museum, Bristol & Gloucester District* (HMSO, 1948)
Kersting, A. F. *Cirencester* (1956)
National Figures of the Agricultural Production of the UK (HMSO, published annually)
Wilshire, L. *The Vale of Berkeley* (1954)

Industry

Daniels, J. S. *The Woodchester Glass House*
Gloucestershire County Council Survey (undated, *c* 1947), by Gordon Payne, Planning Consultant
Gloucestershire County Handbook
Gloucestershire Life (magazine)
Rudder, S. *History of Cirencester*, 3rd ed (1814)
Stroud *Guide*
Stroud Valley Industrial Handbook
Victoria History of the County of Gloucester, Vol 2 (1907)

CHAPTER 5

(Pages 139–77)

Transport : Christopher Cox, Charles Hadfield and David Bick

Roads

Burke, T. *Travel in England* (Batsford, 1942)
Copeland, J. *Roads and their Traffic 1750–1850* (David & Charles, 1968)
Hibbs, J. *The History of British Bus Services* (David & Charles, 1968)
Jackman, W. T. *The Development of Transportation in Modern England* (CUP, 1916; Cass, 1962)
Webb, S. & B. *The Story of the King's Highway* (Longmans, 1913; Cass, 1963)

On Cotswold roads

Finberg, H. P. R. *Gloucestershire: an illustrated essay on the history of the landscape* (Hodder, 1955)

Hadfield, C. and A. M. *The Cotswolds* (Batsford, 1966)

Hudson, K. *Industrial Archaeology of Southern England* (David & Charles, 1965)

Margary, I. D. *Roman Roads in Britain*
Vol I : *South of the Foss Way—Bristol Channel*
Vol II : *North of the Foss Way—Bristol Channel* (Phoenix, 1955, 1957)

Rudder, S. *A New History of Gloucestershire* (1779)

Road maps

BGAS. *A Gloucestershire & Bristol Atlas* (Snell, 1961)

Ogilby, J. *Britannia,* Vol I (1675; and various reprintings as *Britannia Depicta* up to 1753)

Paterson, D. *A New and Accurate Description of all the Direct & Principal Cross-Roads in Great Britain* (1771, and reprinted to eighteenth edition, 1829; from the sixteenth edition of 1822 under the name of E. Mogg)

Directories

Gell & Bradshaw. *Gloucestershire Directory* (1820)

Griffith, S. Y. *History of Cheltenham* (1826)

Local studies

Cox, C. 'Milestones of the Stroud District', and 'Turnpike Houses of the Stroud District', *Trans of the Bristol & Gloucestershire Archaeological Society,* Vols 83 of 1964, and 86 of 1967

Paine, M. J. 'The Cirencester District of Turnpike Roads 1825–1880', copy in Glos Records Office

Rayner, E. *Discovering the Gloucester Road* (Shire Publications, 1968)

Spry, N. 'The Northgate Turnpike' and Bayes J. F. and Roberts J. 'Turnpike Roads from Gloucester to Cheltenham & Tewkesbury', both in *Gloucestershire Society for Industrial Archaeology Journal* (1971)

Canals

Hadfield, Charles. *The Canals of South and South East England* (David & Charles, 1969) gives short accounts of the two canals, and also of their neighbours the Thames Navigation and the Gloucester and Berkeley, Wilts and Berks and North Wilts Canals.

Handford, M. A. *The Stroudwater Navigation* (David & Charles, to be published in 1974)

Household, Humphrey. *The Thames & Severn Canal* (David & Charles, 1969)

Railways

Bick, D. E. *The Gloucester & Cheltenham Railway & Leckhampton Quarry Tramroads* (1968)
Bick, D. E. *Old Leckhampton* (1971)
Gilks, J. Spencer. 'The Cheltenham & Banbury Direct Railway', *Railway Magazine* (August, 1955)
Hadfield, Charles and Norris, J. *Waterways to Stratford* (1961)
Household, H. G. W. 'Sapperton Tunnel', *Railway Magazine* (February, 1950)
Jennings, Paul. *Just a Few Lines* (1969)
MacDermot, E. T. *History of the Great Western Railway* (1927)
Maggs, C. *The Midland & South Western Junction Railway* (1966)
Sands, T. B. *The Midland & South Western Junction Railway* (1959)

ACKNOWLEDGEMENTS TO 'RAILWAYS'

I SHOULD like to thank Roger Burdett Wilson, David Evans and Robert Rainbow for documentary help.

CHAPTER 6
(Pages 178–203)
Wool, Woolmen and Weavers : Lionel F. J. Walrond

Beecham, K. J. *History of Cirencester* (1887)
Bowden, P. J. *The Wool Trade in Tudor and Stuart England* (1962)
Davis, C. T. *Monumental Brasses of Gloucestershire* (1899)
Finberg, H. P. R. (ed). *Gloucestershire Studies* (1957)
Fisher, P. H. *Notes and Recollections of Stroud* (1891)
Girling, F. A. *English Merchant's Marks* (1964)
Hyett, F. A. *Glimpses of the History of Painswick* (1928)
Jenkins, J. G. *The Welsh Woollen Industry* (1969)
Lindley, E. S. *Wotton-under-Edge* (1962)
Lipson, E. *A Short History of Wool and its Manufacture* (1953)
Lipson, E. *History of the Woollen and Worsted Industries* (1921)
Mann, J. de L. *The Cloth Industry in the West of England from 1640–1880* (1971)
Miles, W. *Report of the Assistant Commissioners on Hand-loom Weavers (of Gloucestershire)* (1840)
Morris, G. W. and Wood, L. S. *The Golden Fleece* (1922)
Playne, A. T. *Minchinhampton and Avening* (1915)
Ponting, K. G. *The Woollen Industry of S. W. England* (1971)
Taylor, C. S. *An Analysis of the Domesday Survey of Gloucestershire* (1889)
Victoria County History, vols II (1907) and VI (1965)

Also numerous articles appearing in the following journals :
Folk Life (Journal of Society of Folk Life Studies)

Geographical Journal (October, 1937)
Gloucester Journal
Journal of Industrial Archaeology
Newsletter of Glos Society for Industrial Archaeology
Trans Bristol and Glos Archaeological Society (particularly vol 9, 53, 54, 66, 85, 86)
Textile History, vols 1968–70

ACKNOWLEDGEMENTS

The writer acknowledges help received from Miss J. de L. Mann, and Mr F. T. Hammond, from the staff of the County Records Office and the Museums of the area, from the directors of the firms still engaged in cloth production and from the owners and occupiers of many of the other mill premises, without whose cooperation a great deal of information might not have been available; also Mrs G. I. J. Lewis and Mr D. J. Smith for typing and photographic processing.

CHAPTER 7

(Pages 204–29)

Towns and Villages : Alice Mary Hadfield

ACKNOWLEDGEMENTS

I AM glad to acknowledge the help I have received from many members of staff in the Gloucestershire County Council Planning Department and Record Office, the Gloucestershire Community Council, the Cirencester UDC and RDC, the Librarian of the Bingham Library, Cirencester, Sodbury RDC, Northleach RDC, North Cotswold RDC, and of the Cheltenham Newspaper Co Ltd. Time and information have been most helpfully given.

CHAPTER 8

(Pages 230–49)

Architecture : David Verey

Atkyns, Sir Robert. *Ancient & Present State of Gloucestershire* (1712)
Derrick, Freda. *Cotswold Stone* (1948)
Finberg, H. P. R. *Gloucestershire Studies* (1957)
Jewson, Norman. *By Chance I did Rove* (privately re-published 1973)
Transactions of the Bristol and Gloucestershire Archaeological Society (1876 to present)
Verey, David. *Gloucestershire* (i) *The Cotswolds* (ii) *The Vale and Forest of Dean* in *Buildings of England* (Penguin Press)
Verey, David. *Shell Guide to Gloucestershire* (1970)
Victoria County History

CHAPTER 9

(Pages 250–71)

The Visitor's Cotswolds : John Green

Atkyns, R. *State of Gloucestershire* (1712)
Evans, H. A. *Highways and Byeways in the Cotswolds*
Gibbs, J. A. *A Cotswold Village* (1898)
Hadfield, C. and A. M. *The Cotswolds* (1966)
Rudder, S. *A New History of Gloucestershire* (1779)

CHAPTER 10

(Pages 272–98)

The Planner's View: the Foreseeable Future : Norman Collins

By N. R. Collins and published by Glos County Council :
Camping and Caravanning in the Cotswolds (1970)
Cleeve Common—Its Use and Recreational Potential (1971)
North Gloucestershire Sub-Regional Study (1970)
Outdoor Recreation and the Gloucestershire Countryside (1968)
By N. R. Collins and G. F. McDonic and published by Glos CC and
  Wilts CC :
Cotswold Water Park (1969)
Plan for the River Thames Lechlade to Cricklade (1972)

Index

Principal references are indicated in bold type

Ablington, 162, 214, 240, 254–5; downs, 91
Acton Turville, 228
Adlard, family and business, 129–30
Adlestrop, 211
Afforestation, see Forestry
Agriculture, see Farming
Air Balloon Inn, 42
Akeman Street, 85–6, 88, 91, 93, 101, 140 213
Alderley, 192, 195, 269
Alderton, 41
Aldsworth, 213, 258; Celtic fields, 92
Amberley, 225, 267
Amey Group Ltd (gravel operators), 288
Ampney brook, see Rivers; Park, 46, 220; springs, see Rivers
Ampneys, The, 99–100; Ampney Crucis, 220; Ampney St Mary, 220, 234; Ampney St Peter, 220; Down Ampney, 211
Andoversford, 148, 172, 214, 217
Angles, Middle, The, 94–6; see also Saxons, West
Anglo-Saxons, building, decoration, 233; Christianity, 97–8; settlements, burials, 84, 86, 93–6. See also Angles, Middle; Saxons, West
Archaeology, **76–88**, **91–106**, 109, 219–20 251, 280
Archer, Fred, jockey, 264
Architecture and architects, 162, 221, 224–5, **230–49**, 254, 259, 264–7, 269– 70, 272, 292–7; churches and chapels, 213, 218, 220–1, 224, 228, 230, 233–6, 238–9, 241, 244, 251–2, 254–5, 257, 261–2, 270; Cotswold style, 205–6, 246–9, 255, 259, 295–6; details, 179–80, 222–3, 233–9, 258, 264, 270; manor and named houses, 237, 240–6, 248–9, 253, 255, 259, 264–6, 268– 70, and see also under place names; prehistoric, 78–9, 83; Roman, 87–8; sculpture and sculptors, 233–5; village, 161, 180, 223, 236, 239–40, 255, 259, 262–4, 269, 290, 295–7
Area of outstanding natural beauty (and committee), 75, 110, 259, 272–3, 277, 294–6; wardens, 284
Arlington mill, 198, 236, 255; Row, 214, 236, 255
Ashbee, C. R. (craftsman), 208, 247, 259
Ascott-under-Wychwood, 77, 79
T

Ashton Keynes, 220–1
Asthall, 88, 94
Aston Blank, 211
Aston Subedge, 207, 260
Atkyns, Sir Robert (author), 183, 252
Aulus Plautius, 84
Avening, 77, 148, 201, 225
Avon (Bristol), River, see Rivers
Aylworth, 104–5

Bacon curing, 136. See also Industry, food processing
Badminton, 173, 205, 228, 243–4, 268– 9; 'Celtic' fields, 92
Bagendon, 84, 153, 218; excavations, 84
Baker, Charles (architect), 242
Bakewell, Robert (farmer), 183
Banbury, 141, 171
Banks Fee farm, 45
Barns, old, 236–7, 259, 279
Barnsley, Edward and Sidney, 223, 247– 9, 266
Barnsley, 93, 153, 220, 243; Park, 220 243
Barrington, Great and Little, 103–5, 212, 231–3, 244, 264, 306
Barrow Wake, 42
Barrows, burials, etc, 76–94, 221, 225, 227, 280
Barton farm, Chedworth, 93; Ciren- cester, 94
Basevi, George (architect), 242
Bath, 15, 145, 147–9, 155, 157, 170, 228
Bathurst, Lords, 248, 252, 266; Estate, 121; Park, 219
Batsford Park, 246
Baunton, 218
Beacon, The, Painswick, 242
Beaker folk, 81
Beam-engines, 188, 199
Beaufort, Dukes of, 228, 244, 268; Hunt, 226, 268
Belas Knap, 79, 233
Benedictine monks, Cluny, 233–4
Benson's International Systems Ltd, 135
Bentley Pianos (manufacturers), 135
Berkeley, family and castle, 102, 104, 228, 237, 269; vale of, 44, 226–7, 269
Berkshire downs, 15
Beverstone, 104, 237
Bibury, 15, 46, 68, 99–100, 214, 232, 243, 254–6, 259, 262; 'Celtic' fields, 92; church, 233, 235; races, 263–4; Romano-British sites, 91. See also Arlington mill, Arlington Row

David & Charles publish a range of books on the Cotswolds and the surrounding area. Details of some are given below. For later titles, please ask to be placed on the mailing list.

Sheets 59, 60, 68 and 69 of the David & Charles reprint of the first edition of the Ordnance Survey covers the Cotswolds. They show the personality of the region in the early nineteenth century but with the details of railways which were subsequently added.

THE CANALS OF SOUTH AND SOUTH EAST ENGLAND
CHARLES HADFIELD
$8\frac{1}{2}$ × $5\frac{1}{2}$in 394 pp inc 16 pp plates, text figures and maps
£3·50   4693 8
The story of all inland waterways south of the Thames and of Gloucester, and east of a line drawn roughly from Bristol to Christchurch. Contents: introduction to a pattern; waterways of the South East; the River Medway; the Thames & Medway canal; round London; the London–Portsmouth line; the Basingstoke canal; Hampshire waterways; the River Thames and the canals; the Kennet & Avon canal; the Somersetshire Coal canal; the Wilts & Berks canal; the Stroudwater navigation; the Thames & Severn canal; the Gloucester & Berkeley canal. Appendixes include: summary of facts about the canals and navigations of the South and South East; principal engineering works. Index.
Canals of the British Isles series

CHELTENHAM IN PICTURES
BRYAN LITTLE
$9\frac{7}{8}$ × $7\frac{3}{4}$ in col frontis, 112 pp inc plates
£1·50   4178 2
Pictures and text showing Cheltenham as it was, and as it is today. Main contents: introductory sketch; the medieval church; the early spa; Montpellier; ironwork; Lansdown; the life of the Spa town; the Cheltenham villa; Pittville; workaday Cheltenham; transport; places of worship—19th century; the Victorian town; education; industry in Cheltenham; the modern town. Index.

THE COTSWOLD COUNTRYSIDE AND ITS CHARACTERS
ERIC R. DELDERFIELD
$7\frac{1}{4}$ × $4\frac{3}{4}$in 164 pp inc 16 pp plates, map
$52\frac{1}{2}$p
Stories gathered by the wayside, in the towns, villages and workshops —in places like Kingswood and Stanton, Tewkesbury and Stow-on-the-Wold. Index.

THE COTSWOLDS
ERIC R. DELDERFIELD
Some stories of the Villages and Churches
7¼ × 4¾ in 123 pp inc 16 pp plates, maps and text figures
40p
A description of villages and churches in four main areas of the
Cotswolds—the north, the south-east, the mid-west and the south-west.
Index.
Paper Covered

THE FLOWER OF GLOSTER
1911
E. TEMPLE THURSTON
Introduction by L. T. C. Rolt and New Plates
8½ × 5½in xvi, 244 pp plus 8 pp plates, illustrated
RP 1973   4227 4
A journey made in 1911 through the Thames & Severn Canal from
west to east. Chapters: the discoverer; 'Flower of Gloster'; Oxford;
Joseph Phipkin—owner; the bargain—Oxford; beginning of the journey;
John Aikin and Anna Laetitia; why I would like it to have been Anna
Laetitia; Shipton-on-Cherwell; Somerton; the trade in old bits;
Cropredy; history of Cropredy; spare bootlace; schooldays; pour
passer doucement ma vie; hedgerow philosophy; Warwick; gate into
the Black Country; Stratford-on-Avon Canal; Lowson Ford; Yarning-
dale farm; the compleat angler; Preston Bagot; cure for trippers; an
old nunner; Fladbury Mill; wool-gathering; apple blossom; Tewkesbury; the gold valley; hard-boiled eggs; dietetics; the last lock.
Material added for this reprint: introduction by L. T. C. Rolt, new
plates (the author's originals not used in earlier editions).
David & Charles Reprints

GEOLOGY EXPLAINED IN THE SEVERN VALE AND COTSWOLDS
WILLIAM DREGHORN
8½ × 5½in 191 pp, maps and diagrams
£1·75   4102 2
An 'easy-to-follow' guide to the geology of the Severn Vale, the Cotswolds, and the Malverns: numerous explanatory line illustrations
keyed to the text. Chapters: jurassic system of Gloucestershire; Wain-
lode Cliff; Westbury-on-Severn; Severn Bridge; Severn Bore and Hock
Cliff; Severn terraces; Cheltenham sands; Churchdown outlier; Robin's
Wood Hill; Bredon Hill; Leckhampton Hill; Cleeve Hill; Barrow
Wake; Crickley Hill and Birdlip; the Combes; springs and villages in
the Great Oolite regions; Cotswold tiles and building stones; Painswick area; the northern Malverns; the southern Malverns; May Hill.
Glossary, bibliography, appendix—table of rock strata.

GLOUCESTERSHIRE WOOLLEN MILLS
JENNIFER TANN

8¼ × 5⅞in 254 pp inc 16 pp plates, maps and diagrams
£2·25   4118 9
An account of the development of the woollen industry from 1550 and
its collapse at the beginning of the 20th century. Chapters: the organisation of the Gloucestershire woollen industry; the distribution and
development of the Gloucestershire woollen industry 1550–1640; the
Gloucestershire woollen industry 1640–1802; trade fluctuations and
decline 1802–1900. List of abbreviations, list of directories used, source
notes, gazetteer, index.

OLD COTSWOLD
EDITH BRILL

8½ × 5¼in 192 pp plus 16 pp plates, maps and drawings
£2·50   4223 1
A contemporary study in the local history of the Cotswolds, mainly
concerned with the period since 1750, with a bias towards social and
economic history and special reference to the visible remains of yester-
day. Chapters: Cheltenham Spa; Painswick; the Cotswold hand-loom
weavers; Wooton-under-Edge in the 18th century; the clothier's teazel
and other Cotswold plants; two Campden worthies; Burford in the
coaching era; Cotswold woodlands; Cotswold roofs; Cotswold fulling-
mills; the Tortworth chestnut; Cotswold papermakers; two Cotswold
quarries; some Cotswold masons. Bibliography, index.
Old . . . series

THE SEVERN BORE
F. W. ROWBOTHAM

2nd Edition
8½ × 5¼in 104 pp inc 8 pp plates
£1·25   4746 2
A guide to the origin, size and situation of the Bore. Contents: Talk
of a river; the course and causes of the Bore; when and where to see
the Bore; riding the Bore; the Bore and the barges; photographing the
Bore. Appendixes include: summary of facts and figures; factors
affecting height and time of Bore. Index.

THE THAMES AND SEVERN CANAL
HUMPREY HOUSEHOLD

8½ × 5¼in col frontis, 237 pp inc 16 pp plates, text figures, maps and
diagrams
£2·50   4475 7
A history of a waterway of operational and engineering interest.
Contents: the favourite project; the rivers Thames and Severn; birth

of the company; building the canal; wharves and water; 'conducting a complicated concern'; money and men; links in the chain; zenith of efficiency, 'last of the railway princes'; the death agonies. Author's notes, notes, appendixes, index.

Inland Waterways Histories series